UNDERSTANDING DATA, CULTURE AND SOCIETY

UNDERSTANDING DATA, CULTURE AND SOCIETY

PIETER VERDEGEM

S Sage

S Sage

1 Oliver's Yard
55 City Road
London EC1Y 1SP

2455 Teller Road
Thousand Oaks
California 91320

Unit No 323-333, Third Floor, F-Block
International Trade Tower
Nehru Place, New Delhi – 110 019

8 Marina View Suite 43-053
Asia Square Tower 1
Singapore 018960

Editor: Natalie Aguilera
Editorial assistant: Sarah Moorhouse
Production editor: Ian Antcliff
Cover design: Jennifer Crisp
Typeset by: C&M Digitals (P) Ltd, Chennai, India

Library of Congress Control Number: 2023952319

British Library Cataloguing in Publication data

A catalogue record for this book is available from the British Library

ISBN 978-1-5264-5913-8
ISBN 978-1-5264-5914-5 (pbk)

Contents

About the Author   vii

Part I   Introduction   **1**

1 How to Study Data, Culture and Society   3
2 Data, Algorithms and Society   13

Part II   Structures and Foundations   **33**

3 Capitalism in the Age of Data   35
4 Data, Democracy and Politics   55
5 Data, Identity and Subjectivity   73
6 Data, Machine Learning and AI   91

Part III   Applications and Controversies   **111**

7 Data, Industries and Globalisation   113
8 Data, Tech and Inequalities   135
9 Data, Journalism and Disinformation   157
10 Data, Automation and Work   175

Part IV   Conclusion   **195**

11 Data Justice, Activism and Resistance   197

References   215
Index   235

About the Author

Dr Pieter Verdegem is Reader in Technology and Society and a member of the Communication and Media Research Institute (CAMRI) at the University of Westminster. His research investigates the political economy of media and communication and the impact of digital technologies on society. He is a Senior Fellow of the Higher Education Academy (SFHEA) and teaches core undergraduate and postgraduate modules.

Part I

Introduction

1 How to Study Data, Culture and Society   3
2 Data, Algorithms and Society   13

1

How to Study Data, Culture and Society

Why Study Data, Culture and Society?

London, 2023. At 8:00 a.m., a student's alarm goes off, and they check their iPhone for Instagram notifications and WhatsApp messages. During breakfast, the student is scrolling through the feed of the *Guardian* news app to catch up on current events. The student has a class that starts at 10:00 a.m., and they use their Citymapper app to find the fastest route to the campus. While listening to their professor, the student takes notes on their MacBook, browsing various web pages, and occasionally messaging friends. During their lunch break, they look up information on the Blackboard online learning environment, alternating with scrolling through TikTok posts and checking whether anything is new and exciting on their saved searches on eBay. In the afternoon, project work needs to be done with some classmates, and the group uses Google Docs to record their progress. Because some students are from China, they are also using WeChat. Meanwhile, some online learning materials, e-books and online discussions are consulted too. After the group work is finished, the student is notified to attend a personal tutorial via Microsoft Teams. The student goes to the gym for some exercise after the tutorial and tracks their progress via their Fitbit. Afterwards, they are hungry and decide to order some food via Deliveroo. During dinner, they play music from Spotify and check the latest Netflix recommendations to pick a new TV series to watch and relax. While in bed and before sleeping, they check social media updates and other notifications from digital platforms.

This describes a typical day for a university student in the UK. What this teaches us is how the student's day is characterised by (constant) interactions with digital platforms through electronic devices. Almost every single activity is mediated through digital technologies, producing and leaving multiple data points behind. Even more remarkable is that you, students reading this textbook, are probably unaware of the constant stream of data generated and the continuous engagement with digital platforms. This is how our contemporary societies are organised, and it invites us to reflect on how exactly the digital (and the role of data within it) intersects with society.

Data and the Age of Datafication

We live in the age of *datafication*, a term coined by Mayer-Schoenberger and Cukier (2013), which refers to how many parts of our daily lives are captured and transformed into data, thereby enabling the quantification of social life. Datafication happens in how we nowadays study, work, organise our leisure time and stay in touch with friends and families. The Covid-19 pandemic hooked us even more onto our digital devices and has shown us – whether we liked it or not – that we can continue most of our lives from our homes (when parts of our society are put in lockdown). The question is, what is new about this *data revolution* (Kitchin, 2022), and when did it start? It is crucial to position data in its historical context (Hacking, 1983/2015). Data has always been collected, whether it was for the census or other public records. Historically, there have always been protocols for collecting, representing and sharing data (Bigo et al., 2019). What is new is the amount, speed and variety of data being collected, analysed and stored (boyd and Crawford, 2012). Another innovation is that we – as individuals – are engaged in data production and distribution, which used to be limited to institutions and organisations, such as governments and corporations.

The data revolution is built on earlier so-called revolutions, such as the internet itself, but also social media and mobile media. In their book *Networked*, Rainie and Wellman (2012) discuss the *new social operating system* and elaborate on how the combined influence of the internet, social and mobile media revolution changed how we as individuals communicate with and are connected to people around us. They call this *networked individualism*. This term describes a tendency towards increased individualism, albeit a new type in which we are still connected to others. Beyond the social impact, what is also important to realise is that these connections happen through digital networks, and these interactions generate data. Social media offer the ability to communicate and share with others, while they also offer opportunities for visibility (Meikle, 2016). Mobile media enable us to do these things continuously, as we are constantly connected and *always on*.

The combined impact of social and mobile media contributed to the next hype, the *big data revolution* (Mayer-Schoenberger and Cukier, 2013). According to these authors, big data is a revolution that transforms how we live, work and think. What characterises big data is its volume (*big* datasets), velocity (the speed at which it is produced and can be captured) and its variety (different types of data) (Kitchin, 2022). However, there needs to be an infrastructure that allows this data to be produced, captured and distributed, and this is where platforms come into the mix. Platforms are the infrastructure through which different types of users are connected, and their business model is based on extracting that data (Srnicek, 2017). The *big tech* companies that will be discussed in this book – *GAFAM* (Google/Alphabet, Amazon, Facebook/Meta, Apple and Microsoft) and *BAT* (Baidu, Alibaba and Tencent) – are all active as platform companies. They not only monetise user engagement on their platforms, but also use that data to develop new *artificial intelligence* (AI) services.

The Many Meanings of Culture

Understanding the complex way in which data and society are connected is helped by adding the element of culture. This section explores why the perspective of culture is essential to our critical analysis of data and its impact on society. But first things first, what is culture exactly? Going back to Raymond Williams (1983: 91), the term *culture* has a double meaning, referring to:

- '*A particular way of life*' - in its anthropological sense - and can be seen as a synonym for everyday life.
- Forms of signification (such as novels and films but also advertising and television), including aesthetic intellectual products (*high* culture).

The challenge for studying culture is thus to understand how these two meanings coexist. We first need to acknowledge that there is no such thing as a *culture*, singular. Whenever we talk about culture, we must accept there is always a plurality of cultures at play. So, when using the term *culture*, I refer to the *concept* of culture. Beyond its meaning, what is the traditional role of culture, and how does it function? Stuart Hall, together with Raymond Williams and Richard Hoggart, considered one of the founding fathers of *cultural studies*, argued that culture is formed at very different levels and is linked to the production of everyday meanings. According to Hall (1997), culture is the sum of different classification systems and the *discursive formations*[1] to which our production of meaning relates. Classification systems – a very relevant concept for data, algorithms, and AI – express systematic relationships between signs. Discursive formation happens within specific power constellations. As Williams (1958/1989) noted, culture is the site of historical change and struggle. Therefore, questions about culture are equally questions about power: whoever in society determines what culture is, and what it is not, holds power.

It is essential to understand – when talking about power – that culture is one of the three realms in society, in addition to politics and the economy. Whereas politics is about influencing collective decision-making, and the economy is about the control of use values and what is being produced, distributed and consumed, the power of culture is in the 'definition of moral values and meaning that shape what is considered as important, reputable and worthy in society' (Fuchs, 2014b: 79). The influence of politics and the economy over culture is most clearly manifested in the ideas from the Frankfurt School about the cultural industries. Theodor Adorno and Max Horkheimer (1972) wrote in their famous *Dialectic of Enlightenment* that the culture industry is a filter through which the whole world passes. They stress how the production of culture happens via standardised patterns. The culture industry

---

[1]Discursive formations, as articulated by Michael Foucault, refer to a specific framework or system of language and thought that shapes and structures the way knowledge is produced and communicated within a particular field or domain.

does not only produce commodities; it also creates and dominates the apparatus of production, the culture market and cultural consumption.

What does this mean for the topic of our investigation: data and algorithms? It is essential to acknowledge that technologies such as data-driven systems and AI cannot see that what happens to culture, happens to society. Therefore, recognising the role of culture is essential to understanding how digital technologies are changing societies. Burgess et al. (2022: 27) write: 'It is through culture that we collectively experience, make sense of and contest processes of historical change – including large-scale digital transformations such as datafication.' Shifting to the role of algorithms, when defining algorithmic culture, Striphas (2015: 395) argues that computational processes have taken over from humans doing the traditional work of culture: 'the sorting, classifying, and hierarchizing of people'. This brings us to the final concept to be discussed here: society.

Society and Structures of Human Organisation

We all live in a society, and we all understand what this concept refers to. Definitions of *society* in an encyclopaedia would probably be centred around the idea that a society is a group of individuals living together, involved in some degree of cooperation, communication, and division of labour. Members of a society share a spatial or social territory and are subject to a specific political authority and dominant cultural expectations.

Let us unpack some of the concepts here:

- *Cooperation* and *communication* are central to the ideas of Karl Marx. He saw society as a historical materialist conception of the world and argued that societies are shaped by the economic system and the class relations (and struggle) it generates.
- *Division of labour* is a notion coined by Emile Durkheim, who explored the role of social integration and the division of labour in shaping modern societies. He argued that societies are a system of solidarities characterised by a shared culture.
- *A group of individuals*: sociologist Talcott Parsons defined society as a system of social action characterised by shared values and norms that guide the behaviour of individuals.
- *Political authority* belongs to the thinking of Max Weber, who saw society as a web of social relationships, governed by power and authority. His work focuses on rationalisation and bureaucracy, and he argued that societies are characterised by a complex division of labour and a system of social stratification.
- *Dominant cultural expectations* are central in Pierre Bourdieu's work, which examines how social class, culture and habitus influence individual and collective behaviour.

Just as there are multiple cultures, there are multiple societies too. We can be members of different societies, especially in a world where many people move back and forth.

I hope that by reading this book, you want to be part of the project to help contribute to not just *any* society but a *good* society! What is good or bad depends on different contexts and is part of a normative debate, but I hope that the following chapters help you to think critically about the world we live in, and the role data, algorithms, AI, and other tech play in it. I have written this book to help you understand the complex but fascinating relationship between data and society. I hope it will inspire you to do things with digital technologies that create a better society for all.

Why Use Critical Thinking to Study Data, Culture and Society?

What is *critical thinking*, and why does it matter? Different answers are possible, and they vary according to who is speaking. For starters, we can approach *critical* by looking at its opposite term, *uncritical*. Uncritical thinking can be defined as: 'automatically believing what you read or are told without pausing to ask whether it is accurate, true or reasonable' (Chatfield, 2018: 3). In times when we are constantly surrounded by (dis)information, there is a risk of accepting something because it is easy, sounds plausible or helps to support popular belief. The definition of uncritical thinking thus refers to accepting things too quickly; not asking questions or thinking through something. Following this, critical thinking is all about thoroughly investigating a specific question or phenomenon in a structured way, preferably by evaluating the evidence at hand, with the end goal of understanding what is going on and why this is so.

Media scholar Devereux (2014) goes a step further. To understand the media, he argues, it does not suffice to ask questions, but it is essential to pose *critical* questions. As a student or researcher, you will only thrive and gain more profound insights and understandings of things, how they function and what their impact is, by asking critical questions. Devereux (2014: 35) mentions *healthy scepticism* to elaborate on what *critical* means. Scepticism means we must be critical towards the information we are surrounded with: what ideas are presented, and what evidence are we given to develop our position? How is a story presented, and whose interests are being served? In the context of data, algorithms, and AI, this means asking the following questions:

- What is the data-driven technology being offered, and to whom?
- What discourses and visions exist around these technologies, and who is behind them?
- How will these technologies benefit or (potentially) harm society?

These are crucial questions any critical analysis of technology should start with.

It was sociologist Paul Lazarsfeld (1941) who made an explicit distinction between *critical* and *non-critical* communication research; the latter he termed *administrative research*. Lazarsfeld stated that critical research discusses what the desirable and undesirable effects of communication on society are, and analyses how the desirable effects can be strengthened. Lazarsfeld thus champions a position in which we abandon value-free research: communication and society mutually influence each other, and it is essential to be aware of positive and negative impacts. Critical thinking has a normative dimension and supports research that helps to advance the public good.

According to Marxist media scholar Christian Fuchs (2017a), critical thinking can be distinguished from uncritical thinking in terms of what questions are being asked and their relevance for understanding and improving society. Ultimately, this comes down to questions about power. Power is the central notion as it determines who has resources and can decide what a good society is, how to get there, and how to control it (Fuchs, 2017a: 8–9). Another crucial element, according to Fuchs, is the existence of asymmetries, in the sense that individuals and groups being in power deprive other individuals and groups of that power. The former group is better off, often at the expense of the latter group.

Critical Approaches and Power

If a central feature in critical thinking is power, how can we understand what exactly this is and how it functions in the context of data? A pragmatic definition of power offered by sociologist Erik Olin Wright (2010: 111) can help us. He defines *power* as 'the capacity of actors to accomplish things in the world'. How this plays out in the world of data is that some groups in society have the resources to decide what a *good* data society is, while others have no say in this. Those individuals and groups in society who have power also decide what type of data-driven technologies are being offered and to whom. They develop the discourses and visions surrounding digital technologies such as data, algorithms and AI. As they get to decide what a *good* society looks like, they are in the position to determine whether these technologies benefit society or might benefit some groups in society while disadvantaging or even harming other groups.

In critical social theory, there are many competing theories and concepts of power. It goes beyond the scope of this book to detail this, but a valuable distinction is between *who* and *how*:

- Theories that focus on *who* are mainly interested in which groups in society have power and which groups lack power. Many Marxist theories of power, for example, distinguish between the capitalist class and the working class, whereby the first group owns and controls the means of production. In contrast, the second group owns nothing and needs to sell their labour to sustain themselves (Gilbert, 2020).

- Theories that focus on *how* power works ask questions about how property or social relationships are acquired and maintained. Michel Foucault is a critical thinker who saw power as social technologies for managing and organising human beings. In his work *Discipline and Punish*, Foucault (1979) describes how modern societies use disciplinary technologies of power. Think, for example, about how surveillance cameras and technologies are used to watch people and prevent them from performing certain behaviours.

One final remark about critical theory is that it is inherently interdisciplinary. Critical social theory and critical data studies draw upon various schools of thought. The following section briefly explains why interdisciplinary thinking is essential in data.

Why Interdisciplinary Approaches are Necessary

Data-driven technologies have permeated nearly every aspect of modern life, transforming how we communicate, learn, work and interact with the world and people around us. Understanding the complexities of these technologies and their technological, political, economic, social and cultural impact on society requires an approach that draws upon insights from various academic disciplines. Interdisciplinary perspectives in the study of digital technologies are essential for several reasons:

- The multifaceted nature of data-driven technologies. Contemporary technologies are inherently interdisciplinary, encompassing aspects of computer sciences and engineering, mathematics, arts, humanities and social sciences. To fully grasp their implications, it is crucial to consider these diverse perspectives.
- The increasing complexity of how data and society intersect. Data and society are becoming increasingly complex and interconnected. This complexity makes it difficult to understand data, culture and society using a single disciplinary approach. Interdisciplinary perspectives allow students, researchers and practitioners to draw on insights from multiple disciplines to gain a more comprehensive understanding of these complex phenomena.
- The need to address the opportunities and challenges of data-driven technologies. Data and other digital technologies have the potential to contribute to solving some of the world's pressing problems, but they also raise complex challenges related to ethics, bias, inequalities, privacy, security and societal equity. Interdisciplinary collaboration is essential to develop perspectives that can address these challenges effectively.

Understanding the impact of data on society requires the combination of insights into how data and related technologies are developed, implemented and used. While computer science, engineering and mathematics are at the core of how data-driven technologies are designed and built, disciplines such as *science and technology studies, platform* and *software studies* provide interdisciplinary insights into the technological aspects of data, algorithms and AI. Perspectives originating from *sociology, political science* and *policy studies* allow for an understanding of the political impact of data-driven technologies. Digital technologies are developed by companies to generate a profit. *Economics* and *political economy* are disciplines that help to scrutinise markets, corporations and business models, as well as how this market behaviour impacts society. *Media and communication studies, sociology* and *cultural studies* analyse how technologies impact individual and collective behaviour, societal structures, everyday life and meaning-making processes.

Emerging and new fields, such as *digital humanities, computational social science, digital ethics, human–computer/machine interaction, critical data studies* and *critical AI studies*, embrace the opportunities for interdisciplinarity even more explicitly and push collaboration across disciplinary backgrounds in the critical analysis of digital technologies.

Theory Versus Practice

A final element in the book's approach that needs to be discussed here is theory versus practice. Theory and practice are often seen as separate worlds, creating a distinct boundary. Courses are either theory-oriented or tend to have a clear focus on practice. This can be a challenge for students: when choosing what to study, they often feel the need to decide what their preferred focus is or should be. They might ask questions such as:

- Why is it essential to study theory?
- How will theory enable me to become better at what I'm doing?
- How will theory help me to find a job or help to advance my career?

These are relevant questions, and we need to explain better the contribution of theoretical frameworks and their relevance for practice. This debate is also value-driven. Instructors and students keenly interested in theory sometimes look down on practice-oriented courses. They do so because they think practical learning and skills are less valuable or important. This is incorrect and short-sighted. The dichotomy between theory and practice is unhelpful and creates unnecessary divisions. As a result, we risk losing opportunities to engage with and grasp certain phenomena fully.

But first things first: what is theory? Theory offers a lens to look at an object under investigation. Denis McQuail (2010: 13) defined theory as 'any systematic set of ideas that can help make sense of a phenomenon, guide action or predict a consequence'. This definition makes clear theory is not only about *thinking* but also about *doing*. Theory is about turning something upside down and looking at it from different angles. This can happen from different perspectives and with different goals in mind.

Theory is often seen as abstract and generalised thinking, or the result of this. Theory and practice have their roots in classical Greek philosophy. Aristotle distinguished three types of knowledge: theory, practice and technique. The original meaning of theory is *seeing* or *scrutinising*. Practice (*praxis* in Greek) is the original term for *doing* and relates to action in its broadest sense. Technique, the third type of knowledge according to Aristotle, is the human ability to produce various kinds of objects through art and craft. Following Aristotle, practice/doing is opposed to theory/seeing because pure theory involves no doing apart from itself. But making this separation so explicit means opportunities will be lost or overlooked.

In essence, when we study something, we aim to achieve a thorough understanding of it, and in this sense theory and practice need each other. Theory offers the framework(s) for how to look at a phenomenon, and practice offers the opportunities to apply these frameworks to the real-life context. It was Kurt Lewin, a German-American psychologist who coined the term *action research* – which refers to research leading to social action – who famously said: 'There is nothing so practical as good theory' (Lewin, 1951: 169).

By the time you have finished this book, you will be thinking about theory and practice together, making you a better expert in data and society.

2

Data, Algorithms and Society

Learning Goals

- Appreciate how data is embedded in cultures and societies and how this creates a datafication of society.
- Conceptualise (big) data in its different categories, uses and contexts.
- Understand how algorithms work to make data and datafication so central to our society.
- Recognise the impact of data on how the digital economy is organised, changes political communication and modern democracy, how we are increasingly surveilled and how our identities are being datafied.

Conceptualising Big Data, Algorithms and Their Impact on Society

Data is the new oil is a slogan featuring in the headlines of popular media outlets since the rise of big data. Organisations active in data have adopted the term to refer to the centrality of data in what they do. But should we consider data as oil or instead as the new carbon dioxide, a pollutant affecting everyone? What is the role of algorithms and platforms in this? And what does it mean if a few companies dominate the digital economy? Does this benefit society, or does it mainly benefit these companies?

From Information Society to Data Society

Before engaging in these discussions, we must name our terms and conceptualise what we understand by *data*. How does this concept relate to neighbouring terms such as information or knowledge? What types of data exist? But also, what is the context in which we have witnessed the emergence of big data? How did we move from the big data hype towards the *datafication* of society?

The Information Society Revisited

We live in a society in which we are surrounded by data, which is central to how our social lives and our economy are organised. Despite data, algorithms and AI sounding like very new/contemporary topics, we have been here before. Before discussing what they are and how we conceptualise them, we need to revisit some earlier concepts, such as the *network society* or *information society*.

Sociologist Manuel Castells is among the most cited social sciences scholars. While he has written about various topics, his most important legacy is coining the term *network society*. His *Information Age* trilogy analyses the development of information and communication technologies, mainly how they have been crucial in shaping cultural identities and political communities (Castells, 1996, 1997, 1998). A central idea he develops is how technology, society and space are connected. Castells argues that networks allow geographical boundaries between different places to be overcome, thus enabling a *virtual space*. Communication flows are central to understanding the concepts of *space of flows* and *timeless time*. The former means that physical or temporal limitations no longer bind global transactions. The latter means that time is compressed and de-sequenced. This creates a new type of society, one that is dominated by networks.

Around the same time as Castells, Jan van Dijk (1999, 2006) has also written about the impact of new media and technology on society. In his work, van Dijk analyses the shift from a mass to a network society. He defines the *network society* as: 'a social formation with an infrastructure of social and media networks enabling its prime mode of organization at all levels (individual, groups and organisations)' (Van Dijk 2006: 20). In this book, he documents how relationships among communities are shifting because of interpersonal media. This plays out on different levels, including the economy, politics, social structures, and culture.

Robert Hassan (2008) prefers an *information society* over a network society. The information society is the successor to the industrial society: 'Information, in the form of ideas, concepts, innovation and run-of-the-mill data on every imaginable subject – and replicated as digital bits and bytes through computerization – has replaced labour and the relatively static logic of fixed plant and machinery as the central organizing force of society', writes Hassan (2008: 23). He argues that information technologies are the cause and consequence of globalisation. Hassan sees the information society as a world where personal and collective autonomy gradually diminishes due to an accelerating economy, culture and society. This needs further elaboration, so the next section goes deeper into different perspectives to analyse the information society.

The Omnipresence of Technology

The discussion above illustrates different perspectives from which one can study the information society. Hassan's approach is focused on technology and its impact on the economy. To broaden this out, the information society perspectives of Frank Webster (2014) are constructive. He distinguishes five perspectives one can follow to study the increasing impact of information on society:

- The *technological* perspective mainly refers to the increasing omnipresence of technology in our society and economy. It depicts society as an *information technology society*, *media society* or *data society*.
- The *economic* perspective discusses the *post-capitalist society*, *information economy*, *digital capitalism* or the *fourth industrial revolution*. The focus here is on the emergence of a new mode of production which is increasingly based on knowledge and information.
- Within the *occupational* perspective, the main point of attention is the changes caused by information within the labour market. It therefore proposes notions such as the *postindustrial society*, *professional society* or the *fourth industrial revolution*.
- The *spatial* perspective refers to radical changes in space and time and how those are no longer constraints. This perspective proposes terms such as the *network society*.
- The *cultural* perspective mainly focuses on how fundamental values and practices in society are changing and how this coexists with the increasing importance of symbols and signs. Associated terms are *knowledge society*, *simulation, hyperreality* and *postmodern society*.

This overview can be further complemented with *political* and *anthropological* perspectives, where terms such as the *risk society* or *flexible society* are proposed (Webster, 2014).

Three waves of technological development have had an essential impact on the increasing role that information and data play in society: the internet, social media and mobile media.

The Internet

The early foundations of the internet go back to 1969, when a small computer network was established in the USA. The term *internet* emerged in 1974 as an abbreviation for *internetworking*, networking between different computers (Curran, 2012). Other defining moments in the technical development of the internet have been email, the internet protocol (IP), the first graphical browser, search engines and web directories.

Beyond technical developments, other important dynamics led to the rapid rise of the internet (Curran, 2012): funding from the US military through the creation of the Advanced Research Projects Agency Computer Network (ARPANET), the involvement of scientists using the early internet for sharing files and shaping how the internet was developing, counterculture ideas that would surround the first virtual communities, the European concept of public service, and the commercialisation that started to take off in the mid-1990s. We must be aware of these aspects' combined impact, which has brought about a digital infrastructure on which much of our social interaction and economic activities are now dependent.

We also need to be aware that the idea of cyberspace – a concept popularised in literature by science fiction author William Gibson in the 1980s, in his novel *Neuromancer* (1984) – is a myth. He described it as a graphic representation of data abstracted from every computer in the human system. Of course, now we know that the contemporary internet is not one *global village* (McLuhan, 1962, 1964) but rather a digital infrastructure that can offer freedom and human empowerment while asserting control and contributing to oppression. Above all, we must know that the internet has evolved differently in different parts of the world (Curran, 2012).

Social Media

The next wave in the development of the internet was first called *Web 2.0* and is now known as *social media*. Web 2.0 was first coined by Darcy DiNucci (1999) and later popularised by Tim O'Reilly (2007). It was also called the *social web* and refers to websites that share the following characteristics: user-generated content, a continually updated service to enhance the user experience, decentralisation and user participation, the sharing of data, etc. Web 2.0 was surrounded by widespread optimism and expectations about the positive change the internet would bring. Fuchs (2014b) calls this the Web 2.0 ideology, which he criticises because it ignores aspects such as the business model of targeted advertising, the exploitation of free labour, and corporate dominance. Now we have discussed Web 2.0, what is social media?

In essence, what defines Web 2.0 also holds for social media. Scholars conceptualise social media by pointing at these platforms' opportunities for businesses and users to collaborate, share content and engage in creative production (Fuchs, 2014b; Hinton and Hjorth, 2019). Meikle (2016: 6) provides a more confined definition: 'Social media are networked database platforms that combine public with personal communication.' This definition puts the role of platforms central. These platforms rely on networks and infrastructures to deal with large amounts of data. Platforms function as intermediators between different types of users, thereby mixing public and private communication, which feeds into the business model of digital/data capitalism.

Mobile Media

While social media contributed to an intensification of data collection and analysis, this has been taken to the next level with mobile media and the so-called *mobile revolution*. But let us start by conceptualising *mobile media*. Mobile media are first and foremost associated with the mobile phone. Levinson (2004: 17) refers to mobile media as the 'media-in-motion business'. Mobile media facilitate the portability of communication processes, which also impacts the relationship between the public and private spheres of communication (Goggin, 2006). The mobile revolution refers to the spectacular uptake of mobile devices (first mobile phones but later also personal digital assistants (PDAs), portable music players, smartphones and tablet computers) in the first decades of the twenty-first century.

How did this play out in terms of data? With mobile devices, users were suddenly hyperconnected: they could use the internet and social media services anytime and anywhere, thereby generating data at an unprecedented pace. Simultaneously, another type of data was also being produced: location-based data. Mobile devices shape people's interactions with public spaces, creating new forms of sociability. This results in more data collection opportunities and privacy and surveillance challenges (Gordon and de Souza e Silva, 2011). The mobile revolution, in combination with the affordances offered by social media, results in much more datafied societies. This will only be intensified in the next wave of innovation.

The Fourth Industrial Revolution

The phrase *fourth industrial revolution* was introduced by Klaus Schwab, the executive chairman of the World Economic Forum. He used it in an article written in 2015, and later it became the title of his book (Schwab, 2016). The fourth industrial revolution is called *Industry 4.0* and refers to an economic system dominated by communication and connectivity technologies. Before this, the first industrial revolution (1760–1840) was marked by a transition from manual production methods to modes of production increasingly relying on machines. This was facilitated through the use of steam and water power. The second industrial revolution, also called the *technical revolution*, is the period between 1870 and 1914 that emerged from the installation of railways and telegraph networks. These networks supported a significantly faster transfer of people and ideas, enabled by electricity and transport. Economic growth was realised through an increase in productivity. The third industrial revolution, also known as the *digital revolution*, occurred in the late twentieth century and was characterised by a slowdown of industrialisation and a shift towards technological advancements. This digital revolution, of course, coincided with the spread of personal computing and the internet. The fourth industrial revolution is marked by breakthroughs in emerging technologies such as robotics, AI, quantum computing, nanotechnology, biotechnology, wireless technologies and 3D printing which will increasingly impact our society.

While Golding (2000) criticised the suggested revolutionary change associated with the network society and argued these technological developments are simply a new phase of contemporary capitalism, the same can be said about the revolutionary change circling the fourth industrial revolution. There is also a discussion about the difference between the fourth and third revolutions (Moll, 2021). It is, however, important to talk about the current epoch of emerging technologies, primarily because of the centrality of data in an era where hardware, software and biology will be increasingly intertwined. In the next section we conceptualise data, what types exist, and how to study them.

How to Conceptualise Data

Data has quite a long history, and its meaning has varied across this time (Rosenberg, 2013). What is *data*? This is a straightforward question but also one that, if you ask ten people, you will probably get ten different answers, depending on what these people are doing and how they engage with data. The podcast *Becoming Data* (a collaboration between the Data and Society research institute and Public Books) opened its episodes by asking precisely this question. Despite being experts, some guests struggled to provide a concrete definition. But when they started talking about it, *data* could mean very different things, such as interviews done about someone or something on a massive scale, measurements that are extracted from the flux of the real, the things that a group measures and cares about, something performative (more than just objective units of information); it shows the big picture about something and is critical to both oppression and resistance; representations of people and human subjects, or *data as people*; facts, statistics and attributes, relating not only to people but also to groups, being collected over time; rituals and cultures; a combination of technical and social practices; something taken from things and processes and being made into data; anything.

The Raw Material of Data

Geographer Rob Kitchin (2014a: 1) starts his book *The Data Revolution* by defining data as follows: 'Data are commonly understood to be the raw material produced by abstracting the world into categories, measures and other representational forms – numbers, characters, symbols, images, sounds, electromagnetic waves, bits – that constitute the building blocks from which information and knowledge are created.' The advantage of this definition is that it is clear and comprehensive. Its key elements are raw material, abstraction, categories, information and knowledge. Let us discuss them in more detail.

Starting with raw material, this portrayal suggests that data somehow must be extracted and is based on the activities of users – sharing content and engaging with platforms and other users – that is the natural source of this raw material (Srnicek, 2017). The idea of data as raw material is contested because data does not *just* exist and always has to be produced (extracted, interpreted, abstracted from). Gitelman (2013) talks about raw data being an oxymoron. I come back to this at the end of this section. Turning to abstraction, this can be understood as obtaining or removing something from a source. It is a fundamental concept in computer science and software development, whereby specific physical, spatial or temporal attributes are drawn to focus on more important details (Kelleher and Tierney 2018). In this sense, abstraction is linked to generalisation. Abstraction and generalisation help organise the world into specific categories, also known as *classification* (Gandy, 1993; Lyon, 2002b). This allows humans to organise things, events, ideas or objects and help to make sense of them. Finally, information and knowledge are often used interchangeably with data. Information helps answer a question, and knowledge is understanding something or someone. The following section explains how data, information and knowledge are interconnected.

From Data to Knowledge

A simplified definition of data refers to a set of values of subjects concerning quantitative or qualitative variables (Kelleher and Tierney, 2018). Through this definition, data is commonly associated with scientific research. However, data is collected by a broad range of institutions and organisations. For example, businesses collect and produce a large amount of data (e.g., sales data, data about revenues, profit, stock price). Governments are also data collectors and providers (e.g., unemployment, pandemic infections, literacy rates). In addition to companies and governments, non-governmental organisations, not-for-profit organisations, and charities engage in data collection and analysis (e.g., statistics on biodiversity or censuses of the number of homeless people). Data is measured, collected, reported and analysed, after which it can be visualised using images, graphs or other data visualisation tools.

One wonders what the distinction between data and information is. Data becomes information when it is viewed in context or post-analysis. Information is that which informs: it provides an answer to a question. Floridi (2010) distinguishes three types of information:

- *Factual* refers to information *as* reality (e.g., fingerprints or patterns).
- *Instructional* means information *for* reality (e.g., recipes, commands, algorithms).
- *Semantic* involves information *about* reality (e.g., maps, biographies, train timetables).

In a way, information sits between data and knowledge, as data represents values attributed to parameters, and knowledge signifies an understanding of real things or concepts. Knowledge is an awareness, familiarity or understanding of someone or something acquired through experience or education by perceiving, discovering or learning processes. Knowledge can refer to a theoretical or practical understanding of a subject. It can be explicit (as with the theoretical knowledge of a subject) or implicit (as with valuable skill or expertise). It can be more or less formal or systematic.

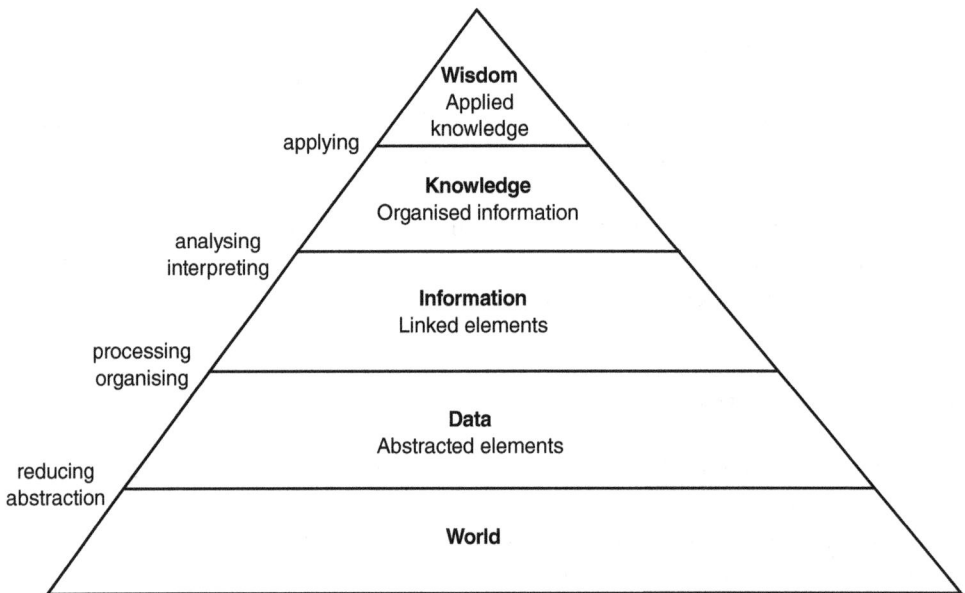

Figure 2.1   The knowledge pyramid (Kitchin, 2022: 12)

The so-called *knowledge pyramid* (Figure 2.1) further conceptualises the relationship between data, information and knowledge (Kitchin, 2014a). The knowledge pyramid is all about making sense of the world. It is a continuum representing the relationships among data, information, knowledge and wisdom:

- The base layer is the *world*, which we aim to understand.
- The first layer in the knowledge pyramid is *data* as abstracted elements. They are captured in the world and have undergone a process of reducing abstraction.
- The second layer in the pyramid is *information*, which can be understood as linked elements. Moving from data to information thus entails processing or organising experiences or observations.
- The third layer in the pyramid is *knowledge*. Knowledge sits higher in the hierarchy because it is organised information. To progress from information to knowledge, a process of analysing and interpreting has to be executed.
- The fourth and last layer of the pyramid is *wisdom*. Wisdom can be seen as applied knowledge, and to progress from knowledge to wisdom there needs to be a process of applying.

The knowledge pyramid, also known as the *DIKW* pyramid, information hierarchy or data pyramid, enabled Milan Zeleny (1987), a management professor, to make the distinction between four types of knowing: know-*nothing* (data), know-*what* (information), know-*how* (knowledge) and know-*why* (wisdom). Now that we have conceptualised data, the following section looks into different types and perspectives on data.

Categories of Data

Data exists in different types and formats. Kitchin (2014a) analyses the diversity of data and states that data can vary by form, structure, source, producer and type.

First, the distinction between quantitative and qualitative data is often made when discussing the data form. Quantitative data can be counted, whereas qualitative data can be observed but not measured numerically. In computer or data science, variables or attributes are very important and are quantitative. Kelleher and Tierney (2018) distinguish the following attributes: nominal, ordinal and numeric. Numeric data can be measured on either an interval or ratio scale.

- *Nominal* attributes take values from a finite set. These values are names for categories, classes or the state of things. Examples are marital status and whether you are vaccinated or not.
- *Ordinal* attributes are similar to nominal attributes. However, they can be ranked, although a specific feature of ordinal data is that there is no equal distance between those values. For example, a survey question can ask you to choose between the categories *totally disagree, disagree, neither disagree nor agree, agree* and *totally agree.*
- *Interval* attributes are measured on a scale with a fixed but arbitrary interval and arbitrary origin. Time and date measurements are examples of interval attributes.
- *Ratio* scales are similar to interval scales, but the measurement scale has a true-zero origin. Distance measurements are examples of ratio attributes.

Second, data can be structured, semi-structured or unstructured. *Structured* data is data that is organised and can be stored in a defined data model (e.g., database). Every instance in the database has the same structure (i.e., a set of attributes) (Kelleher and Tierney, 2018). *Unstructured* data, on the other hand, is data where each instance of the database may have its structure, but it is not identical in every instance. Collections of user data posted on social media platforms are a good example: they can include text, images, videos, likes/shares, etc. Given the lack of structure, unstructured data is challenging to read in its raw form and requires some data processing first. *Semi-structured* data sits somewhere in between structured and non-structured data. This refers to data with no defined data model which, consequently, cannot be held in a relational database.

Third, data can vary according to its source. According to Kitchin (2014a), there are two primary ways in which data can be generated. Data can be *captured* through measurements, such as surveys, interviews, experiments, cameras, sensors and scanners. *Exhaust* data refers to data generated by a specific process or device, but the data itself is some by-product, not the main output of the system. Sales data, for example, tells about what goods or services are being sold but can also provide insights into what stocks need to be filled or even worker performance. *Transient* data is linked to exhaust data, but the difference is that it is not further kept or examined and instead is discarded. This could be because the analysis of this data is too complex, or there are simply no resources for it. Finally, *derived* data is not raw but produced through additional analysis or processing of captured data.

Fourth, another dimension in the typology is based on the producer of data. We can discern primary, secondary and tertiary data (Borgman, 2016). *Primary* data refers to data being collected by a researcher/team of researchers using an original design for data collection. *Secondary* data is primary data made available to other researchers for analysis and reuse. *Tertiary* data is a form of derived data. Examples include statistical results, counts and categories.

Fifth and finally, Kitchin (2014a) states that data is diverse in terms of its type. In this context, he distinguishes metadata, indexal and attribute data. *Metadata* is the most familiar term. It is data that describes other data and, as such, is one of the most common types of exhaust data (Kelleher and Tierney, 2018). Metadata enables us to understand a dataset and its composition and how it should be interpreted and understood. *Indexal* data is a type of data that supports identification and linking, as it includes unique identifiers. Examples are credit card and passport numbers. *Attribute* data represents certain aspects of a phenomenon but is not indexal. Personal data such as age, sex, and weight are examples of attribute data.

The Many Contexts of Data

In addition to different data types, we must be aware of the different contexts in which we position them. Kitchin (2014a) discusses five relevant perspectives for data:

- Data can be framed *technically*, meaning that we pay attention to the methods or procedures via which data is being collected and generated, resulting in clean and accurate datasets. Related technical questions exist around how data can and should be stored, processed, structured, analysed and shared.
- The *ethical* perspective of data concerns how data collection and analysis relates to values such as fairness, justice and equality. When considering data collection and privacy, we deal with the ethical perspective.
- The *political and economic* context certainly influences how data is collected, analysed and used. Data-driven policy-making is on the rise, and contemporary economies are centred around the economic value of data.

- Data is generated in a specific *time and space* context, which refers to the data's temporal and spatial framing.
- The *philosophical* perspective around data asks us to reflect on the epistemology and ontology of data. Epistemology refers to the nature of knowledge and how data can help us understand the world. Ontology is linked to the nature of being and invites us to reflect on what exists and can be observed.

Is Data the New Oil?

This final section revisits the role of data and how we should understand its impact on society, particularly the economy. *Data is the new oil* is one of the most famous slogans in this context, indicating the growing importance of data. The technology magazine *Wired* (2014) first wrote about it in 2014, and *The Economist* (2017) put it on its cover in May 2017. Since then, the metaphor is often used to describe modern times, where data drives economic growth and change, just as oil did in the twentieth century. It suggests that data is behind the creation of new businesses, infrastructures, monopolies, politics and economics. Given its popularity, it is worth debunking the *data as the new oil* metaphor.

This metaphor compares oil and data in the sense that those who can extract oil/data are in the position of establishing (quasi)monopolies, leading to an intense concentration of power. It Is important to interrogate why we cannot so simply compare data to oil.

- The first argument is based on the supply of data. Oil is a natural resource, and while not all of it has been found yet, we know there is a finite amount of oil in the ground. The supply of data, however, is superabundant. Unlike oil, with data, we should be more concerned about *what* to do with it (and *who* can do this) than where to find it. Jeanette Winterson (2021), in her non-fiction book *12 Bytes*, asks whether we should see data as CO_2, a pollutant that affects everyone in society.
- Data can be reused, but different people can use it for various reasons. This has severe economic consequences for all stakeholders involved. Another key difference is about who controls the commodity. Unlike oil, it is much harder to keep track of what data is being collected and by whom it is used. The Snowden revelations and the Cambridge Analytica scandal have taught us about the risks of widespread surveillance by governments and companies and its impact on our democracy.
- A last difference is that the data industry evolves much faster than the oil industry. Companies whose business model is centred on data are engaging with innovation, which means they are constantly developing new services to keep their users active and engaged. This makes the regulation of the data economy much more challenging.

Data is *not* the new oil and will never be. But big data and datafication, in particular, are behind many changes in how society and the economy are organised.

The Rise of Big Data

'The Rise of Big Data' is the title of Cukier and Mayer-Schoenberger's piece written for *Foreign Affairs*. They further expand on these ideas in their book *Big Data* (Mayer-Schoenberger and Cukier, 2013). The growing importance of data and the emergence of big data, in particular, are linked to the internet and later social media and mobile media.

The explosion of data is a relatively new phenomenon: in the year 2000, only a quarter of the world's information was digital. Other information was stored in analogue formats such as paper or film. But the digitalisation of information happened at a very high pace, doubling every three years. By 2013, only 2 per cent of the world's data was non-digital. This is a massive development and has a significant impact. Cukier and Mayer-Schoenberger (2013) even claim that it is changing how we think about the world. And this is driven by the combination of rising computing power and big data. Not only the size of big data is relevant, but also its omnipresence – what Mayer-Schoenberger and Cukier (2013) call *datafication* – should be considered. With all the hype, there are many misconceptions as to what big data is and what it impacts, so we must start with an understanding of what it actually is.

What Is Big Data?

boyd and Crawford (2012) define *big data* as a cultural, technological and scholarly phenomenon that rests on the interplay of technology (using computing power and algorithms to analyse large datasets), analysis (identifying patterns to make specific claims) and mythology (big data as a higher form of intelligence, but also associated with truth, objectivity and accuracy). While this is a valuable definition, one missing aspect is the economic value of big data. This brings us to another – and more comprehensive – way of conceptualising big data. Big data is typically defined using the three Vs: volume, velocity and variety (Kitchin, 2014b). That said, others – particularly in business and management circles – include three more Vs: veracity, variability and value (Gandomi and Haider, 2015). Laney (2001) initially used volume, velocity and variety as three dimensions of challenges in data management. Let us start by looking into these three concepts:

- *Volume* is the most self-evident dimension of big data. The size of big datasets is often expressed in terabytes or petabytes, illustrating that big data are enormous in volume. One terabyte is 1,024 gigabytes (a variable most of us are more familiar with), and one petabyte is 1,024 terabytes. The volume of datasets is relative and depends on the time and type of data. Given rapid developments in data storage, what seemed an enormous volume a decade ago is tiny nowadays. Also, different kinds of data result in other volumes. We are increasingly producing and consuming video, which is much larger than text data.

- *Velocity* refers to the fact that data is being created in or near real time. The proliferation of digital devices enabled data to be produced and collected at an unprecedented rate. In the era of big data, one talks about *streaming* data rather than data collection within a specific and concrete timeframe. However, the speed at which data is analysed and acted upon has changed dramatically. With the rise of big data, we have seen the development of *data analytics* (Beer, 2018). This refers to the processes (and tools) by which raw data is analysed to find certain trends or answer specific questions. And data analytics enables and supports this real-time transformation of data into insights.

- *Variety* is related to the diversity and heterogeneity of datasets. Big data consists of different types of data. Think, for example, about the timeline of your favourite social media platform: this includes text, images, video and engagement with the content (e.g., likes/favourites, shares). Technological developments in data collection and analysis allow us to better deal with this variety of data.

While Kitchin (2014a) lists some more characteristics of big data – big data being *exhaustive* in scope, fine-grained in *resolution, indexal, relational* in nature, *flexible* and *scalable* – I discuss here three additional Vs for the conceptualisation of big data (Gandomi and Haider, 2015).

- *Veracity* refers to the unreliability that is inherent in big datasets. Social media data includes people's opinions, judgements and sentiments, which can be quite challenging to interpret, even though they can potentially contain valuable information.

- *Variability* (together with *complexity*) is a term that represents the variation in the rates at which data is being generated. Earlier, we listed velocity as one of the critical characteristics of big data, but this is not constant and varies according to peaks and lows.

- Finally, *value* is another essential characteristic the business world has assigned to big data. This refers to the (economic) benefit that can be derived from data. While a low-value density characterises big data – the original data has relatively little value compared to its volume (Gandomi and Haider, 2015) – a high value can be extracted by analysing large volumes of such data.

The Big Data Revolution

Cukier and Mayer-Schoenberger (2013) talk about big data creating a revolution. In so doing, they are referring to three related developments that significantly impact how research is conducted and perceived in the era of big data.

The first characteristic is summarised as $N = all$. As traditional data collection is quite expensive, researchers traditionally pay a lot of attention to their research population and how to define a sample representative of the overall population from which they want to conclude. However, big data collection has become much more manageable, convenient and often cheaper, allowing researchers (or big data companies) to collect data on a large(r) scale. For this reason, the research population (N) can potentially be everyone in society, as sampling is nowadays considered less important. This also means that data collection is often started without thoroughly assessing the nature of the research project, which radically differs from traditional research.

With big data, researchers accept much more *messiness* in the dataset. Earlier, we discussed big data characterised by variety, meaning different data types – structured, semi-structured and unstructured – are present in the data collection. Researchers nowadays accept that large datasets have a variable quality and that more work needs to be done in data *cleaning* before the analysis can start. Combining more computing power and algorithms and machine learning allows us to deal with this diversity in the dataset.

Finally, there is a shift *from causation to correlation* in the era of big data. Before, researchers would formulate hypotheses between an independent and a dependent variable, particularly with quantitative research. The hypothesis would suggest that a specific (independent) variable can function as the predictor for a particular behaviour or phenomenon (i.e., dependent variable), hence a (causal) relationship between them. Data would then be collected to be able to either reject or fail to reject the formulated hypothesis. In the big data era, however, more attention is given to detecting patterns within the data – the correlation – rather than explaining why something is happening.

A shift from causation to correlation let some people conclude we live in times in which 'we just have to let the data speak' (Cukier and Mayer-Schoenberger, 2013: 32). Even more provocative was a piece in *Wired* magazine by Chris Anderson (2008), titled 'The End of Theory'. Anderson himself did not coin this statement, but he agreed with it. According to him, the vast amounts of data becoming available and the statistical and computational tools to analyse them offer new ways to understand the world. And this would – according to Anderson – advance coherent models and theories and even make the latter redundant. Scholars have argued that statements like these are short-sighted (see, for example, Bowker, 2014; Fuchs, 2017b; Kitchin, 2014b), but it is clear that we need to look into some of the provocations and misconceptions surrounding big data.

Big Data Provocations

boyd and Crawford (2012) ask critical questions about big data and list six provocations. First, they say that big data changes the definition of knowledge. This refers to the statement above about letting the numbers speak for themselves. In any case, the popularity of big data and the innovative methods we use to conduct big data research (Fuchs, 2017b) invite us to think about epistemology and paradigm shifts in the data era (Kitchin, 2014b).

Second, some claims about big data and objectivity and accuracy are misleading. There is a misconception that (large) numbers are automatically neutral (van Dijck, 2014), which could be problematic if we only pay attention to big data.

Third, bigger data are not always better data. This misconception debunks the myth that larger datasets/samples are always better than smaller datasets/samples. This is a fallacy, as the quality of a dataset or sample is critical. Earlier, I talked about the messiness we tolerate when dealing with big data. We need to be cautious about this.

Fourth, taken out of context, big data loses its meaning. This critical warning is also an invitation to pay attention to the context of the topic under investigation and why combining big data research with small data is crucial (Kitchin and Lauriault, 2015).

Fifth, the accessibility and availability of big data do not necessarily make its collection ethical. This points to critical reflections that need to be made when researchers are collecting data about human subjects. This is part of a more extensive debate within digital research (Zimmer, 2010; Fuchs, 2017b).

Finally, boyd and Crawford (2012) argue that limited access to big data creates new digital divides. In essence, this is about the divides that can emerge between the data *haves* and data *have-nots*, equivalent to discussions about digital inequalities. The point is that certain institutions (governments and corporations) might be the only ones with access to specific data, limiting the possibility of some research findings being replicated or falsified by independent researchers.

Big Data versus Datafication

The big data provocations invite us to reflect on the broader societal impact of omnipresent data. Cukier and Mayer-Schoenberger (2013: 29) have coined the notion of *datafication*, which refers to 'the ability to render into data many aspects of the world that have never been quantified before'. Datafication differs from digitalisation (i.e., converting analogue content into digital information). Datafication is about 'taking all aspects of life and turning them into data' (Cukier and Mayer-Schoenberger, 2013: 35). All digital platforms engage in datafication: Google and Baidu transform our search terms into knowledge and digital data that feeds into targeted advertising; Alibaba and Amazon build specific profiles around our shopping behaviour; and Facebook and Tencent create data around our social interactions and networks. To summarise: datafication is about accessing, understanding and monitoring people's behaviour.

Media scholar José van Dijck (2014) understands datafication – and what she calls *life mining* – as a new scientific paradigm. It is central to the business model of social media platforms to measure, manipulate and monetise online human behaviour. She argues that datafication is part of a big data ideology, which she terms *dataism*. The latter is 'a widespread "belief" in the objective quantification and potential tracking of all kinds of human behaviour and sociality through online media technologies' (van Dijck 2014: 198). Dataism impacts the trust in institutions and is the engine behind *dataveillance* – surveillance through intense data collection.

Datafication, rather than big data, brings change because it has a revolutionary impact: once things, interactions and behaviour can be transformed into data, their goals can be changed, and this information is at the source of new value creation. We live in times where smart environments and devices increasingly surround us. Smart cities, technology, planning, mobility, etc., support intensified data collection and analysis, making us believe that this leads to productivity. But it is also the basis of a new type of capitalism centred around extracting data, controlling our lives and taking over the world (Sadowski, 2020).

Datafication in Practice: Data, Algorithms and AI

This section explores what insights can be gained from data, what algorithms are and their role in this, and how data and algorithms are at the basis of the most critical technology hype of our times, artificial intelligence.

If ... Then: What are Algorithms?

We now shift our attention to another key concept: algorithms. In computer science and mathematics, an *algorithm* is a self-contained step-by-step set of operations (Striphas, 2015). Central in the definition of algorithms are *input* and *output*, also signified by *if* and *then*. Alpaydin (2016: 16) defines algorithms as 'a sequence of instructions that are carried out to transform the input to the output'. We can further explain this with the help of some examples: for instance, we can consider using an algorithm for a sorting project. The input is a set of numbers, and the output is an ordered list. Another example is more mundane: we can see the algorithm as the recipe for cooking a meal. The input is the ingredients, and by following the recipe (or the algorithm, if you like), we will – hopefully – end up with a nice meal as the output.

Media scholar Taina Bucher (2018) applies the definition of algorithms to the world of computers, code and data. She sees algorithms as sets of coded instructions that a computer system needs to follow to perform a specific task. The algorithms are used 'to make decisions, to sort and make meaningfully visible the vast amount of data produced and available on the Web' (Bucher 2018: 3). But Bucher does not see algorithms as neutral artefacts. She argues that algorithms have power – what she calls *algorithmic power* – in terms of how, for example, they rank content on social media platforms. Some content or users will be more visible than others, and algorithms determine this.

Further developing this argument, she investigates the impact of algorithms in our digital and data-driven world, which she terms *programmed sociality*. This concept helps to understand how algorithmic power and politics play a role in the specific programmed arrangement of content and engagement on digital platforms. As we have seen before, our social lives are increasingly datafied, and algorithms play a crucial role in shaping and steering this social interaction.

Understanding Algorithmic Culture

A closely related concept, although broader than programmed sociality, is algorithmic culture. Galloway (2006) first wrote about it but did not clearly define it. In essence, *algorithmic culture* refers to the growing importance of the logic of big data and computation (including algorithms) in everyday life. Communication scholar Ted Striphas (2015: 395) uses algorithmic culture to mark a shift from humans engaging in the traditional work of culture, 'the sorting, classifying, and hierarchising of people, places, objects and ideas', to computational processes, whereby computers are running mathematical formulae for doing so. Digital platforms such as Baidu, Google and Weibo are engaging in the 'enfolding of human thought, control, organisation and expression into the logic of big data and large-scale computation, a move that alters how the category culture has long been practised, experienced and understood' (Striphas, 2015: 396). Social networking platforms such as Facebook and WeChat do much the same work in determining who are one's friends, which of their posts will be featured in others' timelines, etc. The same goes for shopping platforms (Amazon and Taobao), which will offer recommendations based on what products you have bought in the past, or video streaming sites (Netflix, Youku or YouTube). which recommend content similar to what you have consumed before.

This algorithmic culture feeds back to produce new habits of conduct, expression or thought that would likely not exist in its absence. Striphas (2015) calls this a *culture of algorithms*. One of the societal concerns about this is that it reinforces rather than challenges someone's preferences or behaviour. With more data becoming available, algorithms are used to feed personalisation. Eli Pariser calls this the *you loop*. In his book *The Filter Bubble*, Pariser (2011) warns us of the impact of the so-called *relevance paradox*. Mark Zuckerberg, the founder of Facebook, was criticised for his answer when a journalist asked him why the newsfeed of Facebook is so important. Zuckerberg responded, 'A squirrel dying in front of your house may be more relevant to your interests right now than people dying in Africa'. This is a good illustration of the *dark* side of personalisation. There are several problems and challenges surrounding the filter bubble:

- It is invisible, and there is a lack of awareness of algorithms' role in shaping social interaction.
- We – users of digital media platforms – have no agency in deciding to switch off the filter bubble or adjust its settings.
- There is no transparency in precisely what these algorithms entail and by what data they are being fed.
- The availability of more data means that the algorithms – and the filter bubble – become more effective.

There is a discussion about whether filter bubbles and echo chambers exist and their impact on society (e.g., Bruns, 2019). We are surrounded by algorithms that make decisions *about* us and *for* us. We need to understand how they operate.

From Media Logic to Algorithmic Logic

Considering the impact of algorithms on everyday life, we should take a step back and consider how traditional media function and how they differ from digital media. *Media logic* is a concept grounded in media sociology but has acquired an interdisciplinary nature due to numerous applications in different domains. In short, media logic refers to the formats and processes by which the media produce their content (Altheide and Snow, 1979). It concerns the organisational, technological and aesthetic determinants of media functioning, including allocating material and symbolic resources for producing media.

Inspired by this, van Dijck and Poell (2013) coined the notion of *social media logic*. Social media logic is the norms, strategies, mechanisms and economies that underpin the dynamics between social media platforms, mass media, users and social institutions. In grounding it, van Dijck and Poell (2013) have identified four leading principles of social media logic:

- *Programmability* can be defined as the ability of social media platforms to trigger and steer social media users' creative and communicative contributions. They do this through interacting with coded environments, which influence the flow of information and communication on the platform.
- *Popularity* is the principle and technique for filtering out influential people and popular content. Both algorithmic and socio-economic components

condition it. Every platform has its mechanisms for measuring and boosting popularity.

- *Connectivity* is the strategy of algorithmically connecting users to content, users to users, platforms to users, users to advertisers, and platforms to platforms. One of the challenges in this is that the boundaries between human connections and commercially and technically steered activities are increasingly obfuscated.
- *Datafication* is a concept that we have discussed before. It refers to the ability of digital platforms to render into data many aspects that have never been quantified before.

The significant evolution is that the influence of social media logic extends these platforms as society becomes increasingly *platformised*. In other words, algorithmic logic and power increasingly impact society beyond (social) media (Bucher, 2018). And this is not likely to change with the most recent wave of innovation.

AI: Data Meets Algorithms

The most recent hype in digital technology is artificial intelligence. Introducing AI and pointing at the connections between data, algorithms and AI suffices for now. A simplified definition of AI is 'computer programming that learns from and adapts to data' (Verdegem, 2021: 5). One of the problems of AI is that science fiction writers and Hollywood movies portray it as robots that will come after humans. This is a highly unrealistic portrayal, and it distracts from the type of AI we already have and use every day and the discrimination or other negative impacts that exist (e.g., bias in datasets or problematic use of facial recognition).

The currently dominant AI paradigm is *machine learning*. Machine learning means computer systems learn from large datasets, not human input or instructions (Alpaydin, 2016). Let us return to the metaphor of seeing an algorithm as a recipe for cooking a meal. The input is the ingredients, and the output is the meal itself. The algorithm is the recipe, a set of instructions that must be followed to prepare the meal.

Similarly, we could think about how we feed the AI system a lot of data about how to cook a meal based on the available ingredients. After showing the process repeatedly, the AI system learns from the data about how to cook the meal, not from the instructions but from the data. In a sense, this is a bad example because cooking a meal is, in fact, a highly specialised (and creative) activity, and we are far away from AI systems cooking our meals. But the example illustrates how AI, algorithms and data are connected.

We currently see a lot of hype around AI because of the confluence of factors that enable AI to be deployed more extensively. These factors are the availability of computing infrastructure, new techniques and developments in machine learning leading to more sophisticated algorithms, and the growing availability of data to train these algorithms.

Learning Takeaways

- The datafication of society means that all parts of our everyday life are transformed into numbers, which can be the source of value creation.
- Raw data does not exist. It must always be produced (extracted, interpreted, abstracted from). Therefore, there are flaws in calling data the new oil.
- Big data challenges how research is done, but we still need qualitative (small) data approaches, and theory is more relevant than ever.
- Algorithms have their own logic and take over some of the functions of culture. They also play a crucial role in artificial intelligence.

Recommended Reading

Aradau, C. and Blanke, T. (2022). *Algorithmic Reason*. Oxford: Oxford University Press.
Bucher, T. (2018). *If… Then: Algorithmic Power and Politics*. Oxford: Oxford University Press.
Gitelman, L. (2013). *'Raw Data' Is an Oxymoron*. Cambridge, MA: MIT Press.
Jaton, F. (2020). *The Constitution of Algorithms*. Cambridge, MA: MIT Press.
Kitchin, R. (2021). *Data Lives: How Data Are Made and Shape Our World*. Bristol: Bristol University Press.

Recommended Listening

Becoming Data, a podcast series co-produced by the Data & Society research institute and Public Books. https://www.publicbooks.org/category/podcast/public-books-101/season-three/

Part II

Structures and Foundations

3 Capitalism in the Age of Data   35
4 Data, Democracy and Politics   55
5 Data, Identity and Subjectivity   73
6 Data, Machine Learning and AI   91

3

Capitalism in the Age of Data

```
                    Learning Goals
  •  Understand how the era of big data has transformed digital capitalism.
  •  Dissect the structures that organise the data economy.
  •  See the role platforms and big tech corporations play in data capitalism.
  •  Learn how and why to apply a political economy perspective to the study of
     the digital economy.
  •  Better understand the impact of data on democracy and identities.
  •  Envision the future and how data capitalism will shape innovation.
```

How Political Economy Reveals the Structures of the Data Economy

If we want to understand how the digital economy is organised and which companies dominate it, we need to look at the role of data and digital platforms. Platform companies such as Alibaba, Amazon and Uber have embraced data and put it at the core of their business model. Using data and platform mechanisms, they transform and disrupt traditional economies, making them the frontrunners of digital capitalism.

Before examining how the data economy is organised and impacts society, we must introduce the framework to help us with this investigation. Political economy differs from traditional economy as it analyses how economic factors influence government policies and social relationships. It mainly looks at the ownership of communication systems and the consequences for all of us. Political economy helps us with questions about how the data economy is organised and the specific role of data, algorithms and platforms. But it also invites us to reflect on how this leads to a new type of capitalism, which manifestly impacts the lives of people and organisations.

Thinking about the Economy

When thinking about the role of data in everyday life, we need to be aware that data is a crucial part of our contemporary economy. Thus, we must reflect on how the economy and society are connected. Thinkers such as Daniel Bell and Manuel Castells have coined new concepts to illustrate how society is transforming under the influence of technological development (Webster, 2014). Bell (1973) is seen as the most influential theorist of the *postindustrial* society. He pointed out how occupations became increasingly informational throughout his work, marking a shift from an industrial society dominated by manufacturing employment. Castells (1996) observed that electronic highways emphasise the flow of information, giving networks a crucial role in the revision of time–space relations. As such, corporations – and individuals – can organise their way of handling things radically new on a global scale in real time.

The Economy versus Society

Critical historical perspectives on how the economy and society are entangled invite questions about how these connections are organised, what influences happen between the economy and culture, and in what direction. Concerning data, it is clear that the digital economy is affecting digital data practices and society. The following chapters go deeper into this. But first, what is the particular role of the economy, and how does it influence society? A criticism of structural Marxism is that it departs from the proposition of a determining *base* (the economic system) and a determined *superstructure* (cultural and social institutions, policy, education, etc.) (Williams, 1980). This is a reductive, mechanistic and deterministic view of how materialism and social production are connected (Fuchs, 2020), and we need to look beyond this. But we need to have a broad framework at hand, one that offers us a lens through which we can look at societal changes and the role of the economy within it. Political economy provides such a lens.

Political Economy as Framework and Critique

Political economy used to be the name for what we now call *economics*. In the mid-nineteenth century, a division emerged between classic economics and political economy. The latter has always been focused on documenting and understanding social change and historical transformation. Early political economy writers such as Adam Smith, David Ricardo and John Stuart Mill took it as their mission to explain the development of capitalism and its impact on society. While they were interested in the distribution of wealth, Karl Marx's (1859/1975) answer was a radical critique. His contribution was radical in that he was not only interested in studying the central forces of capitalism; he also wanted to reveal its antagonisms (e.g., exploitation and class inequalities) and demonstrate how they relate to political and economic organisation systems.

Vincent Mosco (2009) states that political economy studies control and survival in life. It investigates social and power relations and how they mutually constitute resource production, distribution and consumption. Survival is about managing scarce resources, and control is about who can decide about this, which are political and economic questions. Rooted in the 1970s, the *political economy of communication* is fundamentally interested in understanding the relationship between media and communication systems and the broader society. British scholars Murdock and Golding (1973), two of the discipline's founders, argued that the political economy of communication analyses media and communication as commodities produced by capitalist economies. Political economy is particularly interested in how economic factors influence policies and social relationships (McChesney, 2000). It concerns who can decide about media and communication systems and who benefits from them. To summarise, it investigates how power relations work within media and communication.

The Contribution of Critical Political Economy to Media and Communication

Critical political economy has developed within the political economy tradition and is recognised as a distinct framework (Hardy, 2014). It studies media and communication in the context of power relations, particularly the unequal power distribution. This framework is critical of contexts and practices within which inequalities are sustained and reproduced. Critical political economy is influenced by Marxian political economy, *inter alia*. The latter tradition provides a historical analysis of capitalism, with specific attention to the forces and relations of production, commodification, the production of surplus value, and class and social struggles.

According to Murdock and Golding (2005), critical political economy is holistic and historical, engages with moral questions of justice and equity, and aims to advance the public good. It focuses on the growing concentration and privatisation of media and communication and the impact of commodification and globalisation. Critical political economy analyses the structures and regimes of ownership of media and communication, the relationship between government policies and industry. In particular, it challenges the dominant ideology that legitimises the capitalist system.

Mosco (2009) identifies three central processes in critical political economy: commodification, spatialisation and structuration. These concepts are explained below.

Commodification

Commodification refers to the transformation of goods, services, ideas, nature, personal information or people – valued for their intrinsic use – into commodities, objects of trade that are valued for what they bring in exchange (Mosco, 2009). Commodification is the most visible representation of production in the capitalist sphere. A commodity is a good or service that a company sells on the marketplace to obtain a profit. Profit is obtained by selling it at a higher price than the investment costs. Commodities have a qualitative aspect – the value to satisfy a specific need or want (*use value*) – and a quantitative aspect – the value for which it can be exchanged on the market (*exchange value*). In the commodity form, use value is subordinated to exchange value (Fuchs, 2020).

In the sphere of media and communication, commodification happens on different levels. Mosco (2009) distinguishes between content, audiences and labour. First, commodification has traditionally focused on content: media content is produced to reach a large audience. Second, commodification also applies to audiences. The time and attention audiences spend on content can be sold to advertisers. In the traditional media sphere, this is called the *audience commodity* (Smythe, 1977), whereas this works differently in digital media, where audiences are not only consuming but also active in producing and circulating content. Fuchs (2010) calls this a *prosumer commodity*. Finally, commodification happens in labour, where the production and circulation of content have become the subject of specific job roles, in which some of them are valued more than others (e.g., a computer scientist developing data-driven apps will be valued/paid more than someone working in customer service).

Spatialisation

Spatialisation is linked to geographical space. Mosco (2009) identifies this as an essential element in studying the political economy of media and communication: it refers to how media and communication technologies allow overcoming the constraints of geographical space in social life. Marx (1973) already documented how companies use transportation and communication means to diminish the time to move people, goods and messages through spaces and how this was important to save on distribution costs. Sociologists such as Giddens (1990), Castells (2001) and geographer Harvey (1989) have all studied how shifts in space and time bring about structural changes. Spatialisation here means that our dependency on them is gradually declining. The world is becoming smaller, and people, goods and services can move around more easily. Of course, we should not forget that reducing distance is not available to everyone (immigration is a clear example).

Communication is central to spatialisation, argues Mosco (2009), because it is media and information technologies that support and promote flexibility and control. They have been an essential driver behind globalisation, commercialisation, privatisation and liberalisation. All these concepts refer to a restructuring and increased flexibility of industries and companies, making them less dependent on geographical barriers. Spatialisation plays a vital role in the emergence of global brands and culture, and social media platforms that are – most often – not tight to specific people and regions.

Structuration

The third component of the critical political economy of communication is structuration. This is about the relationship between social structures and human agency. Mosco (2009) refers to structuration as the process of creating social relations, mainly organised around race, gender and social class. The structure versus agency debate is particularly foregrounded by Giddens (1984), who argued that social action takes place within the opportunities and constraints provided by the structures in which it is happening. People's ability to live and make history depends on structures, particularly governmental institutions and companies. The focus on social structuration makes us aware of how media and communication systems and their impact on society depend on structural elements such as class, gender and race.

The political economy of communication has addressed the issue of social class, for example, by looking at what some groups in society have and what others do not. The debate about access to technology has centred on distinctions between so-called *haves* and *have-nots* (van Dijk, 2020). Inequalities, both in access but also in opportunities, are also related to gender. Significant work needs to be done to acknowledge gender inequalities and how this has produced patterns of exclusion and discrimination. Finally, race is also a central aspect in the social process of structuration, and recent scholarship on digital technology, racism and bias has shown how crucial it is to include race in the debate about media and technology.

From Capitalism to Digital Capitalism

Before we can start conceptualising *digital capitalism*, we must be sure we are all on the same page when defining *capitalism*. Earlier, I discussed commodities and commodification, which are central to the capitalist system. In the simplest terms, it refers to a type of economic organisation in which corporations or private individuals use the means available to them to accumulate profits from the sale of commodities (Gilbert, 2020). While commodification is related to transforming use values into exchange values, profit is linked to *surplus value*.

Capitalism: What are We Talking About?

Marx (1867/1976) explains in Chapter 4 of *Capital* how the circulation of commodities happens: C–M–C. A commodity (C) is transformed into money (M) and then into a commodity again (C). Alongside this, another circulation is happening: M–C–M, what Marx calls 'buying in order to sell' (Marx, 1867/1976: 248). Surplus value is represented as $M–C–M'$, where $M' = M + \Delta M$. The latter is the invested sum (M) plus a monetary increment/surplus (ΔM). Profit is the monetary surplus value.

Human labour is essential in the production of commodities. We must acknowledge that no surplus value or profit can be achieved without human labour (or human labour concretised in machinery). Capitalism is interested in producing and selling commodities at a higher price than the invested cost. It invests capital to accumulate profits in the form of more capital. This process is called *capital accumulation* (Gilbert, 2020).

Now it is clear how profit plays a central role in capital accumulation, we need to explain what is different and specific about *digital capitalism*. Dan Schiller (2000), in his analysis of early computer networks and the rise of neoliberalism, coined this notion to refer to the internet as the central backbone of the global market system. As an infrastructure, the internet is crucial in the information exchange within and between transnational corporations. Commodification is increasingly digitised with the internet, and cyberspace has contributed to commodifying communication (Mosco, 2009). We speak of digital capitalism because of the centrality of digital communication technologies, knowledge labour and information commodities (Fuchs, 2020).

Prosumption and Prosumer Capitalism

It is not only technology that is behind the changes in society's dominant economic system. We also need to be aware of the cultural and sociological developments that have led to a new type of capitalism. The futurist Alvin Toffler (1980) wrote about *the third wave*. His idea was that societies had known different waves of economic organisation:

- Pre-industrial societies, characterised by small communities depending on local resources.
- Societal structures centred around markets, clearly separating producers and consumers of goods and services.
- According to Toffler, a new (third) wave was emerging with the rise of the *prosumer*. This notion is a portmanteau of the words 'producer' and 'consumer'. The prosumer society enabled self-determined work, autonomy, local production, and so on (Toffler, 1980).

Media scholar Axel Bruns (2008) was inspired by this when writing about the emergence of blogging, Wikipedia, and early virtual environments. He proposes the notion of *produsage* to describe how the boundaries between production and consumption have become increasingly blurred. According to Bruns, produsage means that more people can be involved in creating and circulating content, there is less hierarchy, people are being rewarded for their contributions, content can constantly be reused and remixed, and digital artefacts can be managed through systems of common property. In the next section, I go deeper into some of the criticisms and limitations of this participatory culture.

The tendency to blur boundaries between production and consumption has also been documented in the work of sociologist George Ritzer (1993). In his book *The McDonaldization of Society*, he demonstrates how every consumer is – to a certain extent – a producer. And this is visible in multiple spheres beyond media and communication. For example, consider airports, supermarkets and restaurants where consumers are asked to embrace the *do-it-yourself* logic (with self-scanning and self-checkouts). Ritzer (1993) analyses how the *McDonaldization* of society is dependent on core principles such as efficiency, calculability, predictability and control. These principles sound familiar to leading concepts of the age of big data.

Participatory Media Culture

Before discussing how this plays out in the data economy, we must examine some of the promises and challenges of participation in the digital culture. Henry Jenkins, an American media scholar, is known for his work on *Convergence Culture* (2006), *Spreadable Media* (Jenkins et al., 2013), fan studies and participatory media culture. A central theme in his work is the celebration of new opportunities for users to be actively involved in the production and distribution of digital content. Whereas *convergence culture* refers to the blurring between media genres and producers and consumers, *spreadable media* stresses the potential (and necessity) for media users to be involved in co-creating, sharing, remixing, and adapting content. By doing so – according to Jenkins – users benefit from artistic expression and civic engagement, allowing them to feel more connected to others.

These ideas have been criticised for overemphasising the participatory potential of users, ignoring the corporate logic behind convergence culture, insufficiently appreciating the broader media landscape in which user participation is happening, and overstating the democratic potential of social media and digital platforms (Hay and Couldry, 2011). Fuchs (2017a) states that the ideas of participatory media culture can be seen as cultural and political reductionism because they do not acknowledge the importance of (capitalist) ownership structures and inequalities among users linked to social class. He also criticises the optimistic Silicon Valley culture as 'white boys with their "participatory" toys' (Fuchs 2017a: 70). Cultural expression cannot be confused with democratic participation. Still, the participatory culture ignores other negative aspects of digital platforms, such as commodification and surveillance.

Prosumer Commodity and Surveillance

To understand surveillance in the digital sphere, we need to grasp how capital accumulation works on social media and digital platforms. Most of the corporate platforms are advertising-based, meaning that the data of users – who can use the platform and its services for free – is being sold to advertisers. Smythe's (1977) notion of *audience commodity* is fundamental here. In a media advertisement model, he argues that consumers pay with their attention to commercial messages and ads in return for getting access to media content. As such, the audience not only consumes content, but is also sold as a commodity to advertisers (Smythe, 1981/2006). Of course, digital and social media work differently than traditional media: users are not only consuming but also actively engaging in producing and distributing content. Fuchs (2017a) explains how capital accumulation works on social media. Rather than an audience commodity, social media platforms generate the internet *prosumers' big data commodity*, producing and selling different types of data to advertisers. In addition to user-generated content, personal data and transaction data – data about their browsing and communication behaviour – are part of the commodities circulated on the platforms, central in *prosumer surveillance*.

This prosumer commodity is at the heart of the business model of what Zuboff (2019) calls *surveillance capitalism*. Her criticism of the Silicon Valley culture, in the aftermath of the revelations made by Edward Snowden and the Cambridge Analytica scandal, is that technology companies are accumulating vast amounts of knowledge *from* us but not *for* us. She criticises how social media platforms use human communication and interaction as free raw material for translation into behavioural data. While Zuboff's analysis is helpful, it also has shortcomings in that she mainly points to the problem of surveillance at the heart of contemporary capitalism while giving less attention to the inequalities and power dynamics sustained by the capitalist system. One of the questions being ignored is whether there is exploitation and who is exploited in the world of digitised commodification.

The Commodification of You and the Question of Exploitation

If it is up to the users of social media platforms to do the work of producing and distributing content while the same platforms monetise our attention and become more profitable and powerful (Moore and Tambini, 2018), this opens the question of whether social media users are exploited. In literature, there is quite some debate about this. Scholars such as Dyer-Witheford (1999) and Scholz (2013) argue that value creation in the digital economy happens by users and – as they are not being compensated for this – they engage in *free labour* (Terranova, 2004) or *digital labour* (Fuchs, 2014a). Inspired by the Marxian *labour theory of value*, Fuchs (2010) argues that social media users are engaged in capital accumulation on behalf of platform owners, thus generating surplus value for them and, consequently, being part of an exploitation process. Other scholars have different thoughts about this and come up with alternative interpretations of value creation in digital capitalism (Arvidsson and Colleoni, 2012), stressing the importance of the conditions of professional cultural labour (Hesmondhalgh, 2010) or arguing for a multifaceted concept of user agency combining cultural and economic roles (van Dijck, 2009).

Less contentious are the practices of extraction and exploitation in the production of digital devices. Fuchs (2014a) has written about the exploitative practices related to the mineral extraction needed to produce smartphones and other digital devices. Qiu (2016) and Chan et al. (2020) provide a powerful analysis of the labour practices in Foxconn factories producing Apple and other popular information and communication technology products. Both the extraction of minerals and the labour for producing digital devices are called *slave work* and are documented by convincing empirical data. Also, Kate Crawford (2021), in her book *Atlas of AI*, points to the patterns of (material) exploitation and extraction in the production and deployment of AI. First, we must examine how the data economy is precisely organised and scrutinise its business model.

Deconstructing the Data Economy

The increasingly dominant role of digital platforms such as Google/Alphabet, Facebook/Meta and Amazon in the Western world and Tencent and Alibaba in China (Moore and Tambini, 2018; Webb, 2019) invites us to reflect upon how the data economy is organised and what the role of data and platforms within it is. The Covid-19 pandemic, which started in early 2020, demonstrated our dependence on these tech companies' digital services. In many places, digital platforms – as private actors – have taken over some of the tasks that used to be the responsibility of governments or governmental institutions in the form of *public infrastructure* (Plantin et al., 2016). Van Dijck et al. (2018) have labelled this tendency *platformisation*, a process in which entire societal sectors are transforming and becoming more dependent on platforms and their internal dynamics.

The Business Model of the Data Economy

Platforms and data are the critical building blocks of the digital economy. The data economy has two key characteristics: the commodification of data and data extraction. Together, they form the engine behind processes that lead to the growth and expansion of digital platforms, which brings about the concentration of ownership. The digital economy has tendencies of monopolisation, with significant consequences for all of us. Throughout this book, I use the concepts of the *digital economy* and *data economy* interchangeably because data is central to the contemporary digital economy.

The Commodification of Data

Data as a commodity has three specific features (Floridi, 2010):

- Data is *non-rivalrous*. This means that data can be possessed and used by different entities simultaneously, unlike material goods.
- Data is *non-excludable*. Data is easily shared, and it takes effort to limit its sharing. Intellectual property rights, for example, are a means to limit that sharing.
- Data has a *zero marginal cost*. Once data is available, the costs of its reproduction are negligible.

Data is also *non-fungible*, referring the inability of one bit of data to be substituted for any other. For all these reasons, data is often seen as a *public good*, meaning that it is available and freely accessible to everyone, like Wikipedia or public libraries.

In the context of data, commodification refers to the processes whereby online and offline objects, activities, ideas and emotions are transformed into tradable commodities, transforming use value into exchange value (Hardy, 2014). In the data economy, commodification is closely linked to *datafication*. The latter concept refers to the ability to render into data many aspects of the world that have never been quantified (Cukier and Mayer-Schoenberger, 2013). Our social relationships, communication patterns, shopping behaviour, etc., are transformed into digital data (Couldry and Mejias, 2019a).

The specific economics of data works particularly well in tandem with digital platforms. For now, *platforms* are intermediaries that connect different types of users and invite them to engage and interact via their digital infrastructure (Srnicek, 2017). Platforms are ideally positioned to function as data brokers: their business model is centred around the possibility of capturing, analysing and extracting the data produced by the interactions on their platform (Crain, 2016; West, 2019). This is why platform companies dominate the data economy.

Data Extraction

The commodification of data works hand in hand with data extraction. Collecting and analysing data is not a new economic activity. Companies and governments have always collected customer and citizen data (Hacking, 1983/2015). What is different is that, in the past, data has been scarce. There were no tools or techniques to collect and analyse data on a large scale. Technological developments, however, led to a transition from data *scarcity* to data *abundance* (Kitchin, 2014a). The combination of two technical advancements supported digitalisation:

- The growing capabilities of digital infrastructures and geo-locational technologies that follow us constantly and track and trace our lives, generating increasingly detailed data about ourselves, our social networks and relationships, and our physical environments (Elliott, 2019).

- The accelerating capacity of advanced computing systems such as algorithms, machine learning and other AI technologies that are needed to generate insights from the massive volume, variety and velocity of data being generated by digitalisation (Coleman, 2019).

These technological advances are combined with an economic trend, leading to new business models in the data economy (Agrawal et al., 2018). The ability to collect ever larger volumes of data and the possibility – because of growing computing power – to analyse and generate insights from it have led to the (economic) opportunity of extracting value from it. This underpins the business model and the centrality of data to these digital platforms. *Data extraction* can be understood in a neutral sense as generating value out of data. However, critical scholars such as Jathan Sadowski (2019: 7) point to the exploitative nature of data extraction, conceptualising it as data that is taken 'without meaningful consent and fair compensation for the producers and sources of that data'.

Expansion and Growth

Data commodification and extraction are the drivers behind the emergence of the data economy. The centrality of data, in combination with the specific characteristics of platforms, led to a massive growth of digital platforms. Two fundamental mechanisms play a crucial role in the expansion and development of these data companies.

First, *economies of scale* are a distinctive economic characteristic for media and other industries where the marginal costs are lower than average (Doyle, 2013). When the cost of providing an extra unit of a good falls as the scale of the output grows, that is, economies of scale are present. That data has zero marginal costs is essential for economies of scale. The latter are profound in data: value emerges once data is compiled in large volumes and processed to provide insights. However, we must add that data is only valuable in its aggregation. This means that individual data is often valueless; only in relation to other data does it become valuable (Sadowski, 2019).

Second, *network effects* mean that the value of a particular network is determined by its size (Katz and Shapiro, 1985). Think, for example, about the internet as a network: the utility for each subscriber increases as others join the network. As a result, data companies become more valuable as more people use their services. Here is the critical role of the platform: engagement and interaction are only possible if there are large numbers of active users on the platform. The power of network effects goes hand in hand with data availability: platforms with access to large amounts of data will grow and become more powerful (Srnicek, 2017). There are also data-driven network effects: more active users on a particular platform means more possibilities for data collection, analysis and extraction. This results in more data that can be used to improve the platform's features and services, which creates the opportunity to attract more users.

Concentration of Ownership and the Risk of Monopolisation

Economies of scale and network effects have led to the so-called *GAFAM* (Google/Alphabet, Amazon, Facebook/Meta, Apple and Microsoft) and *BAT* (Baidu, Alibaba and Tencent) companies dominating the data economy (Kaplan and Haenlein, 2020; Webb, 2019). These companies control markets – sometimes as quasi-monopolies – such as online search (Google and Baidu), social networking (Facebook and Tencent) and electronic commerce (Amazon and Alibaba). Still, they actively pursue strategies to expand their operations to aggregate more significant data volumes and quality. To do so, they use processes of horizontal and vertical integration (Doyle, 2013). *Horizontal integration* means a company will try to increase its market share through internal growth or acquiring another firm with a similar product. Facebook's purchase of Instagram in 2012 is an excellent example of this. *Vertical integration* entails a company expanding its influence in product or service supply to customers. Amazon, for instance, does not only offer audio-visual content through Amazon Prime; it also produces content through Amazon Studios. Vertical integration is often pursued to gain more control over content production and distribution, particularly access to the end-user.

Critical political economy pays attention to the concentration of ownership in media and communications, mainly because it can make a small number of companies or owners of media companies very powerful (Freedman, 2014). Concentration means that progressively fewer organisations or individuals control shares in these companies. Just as researchers are worried about media concentration and its impact on pluralism and democracy in the traditional media landscape (Baker, 2006; Winseck, 2008), similar concerns can also be voiced about the digital landscape (Curran et al., 2016). Questions need to be asked about the fact that one company has such a dominant position in digital services such as search, social networking and electronic commerce – services that are vital in contemporary life (Birkinbine et al., 2017; Fenton et al., 2020).

Pursuing a business model in which data is central, platforms use economies of scale and network effects, contributing to the concentration of ownership. This is why experts warn about the *winner-takes-all* risk of the data economy (Moazed and Johnson, 2016; Srnicek, 2017), whereby only a few tech giants control the market and have the power to push (smaller) competitors out of the market, and also set the rules for how markets and an essential part of the digital economy are run. The latter describes a situation of (near) *monopoly*. This monopolisation is often combined with *enclosure*, meaning that the tech giants aim to strengthen their position – to safeguard their growth and profit – by controlling access to their data and limiting the ability of users to switch to competitors, thereby enclosing more and more of the digital world within their private sphere. This is why scholars talk about *colonisation* in the realm of data (Couldry and Mejias, 2019a).

The Platform Ecosystem

The author of *Platform Capitalism*, Nick Srnicek (2017: 43), defines *platforms* as 'digital infrastructures that enable two or more groups to interact'. They act as intermediaries that facilitate and organise online social and economic interactions between different users: producers and consumers, advertisers, service providers, app developers, and so on. This might suggest that platforms are neutral entities. Still, tech scholar Tarleton Gillespie (2010) reminds us that platforms have specific computational, architectural and political characteristics, which should be considered when studying them. Van Dijck et al. (2018: 4) argue that platforms cannot be seen as single entities and thus need to be analysed as part of a broader (online) setting structured by a specific logic. They use the term *platform ecosystem* to refer to 'an assemblage of networked platforms, governed by a particular set of mechanisms that shapes everyday practices'. Both in the Western world and in China and beyond, the platform ecosystem is mainly operated by a small number of tech companies (GAFAM and BAT), 'whose infrastructural services are central to the ecosystem's overall design and the distribution of data flows' (Van Dijck et al., 2018: 4). This illustrates the point made earlier about the concentration of ownership, but also the crucial role of platforms and data within it.

A Typology of Platforms

Different platforms exist, and we all use several of them on an average day. But it does help to have some typology of platforms. Steinberg (2019) follows a historical approach to defining platforms and distinguishes three types:

- *Product-technology platforms* are part of the first wave, and their label refers to computer hardware and software such as Microsoft Windows. Within this, the platform operates as a layered model, where one layer supports the other. Different examples of this category exist, such as computers and game consoles.
- The second type of platform is what Steinberg calls *content platforms*. The explanation is in its label: these platforms allow and support content sharing, whether video streaming or social networking.
- The third wave of platforms are *relational platforms*. Central to them is the transaction or mediation that is happening there. The platform is a set of products and services that brings together groups of users and providers where people, commodities and money are exchanged.

Srnicek (2017), on the other hand, makes a distinction between five types of platforms:

- *Advertising platforms* such as Baidu, Facebook, Google and Tencent engage in data extraction and use that data for analysis and then sell it to advertisers.
- *Cloud platforms* offer hardware and software infrastructure to digital businesses that rent the service from the platform. Amazon Web Services (AWS), Azure (Microsoft) and Google Cloud are typical examples.
- *Industrial platforms* are similar to the second category, but they offer these services to transform traditional manufacturing into internet-connected processes that lower production costs and transform goods into services. Siemens and General Electric are examples of industrial platforms.
- *Product platforms* are built to generate revenue by transforming goods into services and collecting subscription fees or rents. Product platforms, such as Spotify, often depend on other platforms.
- *Lean platforms* refer to the so-called *sharing economy*, in which the platform does not own many assets themselves but connects owners and consumers of their services, aiming to reduce costs as much as possible. Uber, Didi (Chuxing), Airbnb, and Tujia are examples of lean platforms.

Platform Mechanisms and the Functions of Platforms

Now that we are familiar with different platforms, let us look at how they operate. Van Dijck et al. (2018) explain this comprehensively in their book *The Platform Society*. They distinguish three platform mechanisms: datafication, commodification, and selection.

Datafication is a concept that I have already explained. In the context of platforms, it refers to the ability of networked platforms to render into data aspects of the world that have not been quantified before. Platforms use specific strategies for this:

- *Capturing* means that data is being collected on consumers and citizens. The rise of platforms also means an intensification of the data collection processes.
- Platforms use *circulating*, meaning that the platform ecosystem can only function because data is constantly exchanged among various stakeholders.

Platforms use *commodification* to transform online and offline objects, activities, emotions and ideas into tradable commodities. The platform has different types of currency to value commodities: attention, data, money and users. Commodification and datafication happen in close tandem, mutually reinforcing each other by providing insights into users' needs, interests and preferences (Mansell and Steinmueller, 2020).

Selection is also an important mechanism. In essence, this refers to how platforms combine datafication and commodification to 'steer user interaction through the selection or curation of most relevant topics, terms, actors, objects, offers, services, etc.' (van Dijck et al., 2018: 40). Platforms make use of strategies of personalisation, reputation and trends, and moderation:

- *Personalisation* happens as platforms algorithmically determine users' interests based on various datafied user signals and data analytics. The latter concept means that historical data will predict future choices and trends.
- Platforms decide on certain *reputations and user trends*, which are vital selection mechanisms. However, all platforms also need to invest in moderation, as they need to keep track of what content is being shared on their platform and who can use their services.
- Content *moderation* is quite controversial because of the circulation of hate speech and how platforms account for this. The work of Gillespie (2018) and Roberts (2019) is highly relevant in this context.

Taking into account these mechanisms, Moazed and Johnson (2016) have come up with specific functions of platforms:

- *Audience building* means that platforms are actively investing in building a liquid marketplace by attracting a critical mass of producers and consumers. Srnicek (2017) argues that platforms often develop a series of tools allowing users to build their products, services or marketplaces on the platform, and the platform then monetises these interactions.
- *Matchmaking* refers to connecting the right producers with the right consumers to facilitate interactions and transactions. The platform needs to decide how it will bring the different user types in touch; data is critical.
- Platforms must build *tools and services* that support the core transactions between platform users. They do this by removing entry barriers, lowering transaction costs and making the platform more valuable over time through data.
- The platform faces the critical task of setting *rules and standards*; these guidelines govern which behaviours on the platform are allowed and which are not and how they can be stimulated or discouraged.

The Platformisation of Society

Now that we have a good sense of how platforms operate, we can turn to the impact of platforms on society. Before we do so, it is essential to reiterate that platforms do not exist alone; they are part of a larger platform ecosystem (van Dijck et al., 2018). This ecosystem means that platforms are connected to other platforms, and essential mechanisms exist that support the interactions and data exchanges across platforms.

In the Western world, the platform ecosystem is dominated by GAFAM, along with other platforms such as Uber and Airbnb, while in China, BAT, together with platforms companies such as JD, Meituan-Dianping, ByteDance and others, are taking a leading position in the field.

What is *platformisation* exactly? Helmond (2015: 1) defines this as 'the rise of the platform as the dominant infrastructural and economic model of the social web'. Platformisation also entails the expansion of digital platforms into other spaces, including app ecosystems and other spheres (Nieborg and Poell, 2018). Third parties are increasingly investing in making their data platform-ready. To summarise, platformisation refers to an ecosystem that increasingly impacts society's social and economic developments. In this context, van Dijck et al. (2018: 4) talk about the *platform society*, which is 'a society in which social and economic traffic is increasingly channelled by an (overwhelmingly corporate) global online platform ecosystem that is driven by algorithms and fuelled by data'. With this conceptualisation, they ask questions about the values behind these platforms. This is part of a broader debate about public versus private values (Mansell and Steinmueller, 2020), which is critical because the boundaries between digital platforms and societal structures have become increasingly blurred (Couldry and Hepp, 2017).

From Platform Capitalism to AI Capitalism

The discussion about how the data economy is organised and the role of digital platforms allows us to move on to conceptualising *platform capitalism* itself. According to Srnicek (2017), the term refers to a new phase of capitalism, where – confronted with new technologies, new organisational forms, new modes of production and exploitation – the capitalist system aims to create a new way of accumulating capital. As I have discussed earlier, there is a central role in this for data: the collection and analysis of data and the extraction of value from that data are critical.

When Data and Platforms Meet: Platform Capitalism

The main characteristics of platform capitalism are:

- Instead of creating a new marketplace, platforms provide the primary (digital) infrastructure to bring together different user groups. The benefit is that the platform can position itself – as the middle man – between these users and their interactions happening on their platform, allowing them to benefit (capture, analyse data, etc.) from these interactions.
- Network effects are crucial in platform capitalism as platforms produce and rely on them. Network effects entail that more users on a specific platform

make the latter more valuable for everyone else. Network effects, in combination with data, result in a natural tendency for monopolisation (Moazed and Johnson, 2016; Moore and Tambini, 2018).

- Because of the crucial role of network effects, platforms need to develop specific strategies to attract users and keep them active on the platform. They do this by *cross-subsidisation*, meaning they reduce the price for one service (or make it free – as is the case on many platforms), which is then compensated by charging for other services (Srnicek, 2017).
- Given the crucial role of user interaction and engagement on the platform, it will do everything to keep appealing to its current users and try to grow its user base. It will do this by being creative and adjusting the platform architecture and rules and principles of user interaction.

What Is Data Capitalism, and How Is It Different?

Given the central role of data in this new type of capitalism, some experts rather talk about *(big) data capitalism* instead of platform capitalism. For example, Mayer-Schoenberger and Ramge (2018) herald a new phase in which capitalism is reinventing itself in the age of big data. They depict a very optimistic perspective in which what they call *data-rich markets* lead to a transformation of capitalism: 'A reboot of the market fuelled by data will lead to a fundamental reconfiguration of our economy, one that will be arguably as momentous as the Industrial Revolution, reinventing capitalism as we know it' (Mayer-Schoenberger and Ramge, 2018: 3–4). According to them, big data capitalism is improved and upgraded because data-rich markets are much better than traditional ones. Big data capitalism brings disruption, where firms must reinvent themselves to adapt to the new reality. However, new opportunities emerge, such as flexibility and efficiency. Mayer-Schoenberger and Ramge (2018) even predict that this will mean a move away from money and capital, which offers – according to them – an exceptional opportunity to improve the human ability to coordinate the economy and society at large.

Other scholars offer a less optimistic analysis than Mayer-Schoenberger and Ramge. Sarah Myers West (2019) researches the tech industry and provides a historical analysis of data capitalism. In her approach, she puts power central as she argues that data capitalism is a system in which the commodification of data leads to an asymmetrical power shift which benefits those who have access to and can make sense of data. Like Zuboff (2019), she analyses commercial surveillance, data tracking and mining and raises concerns about the power it gives to platforms and data companies. Sociologist Dave Beer (2019: 7) analyses big data capitalism and sees it as 'a form of capitalism that operates through, is informed by and relies upon data'. He develops the notion of *data gaze*. This refers to the specificity of data capitalism wherein humans are constantly watched over, are subjected to data accumulation and data-led thinking, and data increasingly determines how society is organised.

On the other hand, Fuchs is less convinced about the specific label of (big) *data capitalism*. He argues it is crucial to see capitalism as 'a complex unity of diverse dimensions of capitalism' (Fuchs, 2021: 51). He states that we should see big data not as the only dimension of capitalism and not ignore it nor overestimate its role. From his perspective, he explains how analysing capitalism should pay attention to the exploitation of the working class and digital labour. Big data plays a vital role but is not the dominant aspect. Other aspects that need to be included are the international division of labour, automation and increasing precariousness of labour.

The Future: Data or AI Capitalism?

Data commodification and extraction are central to this new phase of capitalism. Unlike Mayer-Schoenberger and Ramge (2018), Sadowski (2019) is not convinced that data capitalism means a move away from money and capital. On the contrary, he argues that data collection, analysis and extraction are at the core of capital accumulation. By understanding data as a form of capital, we can better understand the consequences of datafication. Let us go back to the role of data in data extraction:

- Data is often considered a raw material. The latter is *constant capital*, the economic value of the materials needed to produce commodities (Fuchs, 2020). Data companies use consumer data as raw material to produce various informational goods and services, what Zuboff (2019) calls *prediction products*.
- Data itself is also a commodity. It is the product of the digital labour of people engaging with applications and services offered by platforms. By engaging in the production and distribution of content on these platforms, their immaterial labour is turned into commodities, taking the form of different types of data (personal data, user-generated content and network data), which is sold to advertisers and data brokers (Fuchs, 2014a).

In addition to seeing data as a raw material or commodity, it makes sense to conceptualise it as a form of capital. Sadowski (2019) writes that data capital is institutionalised in the data collection, storage and processing infrastructure. Data capital is – in some circumstances – convertible into economic capital; as such, datafication adds new sources of value and new tools of accumulation. Sadowski (2019: 5–6) lists six distinctive ways in which value is created from data:

- 'Data is used to profile and target people'. This is linked to data mining and surveillance, where knowing about people results in profit and power.
- 'Data is used to optimise systems'. The second type of value creation is linked to efficiency and the idea that data analysis will allow increased productivity.

- 'Data is used to manage and control things'. This type of data collection can be used to support human decision-making and automated systems.
- 'Data is used to model probabilities'. In combination with powerful algorithms, data is the basis of prediction machines (Agrawal et al., 2018), which can be used for all forecasting applications.
- 'Data is used to build stuff.' Smart technologies are data-driven, and, as such, their performance is dependent on large amounts of data.
- 'Data is used to grow the value of assets'. Adding a layer of data increases the value of infrastructures and tools.

Value creation with data is linked to *artificial intelligence* applications. Let us make clear that data is a crucial resource for developing AI products and services, and it is not surprising that the largest platform companies are also leading the race for AI dominance. This is why some scholars prefer the term *AI capitalism* (Dyer-Witheford et al., 2019).

Given the centrality of data in digital capitalism and the power concentration this results in, one wonders what the future will look like and how we need to deal with this. Sadowski (2020) sees the combination of different strategies. At the core, he argues, is the importance of democratising innovation. This means that more people should be involved in how, why, and for what purposes technology is being developed. This entails two aspects. First, those affected (most) by technology should be allowed to participate in its creation. We need more diversity in the production of data-driven technologies. Second, there needs to be more openness to the opaque operations and processes at the core of intelligent systems. Frank Pasquale (2015) also argued for this in his book *The Black Box Society*, in which he scrutinised information asymmetries.

Of course, democratising innovation needs to be accompanied by other strategies dealing with issues such as the ownership and governance of intelligent systems, data access and sharing, etc.

Learning Takeaways

- Political economy is a framework that helps to understand the structures and regimes of ownership of media and communication systems.
- Commodification, extraction and exploitation are key characteristics of critical political economy.
- Economies of scale and network effects are important mechanisms to control the data economy.
- Different types of platforms exist, and they use different mechanisms to expand and control their markets.
- The biggest platforms are also frontrunners in data/AI capitalism.

Recommended Reading

Beer, D. (2018). *The Data Gaze: Capitalism, Power and Perception*. London: Sage.

Chandler, D. and Fuchs, C. (2019). *Digital Objects, Digital Subjects: Interdisciplinary Perspectives on Capitalism, Labour and Politics in the Age of Big Data*. London: University of Westminster Press.

Coyle, D., Diepeveen, S., Wdowin, J., Tennison, J., and Kay, L. (2020). The value of data. Policy Implications. Bennet Institute for Public Policy, University of Cambridge. https://www.bennettinstitute.cam.ac.uk/wp-content/uploads/2020/12/Value_of_data_Policy_Implications_Report_26_Feb_ok4noWn.pdf

Sadowski, J. (2020). *Too Smart: How Digital Capitalism is Extracting Data, Controlling Our Lives, and Taking Over the World*. Cambridge, MA: MIT Press.

West, S. M. (2019). Data capitalism: Redefining the logics of surveillance and privacy. *Business & Society*, 58(1), 20–41.

Recommended Listening

This Machine Kills, a podcast series about technology and political economy, hosted by Jathan Sadowski and Edward Ongweso Jr., produced by Jeremy Brown. https://soundcloud.com/thismachinekillspod

4

Data, Democracy and Politics

Learning Goals

- Position the role of data in holding power to account, public deliberation and electoral campaigns.
- Ask ourselves whether a networked democracy is putting our democracy in crisis.
- Understand how digital media are transforming political communication and the public sphere.
- Analyse the role of data in political campaigning.
- Envision the emancipatory potential of digital technologies and see the shifts from utopian thinking to more realistic and pragmatic expectations.

Data, the Crisis of Democracy and the End of the Public Sphere

Elon Musk, then the world's richest person, bought the social media platform Twitter (now known as X) in 2022. As an early investor in PayPal, CEO of Tesla and SpaceX, and co-founder of Neuralink and OpenAI, Musk finalised the Twitter purchase for $44 billion in October 2022. While Twitter is not the largest social media platform, its importance for news circulation, digital communication and political campaigning cannot be denied. Twitter radically changed the interactions between politicians, media and audiences, at least in the Western world. The fact that one of the wealthiest people in the world can buy one of the world's most important social media platforms is an astonishing observation and somewhat kills the myth that social media can serve as a public sphere.

The Promises and Challenges of a Networked Democracy

As (big) data is increasingly used for public participation, deliberation and political campaigning, we need to investigate the possibilities and limitations of data-driven digital platforms and their impact on politics.

Is Democracy in Crisis?

The question of whether our democracy is in crisis is a big one but also something that has been asked almost continuously in recent decades (Bennett and Pfetsch, 2018). According to media and democracy scholar Peter Dahlgren (2004), the combined influence of phenomena such as globalisation, the nation-state's changing role, and neoliberalism (which undermines the nation-state's autonomy) profoundly impacted our democracy.

Andrew Chadwick (2006) – who specialises in political communication – analysed the crisis of democracy and came up with several reasons that could explain this:

- We can notice a decreasing number of people participating in the democratic process and going out to vote.
- There is a fragmentation of the political landscape (except in the USA, with its system of two political parties).
- This fragmentation has coincided with the emergence of single-issue politics. Green parties, for example, positioned themselves around the topic of the (protection of the) environment.
- These *new* parties challenged *traditional* political parties and often plunged the latter into a crisis. These conventional parties face hard times with their catch-all ideologies, compared to the new and emerging political forces, which are mobilising around one (group of) theme(s).
- We can observe the professionalisation but also the mediatisation of politics. This *mediatisation* refers to political institutions being increasingly dependent on and shaped by the media.
- The professionalisation and mediatisation also contributed to changes in the finances of political parties, which led to a rise of cynicism and distrust towards political parties.

A common theme is the changes political communication has undergone, particularly the role of the media within them (Coleman and Blumler, 2009; Dahlgren, 2009). Without being an advocate for a media-centric approach to democracy and politics, we cannot ignore the influence of waves of technological development (and their impact on the media and communication systems) on our democracy, for better or for worse. This chapter focuses on the most recent wave of innovation: the role and influence of data and algorithms on politics and democracy. But before we discuss this, we need to look at the promises of networked democracy formulated during the emergence of the internet.

The Early Promises of a Networked Democracy

The uptake of the internet in the 1990s brought about high expectations. Howard Rheingold (1993) referred to the internet as a *democratising technology*. According to him (and other utopian writers at the time), the openness and direct character of communication of digital technologies would result in a revolution for political conversation and debate. The internet, because of its initially democratic and open structure, would facilitate and support deliberative conversation. Unlike the hierarchical model of traditional media – which is unidirectional and does not allow citizens to participate directly – the internet created new expectations for participation and engagement, both with politicians and among themselves. In summary, there was hope for a new and better political system and more democracy supported by digital technology.

The expectations of a better (networked) democracy, created by the emergence of the internet, deserve a bit more elaboration. Expectations existed around three aspects (Hague and Loader, 1999):

- Digital technology would create new opportunities for democratisation of information in production and distribution. The networked democracy would be an information democracy. Information can be freely shared and escape the power of corporate media. In addition, everyone could engage in what Manuel Castells (2009) calls *mass self-communication*. This is the use of digital media – by ordinary users (self-directed, self-selected and self-defined) – to create and share content, potentially reaching a global audience.
- There would be a democratisation of decision-making power and new possibilities for active participation by citizens: facilitated by the availability of information, citizens can be consulted, and representative democracy could even be replaced by direct democracy. Increased opportunities for participation also allow the formation of new interest groups and the mobilisation of people around them.
- The internet would also offer more to facilitate online discussion and deliberation about essential topics relevant to society. This environment would facilitate freedom of speech and association. More opportunities for deliberation also create new expectations for the emergence of a new public sphere (Habermas, 1962/1989; Dahlberg, 2001).

These ideas of a networked democracy are another example of the discourse of technological determinism. Therefore, let us look at the challenges of these ideals.

Then Came the Challenges of a Networked Democracy

The question, of course, is whether these ideals can be realised. This asks for a critique of what Manuel Castells called *informational politics*, a concept similar to networked democracy. In his work, *The Rise of the Network Society* (Vol. 1), Castells (1996) argued that the power of networks and the free flow of information would result in a new type of politics, which is simultaneously decentralised, global and driven by citizens rather than politicians. So, what are the challenges of discourses of a networked democracy or information politics?

We need to question the ability of the internet and other digital technologies to facilitate deliberation. Albrecht (2006), for example, conducted a large-scale study on online deliberation and concluded that optimistic and sceptical perspectives must be contested. Questions need to be asked about the precise influence of technology and the role of individual actors in this.

Additionally, there is the risk of fragmentation of the public. The idea of an all-inclusive, consensus-seeking rational deliberation ignores the tendency of polarisation and the emergence of inter-groups, characterising the digital sphere (Dahlberg, 2007).

In the context of politics or beyond that, we have witnessed how this plays out with the intense polarisation that emerged, for example, around the EU referendum in the UK (the Remain versus Leave camps) and the Covid-19 pandemic (with heated debates between those for and against lockdown and vaccination).

Another aspect relates to the quality of information circulated via digital media. The anonymity of the internet has a shadow side in the sense that questions need to be asked about the accuracy and credibility of information available online. This coincides with the rise of the *infodemic*, a portmanteau of information and epidemic, referring to the rapid spread of accurate and inaccurate information, particularly in the context of pandemics such as SARS and Covid-19.

Several aspects mentioned here touch upon the digital divide problem and the question of who in society can participate in the networked democracy. Here we can point to the unequal access of people to digital technology, but also – and mainly – inequalities that exist in terms of the skills and literacy needed to produce, evaluate and circulate digital content.

Can We Look Ahead to Freedom and Empowerment?

The emergence of the internet coincided with utopian visions about a digital sphere that supports a better democracy or aims to solve its crisis. Cyberspace combines scientific and military developments with counterculture ideas about a new type of society, with virtual communities offering freedom and facilitating empowerment. However, the so-called *Web 1.0* (roughly from 1991 to 2004) mainly consisted of static webpages, in which internet users were passive consumers. This changed with the emergence of *Web 2.0* (and social media platforms), which embraced the idea of the web as a platform (O'Reilly, 2007) and made users active in content creation and distribution (user-generated content). In 2021, the idea of *Web3* (also *Web 3.0*) gained popularity. The term was coined in 2014 by Gavin Wood, a co-founder of Ethereum (a decentralised, open-source blockchain technology). In essence, Web3 criticises how *big tech* has centralised the ownership of data and content, and, in response to this, Web3 propagates the idea of decentralisation, where users can (re)claim the ownership of and control over their data. While Web3 attracted much attention (for a short while) from venture capital firms, the hype seems to have disappeared again.

The Democratic Role of the Media

Having discussed the crisis of democracy, we now need to shift the focus to the complex role of the media in politics. Think, for example, how the shift from mass media to social media has enormously impacted how election campaigns are organised and how media, political and citizen actors engage in this (Larsson and Moe, 2012; D'heer and Verdegem, 2014). But equally importantly, there is also the effect of politics on the media. In this context, scholars often distinguish different categories in the media sphere: news production, content and audiences (Oates, 2008). News production considers the context in which media output is produced, which is impacted by the media landscape, ownership structures, regulations, etc. Content refers to what messages are being circulated and how they are framed (and what influences exist). Audiences focus on the reception of media output and how different categories of audience react to it.

Introducing Power and the Struggle for Resources

The complex relationship between media and politics is determined by power. In simple terms, *power* refers to the capacity of actors to make decisions and realise their will against the will of others.

Sociologist John Thompson (1995) distinguishes four types of power:

- *Coercive* power refers to preventing others from acting in a certain way.
- *Economic* power is related to how specific individuals or groups in society can accumulate resources for productive activity.
- *Political* power is about the authority to coordinate individuals and their interactions.
- *Symbolic* power refers to meaning-making and influencing the actions of others.

In this way, social relationships between people and groups are characterised by struggles over material, economic, political, symbolic and cultural resources (Carah and Louw, 2015).

What do power and struggles over resources have to do with media? Ultimately, media and culture produce meaning, which refers to how we make sense of the world, ourselves and others. Power plays a crucial role in controlling meaning.

To better understand this type of symbolic power, we must introduce three concepts: ideology, hegemony and discourse.

- *Ideology* is – like power – a contested concept. Ideology can have a neutral meaning and refer to the world-views and ideas upon which people act and make decisions. Marxist scholars, however, see ideology as 'the process of the production of false consciousness' (Fuchs, 2020: 180). In that sense, ideology is used to serve the material interests of the ruling class.
- *Hegemony* is a concept popularised by Antonio Gramsci. It is 'a cultural condition where a particular way of life and its associated ideas, identities and meanings, are accepted as common sense by a population' (Carah and Low, 2015: 4). Hegemony thus describes the cultural dominance of a ruling class, which compels the subordination of other groups in society.
- *Discourse* is the vehicle through which ideologies and hegemonies are produced. It refers to a system of thoughts, knowledge or communication that constructs our world experience; it informs a society's rules, procedures, practices and institutions (van Dijk, 2008).

The Impact of Media on Democracy

The impact of media and communications on democracy is part of a long history (Curran, 2011). Elihu Katz (1996) argued that media and communications weaken the foundations of liberal democracy. He saw three main reasons for this. His first reason was that, with the declining influence of mass media, the public has become more fragmented, and, as such, people are less connected to each other. His second explanation was the diminishing role of *public service broadcasting*. A result of this was that people were more entertained but less informed. His third argument was that the declining role of the nation-state, under the influence of globalisation and neoliberalism, weakened national identities. Although much empirical data supports this position, we must also see the nuance of different media systems and political contexts. However, it begs the question, what exactly is the democratic role of the media?

Curran (2002) distinguishes three specific roles for the media in democracy:

- *The media as a watchdog.* In traditional liberal theory, an important role is foreseen for the press to monitor and check on the state and shield citizens from abusing its power. This watchdog role is why the media are called the *fourth estate*, referring to the old European concept of the three estates of the realm (the clergy, the nobility and the commoners). It symbolises the power of the press and media in its direct and indirect role in influencing the political system. The watchdog role is considered the most important of all media functions.

- *Providing information and facilitating debate.* Whereas the first role is somewhat defensive (i.e., protecting the public), this role refers to how media facilitate the functioning of a democracy. Indeed, the media are tasked to brief the people on what is happening in the world and to enable them to exercise their responsibilities as informed citizens and engage in the affairs of their community. The liberal view is that this is best achieved through the free market, where independent media provide a forum to the public.
- *Acting as the voice of the people.* This is the next step after informing the public: the media have a responsibility to offer a platform for different points of view and provide a forum for the expression and exchange of opinion. Ultimately, this is the basis of the formation of public opinion.

Of course, these democratic media roles must be revisited in the era of social media, big data and AI. The following sections will each look deeper into this, consider the impact of data for monitoring power, the potential and limitations of the datafied public sphere, and analyse data-driven campaigning and elections.

Data as Watchdog? or a Watchdog for Data?

The watchdog role is central to liberal media theory. This theory posits that news media should be free to report on societal issues. This is necessary for holding power to account and maintaining a liberal society. Furthermore, this theory believes that free reporting can best be guaranteed by the free market, ensuring independence from government (Curran, 2002). The belief was that once the media and their functioning become subject to intervention from the state (e.g., by media regulation) they would lose their ability to maintain their role as a watchdog. The watchdog role of the media needs to be scrutinised in terms of two aspects:

- How relevant is it still in a completely transformed society where the relationships among media, politicians and citizens have shifted massively due to new developments?
- How should we evaluate the belief that holding power to account can only be guaranteed by the free market?

Challenging the Watchdog Role of the Media

First, the relevance of the watchdog role for the media can be challenged by arguing that contemporary media systems are entirely different compared to the situation of the press when liberal media theory was developed. Waves of innovation, including the internet, social media, mobile media, data and AI, have led to a different landscape, challenging the old-school media watchdog function. Furthermore, empirical data (e.g., Bennett et al., 2007) has shown that the press has struggled to live up to this idealised role because much of its focus has shifted from information to entertainment. The latter can be explained by an increasing commodification of media and news (Hardy, 2014). The datafication of society creates new challenges for citizenship (Hintz et al., 2019), and, as a consequence, the role and impact of media have changed too.

Second, the watchdog perspective can be criticised based on the belief in and dependence on the free market. The free market ideal must be challenged, as market freedom cannot be equated with independence from power. Indeed, the press and news media sector itself have long become part of conglomerates, competing for the attention of audiences and advertisers, and have evolved into large and influential corporations (Bagdikian, 2004). The media have become *big business* themselves, which makes it hard to defend the position that they are less vigilant to corporate power than abuse of state power (McChesney, 2015).

Holding Data and Power to Account

Zooming in on the datafied society, the question is how data and power can be held accountable. In this context, I discuss two relevant cases in terms of misuse of data: the Snowden revelations and Cambridge Analytica.

Edward Snowden, an American computer intelligence consultant working as an employee and contractor for the US National Security Agency (NSA) and the UK Government Communications Headquarters (GCHQ), started disclosing secrets about global surveillance programmes in 2013. He gradually became disillusioned with the programs he was working on regarding the widespread data collection of ordinary citizens. With the help of journalists Glenn Greenwald, Laura Poitras and Ewen MacAskill, Snowden started to reveal classified documents about secret surveillance programmes.

The Snowden revelations have been published in news outlets such as the *Guardian*, the *Washington Post*, *Der Spiegel* and the *New York Times*. These revelations highlighted the unprecedented extent to which our activities on digital platforms are tracked, monitored, analysed and stored by state agencies, as well as the extensive (big) data gathering by social media companies (Lyon, 2014). Particularly interesting is that Snowden revealed to the world how intelligence agencies collect and intercept data from internet and communication infrastructures and the servers from tech companies such as Apple, Google and Facebook, sometimes with their consent (Hintz et al., 2019). To summarise, the Snowden leaks provide us with unprecedented insights into how widespread data collection and analysis are in contemporary societies and how important it is to think about how to fight back.

A second case that shocked the world about the impact of data on democracy is the Cambridge Analytica scandal. In 2018 the *Guardian* reported on attempts to manipulate elections via psychographic profiles created by using Facebook data, collected and analysed without users' consent (Hu, 2020). The scandal was revealed by Christopher Wylie, a whistleblower working for Cambridge Analytica and its parent company, Strategic Communication Laboratories. By scraping the data of an estimated 87 million Facebook users who have filled out a questionnaire on a personality profiling app created by Aleksandr Kogan (who was working at the University of Cambridge), data points were collected to target voters in elections. Cambridge Analytica had used these data points to influence individual voting behaviour in the 2016 US presidential election and the 2016 EU referendum in the UK. Cambridge Analytica is another case warning us about the widespread surveillance culture and the practice of violating individuals' privacy by collecting big data as input for targeting ads in election campaigns (Fuchs, 2021).

Using Data for Scrutiny and Government Accountability

The Covid-19 pandemic has raised questions about media scrutiny and government accountability. A poll organised by *Press Gazette* said that journalists had not properly held the UK government to account during the daily Covid-19 press briefings in 2020–2021. During lockdowns in that period, the UK parliament was shut down to curb the spread of the virus. As such, it was left to journalists to be the only real opposition to the government. Of course, in the case of the UK, the specific media landscape and the close relationships between elite journalists in Westminster and the government need to be considered. But it says something about media power (e.g., the power of the Murdoch family in the UK, Australia and the USA) failing to hold power to account. In addition, media watchdog *Reporters Without Borders* warned that the coronavirus pandemic threatened press freedom worldwide. They said that several governments had used the health crisis as an excuse to take advantage of politics, which was on hold, and the public was distracted and could not organise or protest as in regular times.

To end this section on a more positive note, there is potential for data to hold power to account and offer new opportunities for journalism. There Is great potential for data journalism and using data and AI for investigative journalism.

The (Datafied) Public Sphere

In addition to functioning as a watchdog and holding power to account, the media play a crucial role in providing information and facilitating debate about what is happening in the world. This is important for democracy, too, as people need to be informed if they want to engage in their community and society at large. The work of Jürgen Habermas is central to this. As a prominent member of the Frankfurt

School, his name is connected to the concept of the public sphere. Notably, his work *The Structural Transformation of the Public Sphere* (1962/1989) has influenced numerous studies about the role of the media in democracy, which received renewed attention with the emergence of social media.

What Is the Public Sphere?

It is essential to acknowledge that Habermas's thinking about the public sphere is grounded in Marxian political theory. Inspired by discussions happening in coffee houses in Great Britain and France in the seventeenth and eighteenth centuries, Habermas sketched a model of the *bourgeois public sphere* and then analysed its degeneration in the twentieth century (Calhoun, 1993). The public sphere is a society that engages in critical public debate and sits between the private sphere and public authority. According to Habermas (1962/1989), the *public sphere* has the following conditions:

- It is focused on the formation of public opinion.
- All citizens should have access to the public sphere.
- Citizens should be able to gather unrestrictedly (thereby allowing freedom of speech, assembly, etc. – free from economic and political control) to discuss matters of general interest.
- The public sphere enables debate over the principles of governing social relations.

Habermas argued that private property, influence and skills are crucial for individuals to be heard in the public sphere. As a result, individuals and groups in society who lack this are excluded. The public sphere is thus 'not a true public sphere, but a class-structured political space; it is colonised and feudalised' (Fuchs, 2020: 207). Habermas's public sphere concept has been criticised as not reflecting the interests of the working class. At the same time, the feminist critique positions the public sphere (dominated by educated, wealthy men) in contrast to the private sphere (dominated by women). It is also criticised because of its roots in Western Enlightenment, contributing to cultural imperialism (Fuchs, 2021). While this criticism is valid, Habermas's concept of the public sphere should be seen as an immanent critique rather than an ideal type. As such, it poses questions about how media and communication systems could facilitate a public sphere. In this context, one needs to examine the political economy of media and communication systems and how political communication is organised.

Habermas titled his work *Structural Transformation* as he referred to the degeneration of the public sphere. This degeneration is linked to the rise and transformation of the modern state and capitalist economic production (Calhoun, 1993). Public information became the subject of commodification and media that of market economies. However, the emergence of the internet and later social media provided new perspectives in which the concept of the public sphere became more prominent again.

The Potential and Limits of the Internet as a Public Sphere

Utopian discourses surrounding the internet and later social media argue that people would have better access to political information and more possibilities for self-publication. Simultaneously, anonymity and equality among participants would result in freedom of speech and association (Rheingold, 1993). However, inequalities in access to information and the fragmentation of political discourses also pose severe limitations to the virtual sphere (Papacharissi, 2002).

Dahlberg (1998, 2001) has written extensively about the limitations of the internet to serve as a public sphere. He offers a critique on different levels. First, he points to the increased commercialisation and commodification of the internet, which undermines the condition of being free from corporate control. However, autonomy from state power is challenging, given internet censorship practices and widespread surveillance in large parts of the world. Second, there is the question of whether the rhythm of computer-mediated communication allows rational and dialogical conversation as required within the public sphere. Third, the pace of online communication also jeopardises possibilities for reflexivity. This is challenging in the digital sphere as contributions must be short and often asynchronous. Another aspect deals with people's roles in the virtual world and whether this results in a lack of engagement. Serious questions about productive deliberation in online spaces need to be asked. The latter aspect also feeds into verification problems, meaning that discursive participants must sincerely try to make known relevant information and intentions. Finally, there is a lack of discursive equality and inclusion in the online world. Social inequalities and cultural differences outside cyberspace inhibit online discourses. A particular problem related to the internet and social media is that some participants can make their voices heard more often than others.

In response to the above-discussed limitations, Benkler (2006) argues that, for a *networked public sphere* to function genuinely, it must be organised as follows:

- It should allow universal intake: everyone who wants to contribute should be able to be heard.
- Discussion topics should be filtered for potential political relevance and accreditation; only credible and relevant issues should be selected.
- There should be a system that facilitates synthesis for public opinion: more than the voice of one individual or group.
- The public sphere should be independent of government control.

The question remains: how do we realise this within media and political communication?

Following Habermas' ideas, Fuchs (2021: 213–214) argues that for the internet or social media to be considered a public sphere, one must analyse the political economy of mediated communication and political communication. First, when it comes to the political economy of communication, questions need to be asked concerning ownership (who owns the media organisation and its resources?), censorship (is there political and economic censorship?), exclusion (which viewpoints from elites/ruling classes are overrepresented, and are critical viewpoints present?), and political content production (who can produce political content and how visible, relevant and influential is it?).

Second, when analysing political communication, three aspects need to be scrutinised: universal access (how relevant is political communication and who can access it?), independence (how independent are sites of political communication from economic and state interests?) and quality of political discussion (how sincere, reflexive and inclusive is the political discussion?).

The Datafied Public Sphere

Within algorithmic culture and social media logic, data and algorithms interact to present content to users. The drive for personalisation is behind the social media logic (i.e., offering users a customised media experience). This has implications for the public sphere. Schaefer (2016) states that the datafication of society affects the public sphere as much as it affects our consumption behaviour. A datafied public sphere changes the practices of civic action, political debate and opinion polling. As a result, our understanding of the public sphere, citizenship, democracy and public space is fundamentally transformed in the era of datafication.

If the *filter bubble* concept coined by Eli Pariser (2011) explains how algorithms select what we are exposed to, the *echo chamber* (Sunstein, 2009) is a metaphor for describing a situation where only certain beliefs, ideas or information are shared. As with the filter bubble, there are questions about its existence and impact. Dubois and Blank (2018), for example, concluded the effect of the echo chamber is overstated. However, we should not be blind to the role of algorithms and data in the public sphere. Bunz (2014) argues that digital media has specific functions for the public sphere: a democratising effect in the sense of opening up alternative channels for the public; and allowing alternative opinions to be voiced.

However, we should not forget that this has a shadow side in that when people can be reached more, there is an increased risk of surveillance, too. Kaluža (2022) argues that algorithmic personalisation can lead to the public sphere's fragmentation, polarisation and radicalisation. One of the negative impacts of this is that, as Gurumurthy (2018) states, people have more opportunities to use their voices. Still, they have less agency in being heard and engaging in communicative citizenship, which damages society.

Data-Driven Campaigning and Elections

In addition to being a watchdog, providing information and facilitating debate, there is a third central role of (digital) media in democracy: acting as the voice of the people (Curran, 2002). Capturing and communicating the people's voice is facilitated through different organisational forms, techniques, genres and opportunities for political participation and engagement (Albrecht, 2006; Coleman and Blumler, 2009). While the internet and platforms offer an unprecedented opportunity for people to access helpful information and engage in civic activities, there are challenges and limitations to fully benefiting from this potential.

Participation and Engagement in the Digital Era

Where social media are the most popular contemporary spaces for political participation and engagement, there is a notable shift in our understanding of the role of digital technology and platforms in democracy. The scholarship around this topic has significantly shifted our thinking about participation in the digital era. For example, multiple studies looked at electoral campaigns (see, for example, Anstead and Chadwick, 2009; Kreiss, 2012; Bruns et al., 2016) and protest and social movements (see, for example, Howard and Hussain, 2011; Papacharissi and de Fatima Oliveira, 2012; Poell, 2014). However, there are also studies scrutinising the emancipatory role of digital media, the imposition of restrictions on platforms, and the increased role of censorship and surveillance (Morozov, 2011). The role of social media in the EU referendum in the UK (see, for example, Bastos and Mercea, 2019; Šimunjak, 2022) and the election of Donald Trump in the USA (see, for example, Enli, 2017; Kreiss and McGregor, 2018), as well as the involvement of Cambridge Analytica in this, are some of the most prolific studies in this context.

However, it is essential not to forget that social media platforms are not separate entities (Gurevitch et al., 2009). They are part of a more extensive media system influenced by many elements. Some people make the distinction between *old* media (mainstream media) and *new* (digital/social) media, but studies that examined this conclude that often the most powerful voices in digital media and mainstream media are not that different (Margolis and Resnick, 2000). Andrew Chadwick (2013) also discussed this in *The Hybrid Media System*. In this book, he explores the hybridity and blurring of boundaries between the two categories. He compares:

- Types of media (older versus newer media)
- Media production and distribution (amateur versus professional)
- Voices (official versus informal, broadcast versus conversational)
- Regulations (which are much more complicated for new and emerging media platforms)
- The speed and temporality of the news cycle (the news cycle of digital and social media is much more intense, which asks questions about its potential for deliberation, participation and engagement).

Although *hybridity* is interesting for theoretical and empirical purposes, Chadwick (2103) argues that it is not unique to the digital era and has always been a feature of media systems; they do not replace other media formats but rather complement them.

The Dynamics of Digital Campaigning

The question is how this plays out in contemporary political communication and campaigning and what dynamics are at play here.

First, a notion often mentioned in this context is *identity politics*. In short, this concept refers to a political approach whereby people of a particular gender, race, religion, social class and background, environment and other identifying factors develop certain political agendas based on these identities (Fukuyama, 2018). While the concept has been around for a while, it received renewed attention with the emergence of right-wing authoritarian leaders such as Trump (USA), Putin (Russia), Modi (India) and Orban (Hungary).

Second, identity politics is influenced by the increasingly important role of emotions in politics. Zizi Papacharissi (2015) wrote in her book *Affective Publics* about how combining sentiment, technology and politics leads to a new era. She defines *affective publics* as: 'publics that have been transformed by networked technologies to suggest both spaces for the interaction of people, technology, and practices and the imagined collective that evolves out of this interaction' (Papacharissi, 2015: 125–126). In this book, she analyses the impact of affective publics on the digital footprint, collective action, expression, disruption of political narratives and power.

Third, identity politics and affective publics influence how political messages and stories are designed and distributed. This coincides with the increasing importance of digital storytelling in promoting a specific message to certain target audiences (Couldry, 2008). Digital storytelling links to *mediatisation*, a term used to refer to how media shape and frame the processes and discourses of political communication.

Finally, the power of social media platforms impacts how messages are produced and circulated among audiences. Nielsen and Ganter (2022) argue that platform companies are powerful in three different ways:

- They have hard economic and political power that they can use to influence or prevent certain decisions.
- They exercise soft forms of cultural power that work through attraction and co-opting more than economic or political force.
- Technology companies can exercise certain forms of platform power that publishers and other media organisations cannot.

As such, *platform power* entails the power to set standards, the power to make and break connections, the power of automated action at scale, the power of information asymmetry, and the power to operate across domains.

What is the impact of this? The combined influence of these tendencies opens up important questions about whether digital platforms have their own logic and whether they support collective or connective action (Bennett and Segerberg, 2013). We must also reflect on how crowds and movements are precisely organised and what dynamics are at play (Della Porta, 2015). This new reality invites us to ask questions about the role of affordances of digital platforms and whether we – as citizens involved in democratic processes – are members or followers of these organisations and movements.

Data/Analytic Activism

The campaign to elect President Obama in the USA is often considered a pivotal moment of change in political campaigning. According to communication scholar Daniel Kreiss, the Obama campaign was the prototype of how to win election campaigns that are built around technology. Kreiss (2016) titled his book *Prototype Politics*, in which he analysed *prototype campaigning*. This term refers not only to the emergence of new platforms but also to innovation in the backstage infrastructure: this is where data is collected, assembled, and analysed to develop a strategy for strategic message dissemination, fundraising and media buying.

Kreiss (2016) explains in his book how the combination of network folding and prototyping is crucial in this new type of campaigning:

- *Network folding* describes how and the extent to which professional political networks intersect with professional networks from other areas, such as software development and data analysis.
- *Prototyping*, the constant testing and refining of approaches in electoral campaigning, plays a central role in the innovation processes of political parties.

Data analytics, in particular, is employed to identify well-connected political supporters and use them as advocates to target harder-to-reach voters. However, there are weaknesses in data capture and analytics processes, too: the supporting infrastructure (technologies, knowledge and practices within the organisation) and an extensive network are crucial for the success of prototype politics.

Media and politics professor David Karpf (2012, 2016) has written two books on strategic communication practices and the specific role of internet-related strategies. His book *Analytic Activism: Digital Listening and the New Political Strategy* (2016) explains how the most critical impact of digital technology is not in its capacity for disorganised masses to speak more easily but instead in (civil society and other) organisations listening more effectively. *Analytic activism* refers to three principal developments:

- It embraces a culture of testing about what works and what does not work to guide strategy and practice. This testing culture uses *A/B testing* (or split-run testing), a user-experience research methodology. The relative efficacy of the two designs can be measured by randomly serving visitors two versions of, for example, a website that differs only in the design of a single button element. Karpf (2016) demonstrates how the Obama campaign used A/B testing to gather online traction and understand what voters wanted to see from the presidential candidates. Through A/B testing, staffers were able to determine how to draw in voters and generate additional interest effectively. Data is crucial to be able to perform A/B testing effectively.

- Analytic activism prioritises listening through social media, email and other applications. This can vary from relatively passive mining of metadata to more active seeking and guiding of feedback, although it rarely involves actual two-way conversation. The choice of the word *listening* implies that activist groups want to hear and actively seek to understand and learn from these different signals.
- Crucial in successfully conducting (A/B) testing and listening is a communicative scale. Organisations with large numbers and information about their members (e.g., member lists with personal data) can test more frequently and precisely. Karpf (2016) concludes that analytical activism is a tool for large, established advocacy groups instead of smaller bottom-up connective and crowd-enabled movements. Despite the potential of testing and listening, he also warns about what he calls the *analytics frontier*: the risk that the availability of digital trace data comes to shape the mission and vision of organisations, who should be cautious about this and reflect upon it.

Corrupting the Cyber-Commons?

Reflecting on the critical role of data in digital politics, Gunitsky (2015) wrote an essay entitled 'Corrupting the Cyber-Commons: Social Media as a Tool of Autocratic Stability'. In this piece, he analyses how social media are increasingly used to undermine political opposition, shape public discussion, and cheaply gather information about falsified public preferences. His analysis is based on case studies in China, Russia and the Middle East, where non-democratic regimes have moved beyond merely suppressing online discourses and are shifting towards proactively subverting and co-opting social media for their purposes. Social media thus become not simply an obstacle to autocratic rule but another potential tool for regime durability. Gunitsky (2015) lays out four mechanisms that link social media co-optation to authoritarian resilience:

- *Counter-mobilisation* refers to regimes using digital technology to organise and rally their domestic allies.
- Incumbent rulers can use social media for *discourse framing* (e.g., disseminating propaganda).
- *Preference divulgence* means that autocrats use social media to reveal (in the absence of legitimate elections) information about the strength and identity of their supporters.
- Social media can be used for *elite coordination* (e.g., by sharing information about corruption to inform central elites about the effectiveness of local elites).

In sum, this illustrates the rapid evolution of government social media strategies, which has critical consequences for the future of electoral democracy and state–society relations.

Reality Check: Politics as Usual?

From the high expectations of cyber-democracy to the discussion of corrupting the cyber-commons, it is clear that we have gone through a journey when looking at the impact of digital technology on political communication, campaigning and democracy. First, we must ask ourselves whether increased engagement is always good for democracy. Yes, digital media provide more people more space for participation, people's voices can be amplified, etc. But we need to critically reflect on the assumption that behaviour on social media is always progressive. Even more, we need to ask what has been realised of the radical beliefs associated with digital technology, particularly about the *revolutionary change* it was supposed to bring about.

In this context, we can refer to Resnick (1998), who proposed the *normalisation of cyberspace* thesis. At that time of writing, the dominant discourse surrounding the internet was hope and utopian thinking about its emancipatory potential. However, upon reflection, the realisation came that – with more people and stakeholders entering cyberspace – this would increasingly become a mirror of the offline reality. As such, the traditional power bases in the offline world also started to dominate the online spaces. This became the title of a new book about the cyberspace revolution: *Politics as Usual* (Margolis and Resnick, 2000), a way of thinking about digital technology's change to our democracy. How the story will further unfold remains to be seen.

Learning Takeaways

- High expectations exist of a networked democracy, although it remains to be seen whether it can solve the crisis of democracy.
- Data can be used to hold power to account.
- The datafied public sphere has both potential and limits.
- Participation and engagement are crucial for data-driven election campaigns.
- Data analytics has installed a culture of testing in contemporary campaigning.

Recommended Reading

Fischli, R. (2022). Data-owning democracy: Citizen empowerment through data ownership. *European Journal of Political Theory*. https://doi.org/10.1177/14748851221110316

Macnish, K. and Galliott, J. (2020). *Big Data and Democracy*. Edinburgh: Edinburgh University Press.

Papachararissi, Z. (2021). *After Democracy: Imagining Our Political Future*. New Haven & London: Yale University Press.

Šimunjak, M. (2022). *Tweeting Brexit: Social Media and the Aftermath of the EU Referendum*. Abingdon: Routledge.

Woolley, S.C. and Howard, P.N. (2018). *Computational Propaganda: Political Parties, Politicians, and Political Manipulation on Social Media*. New York: Oxford University Press.

Recommended Listening

Social Media and Politics, a popular science podcast about how social media change the political game, hosted by Michael Bossetta. https://socialmediaandpolitics.org/

5

Data, Identity and Subjectivity

Learning Goals

- Understand the concept of identity and how data and algorithms increasingly shape our digital selves.
- Recognise algorithmic identities and ask ourselves whether we should be worried about profiling.
- Explore how data and algorithms change surveillance.
- Define algorithmic citizenship, reflecting on the challenges datafication poses for governance and regulation.

Datafied Identities in a Pandemic

The Covid-19 pandemic significantly impacted how teaching was organised in lockdowns, how companies and government organisations had to rethink their plans about employees working from home, how international travel was suspended for a while, etc. Another substantial impact of the health crisis was that several countries set up new systems of monitoring their citizens. For example, applications that track with whom you have been in contact after a positive test (also called *contact tracing*), systems that allow or deny citizens entry to venues, the possibility to travel (the so-called *Covid-pass*), etc., have suddenly become commonplace. While there is an argument for using these systems to keep society healthy and safe, especially with an airborne virus that spreads quickly, it also raises questions about what happens with the data when you check into a venue with your Covid-19 app, as well as who can monitor where you have been and with whom you have been in touch, and how accurate these systems are.

How Data and Algorithms Are Impacting Our Identities

This chapter helps you to think about these questions and discusses identity and subjectivity concerning data and algorithms. How we develop our identities on social media platforms is not a new question. Still, figuring out how our identities are shaped in a complex interplay between data and algorithms becomes more interesting and complex. You will learn more about algorithmic identities, digital/data selves and how datafication has intensified surveillance practices, resulting in *dataveillance*. This helps you think about how citizenship is changing in the data era and what opportunities and challenges this creates for governance and regulation.

Identity Singular or Identities Plural?

Thanks to René Descartes, a French philosopher, scientist and mathematician, human beings are considered subjects. His famous Latin aphorism *cogito ergo sum* – translated as 'I think, therefore I am' – led to the common understanding that humans should be recognised as sapient beings, conscious of their existence and selfhood. Descartes asserted that thinking about and doubting one's existence was proof of the presence of a mind, a thinking entity. In the internet era, the famous quote transformed into *blogito ergo sum*, or 'I blog, therefore I am'. The fact that we use weblogs – or posts on other social media platforms – to express ourselves is central to the debate about identity, who we are and how we present ourselves to the world. Digital platforms offer the ability to communicate and interact with the outside world. In this way, as Marshall McLuhan (1964) famously said, 'The medium is the message' – digital media enable interaction and identity construction in ways that traditional media did not support.

But what exactly do we mean by *identity*, or should we instead talk about *identities*? It is a concept with different meanings according to specific disciplines. In social psychology, identity deals with the question, 'who am I?'. Tajfel and Turner (1986) developed the *social identity theory*, suggesting a difference between personal and social identities. The former refers to identities based on our individual personality and interpersonal relationships. At the same time, the latter means that our (collective) identities are determined by the membership of certain social groups, for example, gender and racial identities. There are three mechanisms at play within the social identity theory:

- Identity is constructed based on group affiliation.
- Most people strive towards developing a positive social identity.
- A positive identity is often associated with positive attitudes towards the *in-group* (us) and negative attitudes towards the *out-group* (others).

This *us versus them* attitude is integral to identity construction and plays a particular role in the data-saturated media landscape. It is one of the reasons why social media contributes to polarisation, which seriously impacts our democracy. It also illustrates the normative aspect of identities as their evaluation accompanies them. And most importantly, there are severe psycho-social consequences related to this evaluation. Think, for example, about the pressures on girls and boys to meet specific beauty standards, which are often fortified by social media and their celebrities.

Identity and Performance

What digital media and platforms offer is the ability to *play* with our identities, an expression of our self (Papacharissi, 2010). This concept is linked to but slightly different from identity. Based on the social identity theory mentioned in the previous section, *identity* can refer to the social face – how one perceives others perceive one. *Self* often deals with one's sense of 'who and what I am'. Most importantly, these are not dualistic constructs; the self is expressed as a fluid abstraction. This happens within different political, economic, social and cultural contexts. What is interesting is that technology provides the stage for interaction with different and diverse audiences.

The *New Yorker* magazine famously depicted in 1993 two dogs in front of a computer with the caption, 'On the internet, nobody knows you're a dog'. This cartoon refers to the moment that the internet, as a new technology, could be used for something different than what engineers, developers and academics imagined. The disconnect between *real* and *virtual* identities was crucial to early online interaction interpretations. The main idea is that when digital media users leave their *physical* bodies behind, they can choose and construct their *online* identity. This allows us to escape certain expectations and norms linked to our offline selves. While the depiction of online selves or *avatars* seems related to early online environments such as *Second Life*, they are back in a new shape in the push by Facebook/Meta and its *Metaverse* development.

In the 1950s, Sociologist Erving Goffman wrote the book *The Presentation of Self in Everyday Life* (1956). Several decades later, his insights were rediscovered to study identity and performance in the era of social media. In essence, Goffman analyses self-presentation as a performance. He argues that social interaction is similar to a performance on the stage in front of an audience. This performance/stage can be seen as a *mask*, whereby every individual has multiple faces/masks that can change according to different situations and contexts. For example, I will present myself differently in front of my students than when I am in the company of friends and family. This is a self-presentation whereby most people strive to offer their best selves and please their audience. The performance/stage metaphor helps as the backstage is where we can be our true selves, in hidden or private spaces, liberated from societal pressures (Goffman, 1956). It offers a space for freedom and experimentation (e.g., with gender or relationships).

Identity and Modernity

Anthony Giddens, a sociologist primarily known for his *structuration theory*, wrote about identity in the context of modernity (Giddens, 1984). His structuration theory is an attempt to overcome the dichotomy between *structure* (how our society is organised and what societal structures determine everyday life) and *agency* (the possibility of individuals acting and living according to their wants/needs). This theory is a relational approach, connecting structure and agency and thereby integrating micro and macro levels of analysis, combining objectivity and subjectivity. Giddens (1984) argues that societal structures result from continuous repetition of the behaviour of individual beings within a particular context, with its norms and laws. Giddens and fellow sociologists Ulrich Beck and Scott Lash also introduced the notion of *reflexive modernity* (Beck et al., 1994). This refers to a modernisation process whereby norms and laws are changing and evaluated. This happens through *reflexive feedback*. Reflexive modernity is an attempt to counterbalance the idea of the postmodern society. Beck et al. wrote about realising new ideals and how societal institutes (e.g., states) can deal with economic and cultural globalisation (neoliberalism and the shift from the collective to the individual within it).

What is the role of identity in this? Giddens (1991) connected the formation and expression of identities with processes of modernity. He argues that identities are dynamic and subject to constant change and development – similar to Bauman (2000), who had written about *liquid modernity*. Giddens (1991) coined the notion of *life histories*, by which we constantly create and revise the narratives about our lives based on the social environment in which we operate.

Identity and Self-Communication

Henry Jenkins's name is mainly connected to convergence, fan and participatory culture. When analysing Web 2.0 and social media, he also discussed *self-identity*, which he saw as a process (Jenkins, 2006). Self-identity happens in public and private life via multiple and diverse types of interaction and networks. Digital technologies offer the stage for this interaction, thereby linking individuals with audiences. Social network platforms offer these possibilities for self-presentation and identity negotiation (Papacharissi, 2010).

Manuel Castells, whose name is connected to the *network society*, wrote about social media's affordances to present ourselves and connect us to others. In his book *Communication Power*, Castells (2009) proposes the concept of *mass self-communication*, which he sees as a new type of communication that replaces mass communication. He defines mass self-communication as follows:

> It is mass communication because it can potentially reach a global audience …
> At the same time, it is self-communication because the production of the

message is self-generated, the definition of the potential receiver(s) is self-directed, and the retrieval of specific messages of content from the World Wide Web and electronic communication networks is self-selected. (Castells 2009: 55)

This transformation has massive consequences as we – as individuals – can reach global audiences via which we present ourselves to the world. Or at least, this is how it is in theory. Some people/groups have more visibility on digital platforms than others.

Identity and Subjectivity

Finally, the contribution of Michel Foucault, a French philosopher, historian, activist and critic, is crucial when thinking critically about identity, modernity and subjectivity. In his work, Foucault gave special attention to social institutions, power, knowledge and discourse. He especially stressed how identity and power are connected. According to Foucault (1980: 156), power results from different relationships and how they are interconnected: 'Power is no longer substantially identified with an individual who possesses or exercises it by right of birth; it becomes a machinery that no one owns.' This quote illustrates Foucault's thinking on how power goes in different directions. His later work made more explicit how even powerful individuals or groups are *governmentalised* and caught under the influence of power (Foucault, 1991). Foucault's work stresses how power should be seen as a vehicle for disciplining individuals and society, highly relevant in the context of surveillance, which I discuss in the following section.

The notion of subjectivity shapes Foucault's thinking about power and identity. According to Foucault, this refers not to a state of *being* but rather a *practice*, an active being. Unlike other philosophers who consider subjectivity as how we become unique individuals and selves and distinguish ourselves from others, Foucault (1983) believes subjectivity is a construction created by power: power creates subjects while oppressing them using social norms. Within the development of subjectivity, specific techniques and habits are at play:

* What he calls *technologies of the self* are practices – that are not neutral – by which we can understand and shape ourselves (Foucault, 1988).
* We develop subjectivity through *power discourses*: these are socio-historical circumstances that impact how we position ourselves with a particular socio-political system.

Surveillance Culture

There is a critical shadow side of the possibilities to present ourselves to the world and shape our identities online: someone – an individual or organisation – can be watching, listening, following, etc., how we engage with the platform and its users.

However, surveillance is not exclusively connected to digital media. Even before the big data hype started, scholars were investigating surveillance. But what does this concept exactly mean?

What Is Surveillance?

Surveillance comes from the French verb *surveiller*, which refers to watching or observing. It is a container concept to describe the monitoring of activities, behaviour and information. One of the founders of surveillance studies, David Lyon, offers a comprehensive definition of surveillance. According to him, surveillance is 'a cross-disciplinary initiative to understand the rapidly increasing ways in which personal details are collected, stored, transmitted, checked, and used as a means of influencing and managing people and institutions' (Lyon 2002a: 1). It is thus essential to see surveillance as an umbrella concept. Lyon's definition clarifies that it is linked to several disciplines, from sociology to information science and from computer science to media studies. The words *personal details* may suggest surveillance mainly deals with personal data, but it is broader than that: our faces, behaviour, interactions, etc., are observed and monitored. Surveillance is more complex than just watching, listening or observing: it is also essential to question what happens to the personal details once collected – their processing, distribution and deployment. We must also pay attention to the consequences of surveillance: how this is used to influence the behaviour of individuals and groups in society.

In reflecting on the impact of surveillance, Gary Marx (2002) argued that the traditional (dictionary) definition of surveillance as the close observation of someone, often a suspected person, is deficient. His criticism is not only about the *suspected person* (which has changed massively in the aftermath of 9/11 – suddenly, everyone is potentially a suspect) but also about the clear distinction between the object of surveillance and the person (or organisation) responsible for it. He also disagrees with the term *close observation*, as a lot of monitoring happens remotely via satellites, drones and other (digital) communication systems. Instead, Marx (2002: 12) proposes to define surveillance as 'the use of technical means to extract or create personal data'. This conceptualisation is vital for our investigation.

Positive, Critical and Neutral Perspectives on Surveillance

People and organisations have different attitudes towards surveillance, depending on their societal position and relationship to power. Attitudes can be positive, neutral or negative. A positive take on surveillance would be that it can enhance efficiency and increase productivity. A neutral position towards surveillance is that it is inherent to the context of how organisations and institutions are organised, especially the bureaucratic context. Negative attitudes are at the centre of a critical analysis of surveillance, which argues that it leads to disciplining and discrimination. For example, Oscar Gandy Jr. (1993) refers to surveillance as *social sorting*. According to him, social sorting (or *panoptic sorting*) is a surveillance system that identifies, classifies and assesses personal data for strategic ends. He considers it a discriminatory technology that allocates options and opportunities based on those measures and the administrative models they inform. Lyon (2003) concludes that this leads to patterns of profound discrimination.

To offer a more comprehensive understanding of its role and use, Lyon (2001) introduces four distinguishable perspectives on surveillance:

- Protecting the security of citizens and the state
- Control as part of rationalisation
- Techno logic.
- Commercial logic.

The 9/11 attacks in 2001 have been pivotal in the extent to which surveillance practices are used in society. After the attacks on the World Trade Center towers in New York, policy-makers in the USA (but also elsewhere) argued that they need to be able to observe and follow everyone – no longer only *suspected* individuals – to keep everyone safe. This surveillance perspective thus portrays surveillance as the *necessary evil* to enhance security and protect citizens and the state from attacks (Lyon, 2003). The argument can be criticised, though, because several attacks and incidents have happened (e.g., terrorist attacks in the UK, France, Belgium and elsewhere) since 9/11, *despite* the increased adoption of surveillance in our lives. The revelations made by Edward Snowden and published in major Western newspapers have shown how widespread and far-reaching the surveillance by government agencies such as the NSA and GCHQ is. One of the more shocking details in these revelations is how companies are well aware of their contribution to the systematic monitoring of citizens (Hintz et al., 2019).

Surveillance is central to the capitalist system's search for efficiency and productivity (West, 2019). Bureaucratic structures are set up to facilitate rationalisation. For example, students and employees need to swipe ID cards before entering a campus building or their workplace. The sociologist Max Weber (1978), who studied the development of modern societies and organisations in particular, argued that organisations have three main characteristics: logical, rational and efficient. Surveillance technologies are then used as they should improve workplace efficiency or population management (think, for example, of the context of traffic or transport).

The *techno logic* surveillance perspective is an upgrade from the search for efficient and productive systems and organisations. Still, it makes intensive use of monitoring through the further development of automation and digital technologies (Lyon, 1998). Surveillance scholar Mark Andrejevic (2019a) talks about *automating surveillance*, which results in practices of monitoring and watching that are so widespread and omnipresent that the subjects of this surveillance no longer inter-nalise the monitoring gaze (i.e., the fact that they are being watched). He refers to it as a 'total information capture', whereby monitoring is constant and ubiquitous (Andrejevic, 2019a: 9). Airports are typical examples of this, but modern cities, such as London and Beijing, are also equipped with many CCTV cameras.

Finally, surveillance also has a clear *commercial logic*. This means that different surveillance practices are inherently part of the capitalist system and are used to optimise capital accumulation and increase profit (Fuchs, 2021). This commercial logic exists in different types and systems, from digital video recorders that capture audiovisual consumption so as to provide customised advertising messages, to monitoring shops and organising the placement of products on shelves to maximise purchasing behaviour, via social media platforms whose prime business model is targeted advertising (Andrejevic, 2007; Turow, 2006, 2011).

A Closer Look at Corporate Surveillance

After discussing surveillance as protection, rationalisation, techno and commercial logic, this section looks closer at how these aspects are combined in practices of corporate surveillance. A critical and often-used argument about data (personal and other) collection – whether on digital media platforms or offline settings – is to make services more effective and efficient (Turow, 2006, 2011). A specific type of service that data can optimise is marketing campaigns. Marketing efforts will be more *effective* through being able to reach specific segments of the population. Unlike exposing everyone watching a particular TV show (or any other cultural product) to an advertisement of laundry products, for example, you can filter out who would be responsible for the purchasing decision to buy those products (and influence them in that decision). In the same vein, marketing campaigns will be more *efficient* as you no longer have to spend marketing resources on the overall population but can filter out and target those likely to decide to purchase your product. Of course, to do so, one needs more information about who your customers are and their consumption habits. That is where data comes in the mix.

It is essential to understand that this process of *datafication* is not only related to the digital era. Think, for example, about loyalty cards in supermarkets or other shops. In exchange for extra information about yourself, you are promised a better deal on purchases. Social media have optimised this model as they have much greater means to collect data and link it to those you are connected to and your engagement on the platforms. The business model of social media companies is based on targeted advertising built around what Fuchs (2017a) calls the *prosumers' big data commodity*. In essence, on digital platforms, users not only pay attention to commercial messages but also are actively involved in their production and dis-tribution. But one could ask: what is the problem with targeted advertising? At least we are no longer bothered by general ads that are not relevant to us. While this might be true to some extent, it does not paint the complete picture. Table 5.1 lists some of the advantages and disadvantages of user profiling (Lyon, 2014; Tufekci, 2014; Ibrahim, 2021).

Table 5.1 Advantages and disadvantages of user profiling

Advantages	Disadvantages
A more customised media experience	The idea of *prosumer commodity* suggests that targeted advertising *creates* rather than *observes* our identities (which contributes to a further commodification of society)
We are no longer exposed to general (and therefore irrelevant) content and advertisements	User profiling leads to decreased personal autonomy
Marketing campaigns can be more effective and efficient	It contributes to the blurring between the public and the private (the digital consumer is neither anonymous nor private)
Campaigns can be automated using networked technologies	User profiling contributes to normalising surveillance

These disadvantages of user profiling also result in broader risks to the surveillance society. Lyon (2001) discusses several risks related to this:

- Individuals may be disadvantaged because of the information that is shared involuntarily (e.g., information about political or sexual preferences).
- The information collected can be used *against* individuals, especially when that information is collected for other purposes.
- Information can be incorrect and incomplete.
- Information in the digital era exists for ever.
- Information collected by private entities might be handed over to governmental organisations (the Snowden revelations have demonstrated this).
- There is a risk of oversurveillance, meaning that individuals are becoming aware of the constant surveillance and will adapt their behaviour.

Data(sur)veillance

The question remains where the role of data sits in all of this. Before the *big data hype*, scholars were already writing about *dataveillance*. Clarke (1988: 499) introduced the concept – a portmanteau of data and surveillance – as 'the systematic monitoring of people's actions or communications through the application of information technology'. By its very nature, dataveillance is intrusive and threatening and can be deployed for personal and mass surveillance purposes. The former aims to target individuals, whereas the latter is about the dataveillance of groups of people to identify individuals.

Dataveillance received increased attention after the Snowden revelations. Raley (2013) wrote about dataveillance as a form of continuous and intensified surveillance made possible through the use of (meta)data. Van Dijck (2014) considers datafication and *life mining* (observing and keeping track of how we engage with digital platforms and share things with friends and connections) a new scientific paradigm, which she terms *dataism*. The latter should be seen as an ideology characterised by 'a widespread belief in the objective quantification and potential tracking of all kinds of human behaviour and sociality through online media technologies' (van Dijck, 2014: 198). The implied objectivity of this datafication should be critiqued, alongside the belief that (meta)data are just *raw material* that can be analysed and processed into algorithms that predict future human behaviour (Gitelman, 2013).

However, the centrality of data(sur)veillance in the business model of the digital economy has received increased attention through Shoshana Zuboff's (2019) work on *surveillance capitalism*. One critique of Zuboff's analysis in that she sees surveillance's centrality in the digital economy's business model as the main problem. At the same time, she pays less attention to the power dynamics of contemporary capitalism (and the resulting inequalities) in itself.

Datafication and Subjectivity

In *McQuail's Mass Communication Theory*, Denis McQuail (2010) reminds us that we need to distinguish between the process of mass communication and the actual media (technologies) that facilitate this: humans have exchanged messages since long before the emergence of professional media, but a lot has changed since their arrival.

From Mass Media to Mass Customisation

In simple terms, *mass communication* refers to disseminating and transmitting ideas to mass audiences. Examples of these traditional (mass) media are print media such as books, newspapers and other press, film, broadcasting, and music. It is an institutionalised communication process whereby a communicator uses a medium to send a message to a receiver, whereby minimal feedback from the latter is possible (Carah and Louw, 2015). Therefore, mass communication is *top-down*, as it is a select group of communication professionals who produce and distribute meaning on a large scale. Furthermore, it is also *unidirectional*, as one group speaks and another listens. As such, the flow of messages is *one-way*; there is little scope for input or feedback. In principle, mass media are funded through advertising, subscription, public funding, or a combination.

The Internet as a communication medium fundamentally disrupted the mass media communication logic. McQuail (2010) discusses several essential features of the internet, such as the centrality of computer- and network-based technologies, the hybridity in terms of private and public functions that simultaneously facilitates mass and personal communication, the ubiquity, the possibility to overcome distance, as well as the low degree of regulation. In an update of McQuail's original work, Mark Deuze states that there are two significant implications of the (internet) communications revolution (McQuail and Deuze, 2020: 52–53):

- *Traditional* media have both benefited from new media innovations and experienced profound challenges to their business models and production processes.
- There is a shift in the *balance of power* from the media in two directions: first, new forms of communication are essentially interactive, and this gives way more opportunities to audiences; and second, 'power has shifted from those who control the means of production and distribution … to those who have successfully monetised the place and moment of (digital) consumption'. The latter refers to the companies that control and manage the platforms on which communication (and data collection, analysis and distribution) happens.

With interactive media, users thus become more active but also more customised (Andrejevic, 2013; Turow, 2006, 2011). With *segmentation* techniques, the population is divided into subgroups of users/customers who can be offered specific content tailored to their preferences. This segmentation enables the shift to targeted advertising. Looking back, we can thus notice an evolution from mass media to mass customisation in content and advertising strategies. This shift has been made possible by *datafication* and *dataveillance*. How this works exactly is further explored in the following sections.

Digital Selves versus Data Selves

Social scientists have argued that *datafication* (the process through which people's bodies and activities are rendered into digitised information when they are online or engage with digital devices) (Mayer-Schoenberger and Cukier, 2013; van Dijck, 2014) and *dataveillance* (the systematic monitoring of people's actions and communication through the application of information technology and the use of these data to watch people (Clarke, 1988; Raley, 2013) increasingly determine people's concepts of selfhood, forming what can be called:

- *Numbered lives* (Wernimont, 2019)
- *Digital selves* (Cheney-Lippold, 2017)
- *Data selves* (Lupton, 2020).

These terms have in common that they analyse and explain in detail how data generated on digital platforms has many benefits but can also be exploited by third parties. More specifically, Wernimont (2019), Cheney-Lippold (2017) and Lupton (2020) explore the impact of data and algorithms on our identities.

Communication scholar Cheney-Lippold (2017) contends in his book *We Are Data: Algorithms and the Making of our Digital Selves* that knowledge – which shapes our digital selves and the world we operate in – is increasingly built by data, algorithms and the logic behind them. The data we generate and the digital traces we leave behind (e.g., when planning meals, tracking steps, managing our finances or seeking entertainment) are algorithmically interpreted, categorised and employed by state security programs and for-profit corporations (among others). They do this on their terms, for their purposes and according to their private and proprietary algorithmic logic. The *digital selves* (or *numbered lives* or *data selves*) that are assigned by algorithmic systems, operated by the state and by capital, emerge in and are the subject of a dynamic interplay between the data we produce and the different state and corporate powers that engage with and produce outcomes based on that data.

Confronted with this, we need to be aware that it is not just we who can decide to go online and start using digital services offered by platforms; the interplay between data and algorithms has a crucial role in this and contributes to algorithmic identities, including the infrastructure and guiding principles that generate them.

Algorithmic Identities

How can we understand *algorithmic identities*? Cheney-Lippold (2017: 25) argues that they 'emerge from a constant interplay between our data and algorithms interpreting that data'. This adds a new layer to identity construction compared to what I discussed earlier. How we present ourselves (or, more correctly, how we are presented) to the world depends on our data and how algorithms make sense of that data. Mark Andrejevic (2019a) follows the same line of thinking but stresses the centrality of surveillance in this: he argues that our data is constantly watched by and interacts with algorithmic machines. To summarise, our algorithmic identities are based on (near-)real-time interpretations of our data. And as we produce more data points, these interpretations evolve and become more sophisticated.

For the conceptualisation of algorithms (and how they shape our identities), Cheney-Lippold (2017) uses the term *measurable types*. This term is inspired by what Max Weber (1904/1949) called *ideal types*. An ideal type is formed by the (single-sided) emphasis of one or more points of view, according to which concrete phenomena are arranged into an analytical construct. It refers to *some* characteristics and elements of a given phenomenon but is not meant to correspond to *all* of its features: it stresses certain parts common to most cases of the given phenomenon. Using ideal types can thus be problematic as it tends to focus on extreme, one-sided phenomena while overlooking the connections between them and how the types and their elements fit in larger social systems. Inspired by this, Cheney-Lippold (2017: 47) sees measurable types as technical constructions (classification systems), which are fabricated using data: 'A measurable type is a data template, a nexus of different datafied elements that construct a new, transcoded interpretation of the world ... These measurable types are ultimately classifications, empirically observed and transcoded as data, that become discrete analytical models for use in profiling and/or knowledge abstraction.' Of course, a central question in this is who develops the data templates/classifications, what they look like and for what purposes they are being used.

In his book, Cheney-Lippold (2017) uses a quote from a former NSA chief who states that people are being monitored, captured and sometimes even killed based on metadata. What is *metadata*? In the context of communication, it refers to data about where you are, from where you send a text, and to whom that message is sent. This also contains data about when the message was sent and what device was used for it. The metadata of someone can be compared to pre-existing patterns, which form the basis upon which someone can be labelled a *terrorist* and can potentially become the subject of a surveillance operation or even the victim of a drone attack.

A more innocent example is the viral trend *Who does Google think you are?* Every Google account has a feature with a demographic estimate of your gender and age. This estimate is based on the websites you visit, basically developed on the data that Google uses to personalise search results.

From Personalisation to Profilisation

Personalisation and profilisation are central to understanding how measurable types are used in data-driven and algorithmic systems. *Personalisation* can be defined as 'the large-scale manipulation of what and how information, people, goods and services are selected, arranged and presented to individuals' (Webster, 2023: 2141). It is often based on socio-demographic and socio-economic parameters, such as gender, race, class, education and income. However, Cheney-Lippold (2017) states that personalisation – the assumption that you, as a user, are distinctive enough to receive content (or recommendations or ads) based on you as a person with a history and individual interests – essentially does not exist.

Instead, we are communicated with through what Cheney-Lippold (2017: 87) calls *profilisation*. This refers to the 'intersections of categorical meaning that allow our data, but not necessarily us, to be "gendered", "raced" or "classed"'. The important nuance here is his distinction between *us* and *our data*. Cheney-Lippold explicitly acknowledges this difference, and it is essential to consider this. When talking about identity, surveillance and subjectivity, we thus need to stress that our data – and not necessarily ourselves – is part of a process of profilisation. This is also important when discussing algorithmic profiling.

Algorithmic Profiling

Public and private sector organisations are interested in building reliable inferences that can guide their decision-making. They do this by profiling, which can be defined as the systematic and purposeful recording and classification of data related to individuals – a *profile* is thus a compilation of data referring to an individual (Hildebrandt, 2008). Moving into the digital age transformed profiling into algorithmic and automated profiling. *Algorithmic profiling* uses data and algorithms to detect patterns and make decisions based on them (Mann and Matzner, 2019). The big data era enabled the creation of profiles based on more extensive data sources. Some of the core drivers of this development of algorithmic profiling are:

- The increase in digital data availability
- A shift from demographic to individualised targeting
- Real-time experimentation
- Platformisation.

Automated algorithmic profiling, on the other hand, is the result of deploying algorithms in a data mining process. It uses the method of inferential analysis to identify patterns or correlations within datasets to be used as an indicator to classify a subject as a member of a group (Hildebrandt, 2008).

The corporate sector, but increasingly also the public sector, is interested in classifying data points that relate to a specific user, or a specific category of users (Cheney-Lippold, 2017). Examples include data relating to online and offline purchases, census records, online surfing behaviours and interests, and location data. Such data are valuable as they allow for creating profiles that enable a service provider to target individuals through ads or a product/service placement.

The problem with algorithmic profiling is that it can result in social sorting and disadvantaging marginal groups in society. *Social sorting* is a discriminatory approach to profile and target marginalised communities based on gender, social class or race/ethnicity. Algorithmic profiling perpetuates hierarchies based on identity characteristics. This contributes to self-enforcing feedback loops, where datasets disproportionately contain data about specific groups, which can be used, for example, in surveillance and policing activities.

Algorithmic Citizenship

In the summer of 2020, A-level exams in the UK were scrapped because of the Covid-19 pandemic. The UK government used instead an algorithm to assign exam grades. These exams are crucial as they impact what offers students get from which to choose their university for higher education. The algorithm replaced teachers' assessments of students. The model was designed to produce results that looked fair on the headline measures (the averages could look similar to teachers' exam grades). However, the system was flawed, placed constraints on how many pupils could achieve specific grades, and based its output on schools' prior performance, downgrading around 40 per cent of predicted results. This led to a significant protest, during which A-level students chanted 'Fuck the algorithm'. This case demonstrates the limitations of governance by algorithms and illustrates the encoded bias in them.

The question of algorithmic citizenship brings us back to earlier discussions about identity and subjectivity. *Identity* is how we present ourselves to the world and *subjectivity* is how we become unique individuals and distinguish ourselves from others. By adding datafication to the mix, we explore how the world, including governmental, corporate and educational organisations, think about who we are through the data that represents us.

From Citizens to Algorithms

Before talking about algorithmic citizenship, let us look at what citizenship in the digital era entails. Hintz et al. (2019: 21) argue that while citizenship has traditionally been defined through membership of nation-states, digital technologies have transformed citizenship negatively 'from something we use to the environment in which we live, and it enables new governance models based on omnipresent data collection and analysis'. This negative change refers to power and control shifting away from citizens to governments and tech companies. In this sense, digital citizenship can be defined as enacting people's societal role through digital technologies. As the quote above illustrates, this includes empowering and democratising characteristics, as well as challenges, such as monitoring citizens and how this brings about a power balance shift.

Cheney-Lippold (2017) mainly focuses on how citizenship is changing through interaction with data and algorithms. In his book *We Are Data*, he investigates the theoretical problems and issues encountered when our online datafied selves coexist with our offline subjective selves as if they are mutually inclusive. These new digital forms of subject relations thus add a layer of existence without self-determining agency: this is non-negotiable and happens above our heads, and we – citizens – have no say in it. The *measurable type* (explained in the previous section) interpretations conducted by a multiplicity of algorithms online become components of an identity construct that remains an invisible *moving target* within a non-human world.

Cheney-Lippold (2016) coined the notion of *jus algoritmi*, which he uses to describe a new form of citizenship produced by the surveillance state, whose primary mode of operation is controlled through identification and categorisation. Jus algoritmi – 'the right of the algorithm' – refers to the increasing use of classification systems and software to make judgments about the citizenship status of individuals, which also determines a decision about what rights one has and what operations can be permitted on them. In his book, Cheney-Lippold (2017) gives examples of how this algorithmic citizenship exists in reality (e.g., about NSA and military operations). In short, our rights as citizens – Hannah Arendt (1951: 296) famously wrote, 'citizenship is the right to have rights' – are under threat, as the example of the NSA makes clear that we are all *foreigners* (or *terrorists*, to give a more extreme example) until we can prove our citizenship.

Calzada (2022) further argues that there are more emerging citizenship regimes than algorithmic ones. He adds *pandemic* (techno-politicised and regionalised digital citizenship regimes under the influence of the Covid-19 pandemic), *liquid* (driven by *dataism*), *metropolitan* (urban versus rural, revindicated by, for example, Brexit) and *stateless* (caused by devolution independence movements) citizenship. The centrality of data is crucial in these emerging citizenship regimes.

Algorithmic Regulation and Governmentality

The conceptualisation of algorithmic citizenship – particularly the subjective situation of being a citizen while not having citizenship – creates challenges for regulation and governance. This section explores algorithmic regulation and explains what scholars have termed *algorithmic governmentality* (Rouvroy, 2013). It is crucial to keep in mind that the regulatory environment is not static but instead evolves and is influenced by (the combination of) political change, societal debate and technological development.

Crises, such as the Snowden revelations about mass surveillance, inspire policy debates and can change regulation and governance (Hintz et al., 2019). The context determines the regulatory environment and the stakeholders involved in this. Given the global character of the digital economy, Raboy (2002: 6–7) writes that 'media and communication policy is a complex ecology of interdependent structures'. In addition to national governments, supranational organisations (such as the European Union) or international institutions (such as the United Nations) contribute to debates and policy development. This multi-stakeholder approach also involves the business sector, regulatory bodies (e.g., the Internet Corporation for Assigned Names and Numbers) and civil society (e.g., non-governmental organisations and activist groups). The question, though, is how regulation itself can change under the influence of data and algorithms.

Although Silicon Valley entrepreneur Tim O'Reilly (2013) was one of the first to popularise *algorithmic regulation*, he did not elaborate on what it means. He mainly proposed the idea for governments to embrace the potential of big data. Legal scholar Karen Yeung (2018: 505) defines it as 'decision-making systems that regulate a domain of activity in order to manage risk or alter behaviour through continual computational generation of knowledge by systematically collecting data … in order to identify and, if necessary, automatically refine … the system's operations to attain a pre-specified role'. In simple terms, algorithmic regulation refers to governance systems that use algorithmic decision-making.

Mireille Hildebrandt (2018) distinguishes between code-driven and data-driven regulation. *Code-driven* regulation refers to computational algorithms that depend on pre-coded decision trees such as *if this, then that*. *Data-driven* regulation refers to predictive algorithms that infer standards to monitor, better predict, or influence behaviour based on data analysis (driven by machine learning). In other words, data-driven regulation means that 'the code is informed by the data on which it has been trained instead of being informed by legal experts that have translated their insights into code' (Hildebrandt 2018: 2). To summarise, algorithmic regulation is a new type of regulation whereby data and algorithms (in a complex interplay) are deployed to engage in changing behaviour and social ordering.

However, scholars also encourage us to be critical towards algorithmic regulation. Delacroix (2019), in particular, argues that we need to stop confusing algorithmic regulation and regulatory power. In doing this, she points at two main problems:

- Digital platforms do not regulate us, but they have regulatory power over us.
- The influence exerted by platforms is not only non-inclusive (as users, we have very little to say about this) but also covert. As such, it threatens our freedom but also compromises our commitment to moral equality.

Algorithmic governmentality is a term proposed by Rouvroy (2013). This is a broader concept and an interpretation of *governmentality*, which Michel Foucault developed as a new understanding of power. To explain the concept of *algorithmic govern-mentality*, we first need to introduce *data behaviourism*. Rouvroy (2013: 145) refers to this as the emergence of a new *truth regime*, which centralises data mining and profiling and is built on the factual availability of enormous amounts of raw (digital) data. She then conceptualises algorithmic governmentally: 'The spread of data behaviourism accompanying the deployment of data mining and profiling systems in a diversity of applications inaugurates an unprecedented regime of power' (Rouvroy, 2013: 150). This refers to governance based on the algorithmic processing of big datasets rather than politics, laws and social norms.

Unlike the more neutral conceptualisation of algorithmic regulation, this approach to algorithmic government explicitly mentions power and subjectivation: 'algorithmic governmentally is without subject: it operates within infra-individual data and supra-individual patterns without, at any moment, calling the subject to account for itself' (Rouvroy, 2013: 144). This means that digital traces of a specific individual are not algorithmically relevant; they only become valuable and relevant through their processing and interlinking with other data points. Rouvroy is critical of algorithmic governmentality as it allows governments (and other holders of power) to hide themselves and the accountability of their decisions behind the algorithms and data systems that produced them.

Are We Data?

This leaves us with the question, *are we data*? Answering this question is about reflecting on processes of algorithmic identification about *you* and *us*. But it also opens new questions about (algorithmic) visibility; for example, why are some posts and profiles more visible than others on social media platforms, and what is behind this? Cheney-Lippold's (2017) analysis of algorithmic regulation, visibility and related aspects, particularly the examples provided, is a bit dire and scary. However, this analysis is critical in understanding how data and algorithms impact our lives and how they shape us. In the final chapter of his book, Cheney-Lippold (2017) offers some hope by sharing strategies about how to fight back and what we can do to challenge the limitations of our digital selves. For example, when discussing privacy and control, he endorses the strategy that privacy scholar Helen Nissenbaum calls *obfuscation*: flooding an algorithmic system with arbitrary data to compromise its predictive capabilities (Brunton and Nissenbaum, 2016). But there is hope in how to take up the challenge of fighting back against structures of power in digital and data environments, and building more humane uses of data – which is how we will end this book.

Learning Takeaways

- Identities can be looked at from multiple perspectives: from performance to subjectivity.
- Dataveillance brings the systematic monitoring of people's actions to the next level, using data and algorithms.
- Personalisation and customisation lead to algorithmic identities, which are interpretations of our data.
- Algorithmic citizenship asks questions about how institutions think about who we are through the data that represent us.

Recommended Reading

Amoore, L. (2020). *Cloud Ethics: Algorithms and the Attributes of Ourselves and Others*. Durham, NC: Duke University Press.
Barassi, V. (2020). *Child Data Citizen: How Tech Companies Are Profiling Us from Before Birth*. Cambridge, MA: MIT Press.
Browne, S. (2015). *Dark Matters: On the Surveillance of Blackness*. Durham, NC: Duke University Press.
Lupton, D. (2020). *Data Selves: More-than-Human Perspectives*. Cambridge: Polity Press.
Wernimont, J. (2019). *Numbered Lives: Life and Death in Quantum Media*. Cambridge, MA: MIT Press.

Recommended Listening

Data and Society, a podcast series about the power of technology that bridges interdisciplinary research with broader public conversations about the societal implications of data and automation. https://listen.datasociety.net/

6

Data, Machine Learning and AI

Learning Goals

- Learn the long history of AI to understand why we currently are seeing so many stories of AI hype.
- Understand how contemporary AI operates through machine learning, deep learning and artificial neural networks.
- Investigate some of the limitations of these technologies by looking at their applications.
- Critically assess both the opportunities and controversies surrounding AI.

AI Becomes Mainstream News

Artificial intelligence became mainstream news in 2022. First, a Google/Alphabet engineer was fired for causing a media controversy by claiming that the large language model AI system he had conversations with had become sentient. Later in the same year, the AI research company OpenAI launched AI interfaces, ChatGPT and DALL-E, allowing everyone to experiment with text and image-generating software. These AI services, along with systems offered by other companies, led to an explosion of attention for AI. What is remarkable is the rapid uptake of this software by the general public and the observation that responses to prompts to these interfaces are surprisingly realistic and offer good-quality images, designs, etc. Simultaneously, this AI hype moment also accompanied hyperbole such as 'this is the end of journalism' (or even writing) and 'artists have no future'. The hype continued and intensified in 2023 when some people in the AI world claimed that artificial *general* intelligence (an autonomous system that surpasses human capabilities) could be closer than ever. Whether these expectations are part of a hype cycle or will be realised remains to be seen, but what is now needed more than ever is a critical and profound understanding of what AI is and what it is not, as well as more insights into how it functions, how we can benefit from it, but also what challenges exist in its development and application.

But First, a Brief History of AI

Even though we often associate AI with science fiction stories about the future, it is essential to start with the history of AI. AI is already here, and we need to know what type of AI we have and how we got here. The historical context is necessary to face the challenging task of defining AI and explaining key concepts you need to know. Different AI applications have strengths and weaknesses, and critical thinking can help us look at the many AI-related controversies and how we – as a society – need to work to develop AI that benefits humanity and its diverse communities.

The Long History of AI

It is easy to forget that AI has existed for over 60 years; it is not new. The term *artificial intelligence* was coined in the mid-1950s at a series of academic workshops organised at Dartmouth College (New Hampshire, USA); however, its foundation dates back much earlier. As early as the seventeenth century, philosophers such as Descartes and Hobbes were busy analysing and comparing the bodies of living animals to complex machines. In his famous work *Leviathan*, Hobbes (1651/1996) argued for a mechanical way of thinking, comparing the human mind to machines combining different modules to gain further functionality. Around the same time, German scientist Gottfried Leibniz proposed using binary numbers to reduce human reasoning to mechanical calculations. The theoretical foundations of computer science, and thus AI, were developed in that period. British mathematician Thomas Bayes (1763) would play a crucial role in this, too: his famous *Bayes' theorem* would serve as a basis for developing *machine learning*. The theorem is a mathematical method to describe an event's probability: it predicts future events' success based on past experiences and new evidence.

A century after Bayes, another British mathematician, George Boole, inspired by Aristotle's ideas of deductive reasoning, added a mathematical foundation for modern computer logic: *Boolean logic*. Boole thought that laws govern human thinking, and mathematics can describe these laws. Boolean logic is a branch of mathematics that uses symbols to represent true and false (Boole, 1854). The nineteenth century saw the development of the first so-called *programmable machines*. Charles Babbage and Ada Lovelace originated the concept of a programmable calculating machine called the *Analytical Engine*. Ada Lovelace would later publish a series of commands for the Analytical Engine to calculate numbers automatically. In our times, we call such a series of commands an *algorithm*. It demonstrates how crucial Ada Lovelace's contribution to computer science has been. Her work would also inspire further developments in the twentieth century, leading to AI's emergence as a separate discipline.

Alan Turing, Dartmouth College and the Emergence of AI as a Field of Study

Before the name *artificial intelligence* was coined, mathematician and computer scientist Alan Turing invented a simple device in the 1930s, which he called the *automatic machine*. This machine, later called the *Turing machine*, is a computing device capable of performing any conceivable mathematical computation using symbols as simple as 0 and 1. The idea was that if thoughts could be reduced to algorithms, machines would have the capability for human thought. This then became the theoretical concept of modern computers. Turing's most significant contribution to the development of AI was his seminal essay 'Computing Machinery and Intelligence' (Turing, 1950). In this essay, he dealt with the question of whether machines can think. Crucial here is how to define thinking and intelligence. His solution to conceptualising *intelligence* was to propose an imitation game; this is a thought experiment that later became famous as the *Turing test*.

The Turing test holds that a machine can be considered intelligent if a human interrogator cannot distinguish it from a human through conversation. There is disagreement about whether the Turing test could be used to determine whether a machine can think. Searle (1980), in a paper entitled 'Minds, Brains, and Programs', proposed the *Chinese room* thought experiment as an alternative. He argued that software could pass the Turing test by manipulating symbols it did not understand. The Chinese room experiment takes Chinese characters as input and, following an algorithm (the instructions of a computer program), produces other Chinese characters as output. The computer passes the test if it can convince a Chinese speaker that the program itself is an authentic Chinese speaker. The Chinese room experiment, just like the Turing test, is simultaneously endorsed and criticised. But Turing's main contribution was to explore computational methods that simulate human intelligence and gain insight into the human mind by mimicking it with algorithms.

In 1956, a group of mathematicians, engineers and computer scientists, including John McCarthy, Marvin Minsky, Claude Shannon, and Herbert Simon, convened for the *Dartmouth Summer Research Project on Artificial Intelligence*. John McCarthy, then a young mathematics scholar at Dartmouth College, picked the name *artificial intelligence* for the conference aimed at developing ideas about thinking machines. Throughout a series of workshops, they discussed the theory of computation, abstraction, creativity, natural language processing, neural networks, etc.

This Dartmouth College workshop series is considered the birthplace of artificial intelligence. McCarthy et al. (1955/2006) defined it as: 'Making a machine behave in ways that would be called intelligent if a human were so behaving.' Of course, this definition does not answer what needs to be understood under *intelligence*.

The Dartmouth College workshop participants thought – perhaps naively – that fully intelligent machines/robots would be within reach soon. While not realised then, this period is marked as the foundation of AI as a separate field within computer science. It was in the period from the mid-1950s to the mid-1970s that the foundational research interests of the field crystallised and started to be popularised. The early generation of AI researchers was invested in refuting sceptical claims that machines could not perform specific human tasks. In response to this, they were engaged in research projects that are called *toy problems*. In computer science, this refers to simple and pared-down versions of real-life tasks used to test AI algorithms. The successes and failures of some of these tests, projects and experiments would see a period of hype alternating with disillusionment, discussed in the following section.

AI Breakthroughs versus AI Winters

In the 1960s, the first AI applications were knowledge-based programs. They called upon a bank of programmable knowledge to reason about and solve complex programs. The best-known examples of this type of AI paradigm were so-called *expert systems*. These systems are programs with particular expertise in a specific domain. Joseph Weizenbaum's *ELIZA* was a famous example of this. It was a *natural language processing* computer program capable of engaging humans in a conversation resembling one with a psychologist.

Throughout the history of AI, we can notice a sequence of periods of hope and excitement, coinciding with large amounts of funding available, followed by periods of disappointment, characterised by projects not delivering their expectations and, as a result, research funding slipping away. These periods of disillusionment are often described as *AI winters* (Floridi, 2020). This term first appeared in 1984 as part of a debate at the *American Association of Artificial Intelligence*.

After the initial period of AI excitement – particularly around the AI expert systems – the first AI winter started began in 1974 and lasted until 1980. It was caused by several problems, most notably hardware issues (computer memory and available processing speed could not sustain the increasing needs of AI algorithms) and what is called *combinatorial explosion*. This concept refers to the exponential growth of a problem as it becomes more complex. This is linked to the problem of insufficient hardware, as increasing computing time and resources are necessary to deal with more complex issues.

However, in the early 1980s, Japan funded its *Fifth Generation Computer Systems* project. This project launched in 1982, aiming to develop powerful computers with capacities similar to the supercomputers we have today. The hope was that this would lead to a new computing architecture that could serve as a hardware platform supporting the development of new powerful AI programs. In response, Russia (then the USSR) began to show interest in future-generation computers and AI systems. Consequently, there was growing concern in the USA that its technology could be leapfrogged, resulting in a boom of funding into AI research, particularly by the US Defense Department. This new period of hype saw a renewed interest in expert systems, driven by the assumption that the ability to use large amounts of data would revolutionise intelligent thinking. The dominant AI paradigm of the time was *good old-fashioned artificial intelligence* (GOFAI). GOFAI is an umbrella term for AI algorithms that rely on manipulating symbols and rules, which serve as the basis for expert systems. However, by the late 1980s, the new generation of expert systems started to run into problems: smaller systems proved too computationally limited to help with real-world issues, and the problem of adequate data to solve this was real, too. As a result, the *Fifth Generation* project failed to meet its goals, and interest in expert systems deflated. A second AI winter (mainly between 1987 and 1993) descended.

AI: What's in a Name?

In the 1990s, AI researchers moved away from expert systems and GOFAI, instead turning to algorithms that are better capable of dealing with change. The widespread adoption of the internet (predominantly in the Global North) heralded a new age for AI research. With the internet, hardware capabilities and available data grew exponentially.

Twenty-First-Century Breakthroughs and Hype

In the early twenty-first century, data availability and technological breakthroughs resulted in significant developments in the field of (contemporary) AI. Pivotal moments are the DARPA Grand Challenge and the release of ImageNet.

The *DARPA Grand Challenge* is a race for autonomous vehicles sponsored by the US Department of Defense. Stanford University's autonomous vehicle Stanley won the race in 2005, and this victory triggered commercial interest in the development of self-driving cars, which is considered one of the most iconic AI ambitions/applications. Again, Stanford University released *ImageNet* in 2009, an extensive visual database for training computer object recognition algorithms. Although ImageNet is controversial in terms of its role in producing algorithmic bias, this was a critical AI milestone as it provided sufficient data for further developing multi-layered *artificial neural networks*. Data from ImageNet supported an essential breakthrough in *computer vision*, one of the significant AI applications, in 2012. This contributed to the further development of *deep learning*.

Other significant events in the deep learning revolution happened between 2011 and 2016. In 2011, there was an iconic victory of *Watson* – an IBM supercomputer that uses AI – in the television show *Jeopardy!* This show tests contestants' knowledge on a wide range of subjects, and Watson had beaten Ken Jennings and Brad Rutter, two of the best players in *Jeopardy!* Another pivotal moment leading up to the current period of AI hype was the victory of DeepMind's *AlphaGo* over multiple world champion Lee Sedol in the ancient board game *Go*. Go, invented in China over 2500 years ago, is an abstract strategy board game in which a player must surround more territory than their opponent. What was striking about AlphaGo's victory is that DeepMind had developed a self-taught system that learns new strategies by playing the game Go. It uses *brute force* methods, a problem-solving technique that systematically enumerates possible solutions to a problem and checks every candidate solution before reaching a result.

Behind these breakthroughs are further (technical) developments in machine learning, deep learning and artificial neural networks, which will be discussed in this section. These breakthroughs in machine learning techniques, supporting the development of more sophisticated machine learning and deep learning models, including artificial neural networks, together with the growing availability of data with which algorithms can be trained, as well as the increasing availability of powerful computing capacity, are behind the current period of AI hype (K.-F. Lee, 2018). However, before going deeper into this, we need to make a critical – conceptual – clarification about AI.

Artificial General Intelligence versus Artificial Narrow Intelligence

Popular understandings of AI are fed by science fiction literature, Hollywood movies and sensational newspaper articles that declare that we are reaching *superintelligence*, a concept coined by AI and technology philosopher Nick Bostrom (2014), which warns of the impact when machines overtake humans in intelligence. In this context, it is helpful to distinguish between strong and weak AI. *Strong AI*, also called artificial *general* intelligence, refers to computational systems with *general* cognitive abilities which have the future potential to surpass human intellectual capacities. This can be seen as an attempt to mechanise human-level intelligence. Computer scientists and philosophers disagree on whether this is possible (Coeckelbergh, 2020): some directly reject this scenario, while others think that – if theoretically possible – it is not likely to happen any time soon in practice (Boden, 2016). This is why it might be better to focus on advancements in *weak AI* or artificial *narrow* intelligence, as this type of AI already impacts everyday life on a massive scale. Weak/narrow AI performs *specific* tasks requiring intelligence in a human being – machines aiding human thought and action. Narrow AI is a statistical method trained on data for prediction (Agrawal et al., 2018; Broussard, 2018). Such systems can be extremely powerful but are limited in their range of tasks.

Artificial general intelligence should not be confused with *generative artificial intelligence* (generative AI or GenAI), popularised by services such as ChatGPT. This label refers to AI capable of generating text, images, code or other media using generative models. These models learn the patterns and structure of their input training data and generate new data with similar characteristics.

Our understanding of and attitudes towards AI is influenced by famous science fiction literature and movies or television series such as *Blade Runner, Terminator,* HAL 9000 in *2001: A Space Odyssey, Ex Machina* and *Westworld*. It is best to understand *robots* as the product of fiction; often, they are portrayed as biological creatures that are human-like in both material and shape. A good operational definition of robots is provided by Bekey (2005): 'A robot is a machine that senses, thinks, acts.' Winfield (2012) adds to this three qualifying characteristics for a robot:

- It is an artificial device that can sense its surroundings and purposefully act on or in that environment.
- It is an embodied artificial intelligence.
- It is a machine that can autonomously carry out helpful work.

Before moving on to a more detailed discussion of the technical breakthroughs behind the current period of AI hype, it is essential to briefly talk about superintelligence and the controversies around robots and intelligent machines. The idea of superintelligence relates to what Google futurist Ray Kurzweil (2005) calls the *singularity*. This concept refers to a hypothetical point in the future when technological development advances to such an extent that it becomes uncontrollable and irreversible, leading to unforeseeable changes to human civilisation. Bostrom (2014) argues that an *intelligence explosion* would cause this. According to Bostrom, superintelligence might happen soon after reaching *human-level machine intelligence*. However, there is no agreement on whether this is possible and when it would happen, but it certainly keeps scientists busy thinking about its (potential) consequences. Bostrom (2014) discusses different paths and types of superintelligence and how we – as humanity – should reflect on this.

An illustration of the relevance of this debate is a controversy that emerged in mid-2022 when a Google/Alphabet AI researcher declared on his website that – after conversing with an AI system for a while – he was convinced the AI system had become sentient. There has been pushback on this story, mainly criticising the hype created for its lack of understanding and nuance about concepts such as language, intelligence and sentience. However, it illustrates how hype (and moral panic) is often created around developments in the field of AI.

The Technicalities Underlying AI

To better understand the controversies surrounding AI, we need to look into some of the technical breakthroughs behind the current AI hype. First of all, Russell and

Norvig (2016) argue that for a machine to be intelligent – passing the Turing test – it needs to possess the following capabilities:

- *Natural language processing* (communicating successfully)
- *Knowledge representation* (storing what it knows or hears)
- *Automated reasoning* (using the stored information to answer questions and draw new conclusions)
- *Machine learning* (adapting to new circumstances and to detect and extrapolate patterns).

The currently dominant AI paradigm is machine learning AI. Advances in machine learning have been the most potent contributor to the development of AI in the past two decades (Asaro, 2019). While often seen as a single approach, machine learning is an umbrella term for diverse statistical strategies that aim to solve specific problems. It is a paradigm that allows software programs to automatically improve their performance on a particular task by learning from vast amounts of data (Broussard, 2018; Russell and Norvig, 2016). Machine learning is based on correlation and detecting statistical patterns in large datasets, and it began to be used in the late 1980s and early 1990s. Earlier versions of machine intelligence (e.g., expert systems) were primarily rule-based, using symbolic logic and involving human experts, generating instructions codified as algorithms (Agrawal et al., 2018). The problem was that they could not cope with the complexity of most applications and tasks. Unlike expert systems, powerful machine learning algorithms learn from the ground up, not from humans but from data (Alpaydin, 2016). The rise of machine learning can be explained by more robust and reliable computing infrastructure, which has made possible the development of systems driven by real-world data (K.-F. Lee, 2018). The availability of significant amounts of data further enables the development of learning algorithms that derive solutions using statistical methods.

Within machine learning, three types of learning need to be distinguished (Boden, 2016; Broussard, 2018):

- *Supervised* learning refers to a situation where a defined set of desired outcomes trains the system for a range of inputs (e.g., the system is fed pictures of roads – these are labelled examples) and continually provides feedback about it. The learning system generates hypotheses about the relevant features, and when it classifies incorrectly, it amends its hypothesis accordingly.
- In *unsupervised* learning, the system is not fed any specific outcomes or error messages: the learning is driven by the principle that if features occur together, it creates the expectation that they will do so again. This type of learning is often used to find patterns/clusters in data to discover knowledge.
- *Reinforcement* learning is a type of learning driven by reward and punishment: a feedback mechanism informs the system about what was good/correct or

bad/wrong. Rather than binary, this reinforcement is given in terms of specific scores that tell the system to what extent its decisions lead to success.

Deep learning is the driving force behind machine learning today (Broussard, 2018). The technique is rooted in *artificial neural networks*, computing systems inspired by biological neural circuits that support human thought. A neural circuit comprises a population of neurons that perform specific functions when activated. An artificial neural network is based on a collection of connected units or nodes called *artificial neurons*. Like synapses in a biological brain, each connection can transmit signals to other neurons. An artificial neuron receives signals, processes them, and signals other neutrons connected to it. The signal in a connection is an actual number. In the early 2000s, machine learning pioneer Geoffrey Hinton and colleagues demonstrated the power of deep learning neural networks (LeCun et al., 2015): these allow the automatic processing of unlabelled data, which is used in nearly every contemporary AI application and makes them much more effective.

A Comprehensive Conceptualisation of AI

These *technical approaches* to AI are only one part of conceptualising AI. We must be aware that AI simultaneously refers to technical approaches, social practices and industrial infrastructures (Crawford, 2021).

The *social practices* of AI refer to the classification systems developed by humans, which are behind algorithms, machine learning/deep learning models and AI systems. Crucial questions we need to ask here are as follows:

- Who is involved in developing these classification systems?
- Who decides what classifications are used?
- What do they look like?

Ultimately, these are questions about power as political power impacts inclusion and representation. Essential challenges exist around fairness, bias and discrimination. How representative these classification systems are is a crucial question. Avoiding bias and supporting inclusion in AI systems are critical political issues that urgently need to be addressed (Brevini and Pasquale, 2020).

The *industrial infrastructures* of AI refer to the computing power, algorithms and datasets that are the source of knowledge and production. This infrastructure entails the possibility of collecting vast amounts of data needed to train algorithms and the computational power to develop and run machine learning and deep learning models. Few companies have access to the required datasets, possess the computational power to run machine learning/deep learning and can attract the brightest AI scientists. As a result, we are witnessing a concentrated industrial AI infrastructure, leading to AI oligopolies/monopolies (Dyer-Witheford et al., 2019). This puts a lot of economic power in the hands of a small number of corporations (Verdegem, 2022).

The conceptual clarification that AI also refers to social practices and industrial infrastructures is necessary for understanding its impact on society, especially when looking at AI, power and inequalities. This brings us closer to an operational definition of AI. In basic terms, AI is 'computer programming that learns from and adapts to data' (Verdegem, 2021: 5). A more elaborate version sees AI as a cover term for 'any computational system that can sense its relevant context and react intelligently to data' (Elliot, 2019: 4). It is important to keep in mind the centrality of data processing and automated data analysis in this, to perform specific tasks and achieve specific goals, based on relevant parameters.

AI Applications Are Here

We use AI and automated systems every day; it is not some far-away future scenario. Although these systems operate (mainly) in the background and can be very complex, they can be deconstructed as simple input–output relationships. Let us take a look at some examples:

- We all use email daily. Whatever email client or provider you use, your messages are sorted and classified. One specific type of email is filtered out: spam. AI is behind spam filtering; the input here is your email, whereas an email labelled spam is the output.
- A second example is online advertising. When browsing the internet, we are presented with advertisements customised according to specific user data. This input for an AI system predicts whether or not we will click on a particular online ad (output).
- *Machine translation* is a third example. Imagine we travel to China but do not speak Mandarin. We can use online services whereby AI translates English (input) into Mandarin (output).
- A final AI application used by millions of people is based on *speech recognition*. We give commands to Amazon's *Alexa*, Baidu's *Zaijia* or Apple's *Siri*. In this case, the input is a voice command, and the output is a text transcript, which puts in motion any command we have given (e.g., playing a song, calling a friend or ordering something online).

These examples use a range of AI applications. In the literature, there exist different overviews of subfields of AI (see Table 6.1).

Table 6.1 Classifications of AI subfields

de-Lima-Santos and Ceron (2022)	Dignum (2019)
Machine learning	Problem-solving
Computer vision	Knowledge and reasoning

de-Lima-Santos and Ceron (2022)	Dignum (2019)
Speech recognition	Machine learning
Natural language processing	Interaction
Planning, scheduling and optimisation	Natural language processing
Expert systems	Perception
Robotics	

Computer Vision

In simple terms, computer vision makes it possible for computational systems to *see*. However, this is a misleading term, as computers do not understand visual images or other stimuli like humans (Boden, 2016). A more accurate description is that AI applications can replace some of the functions of the human eye (e.g., scanning text, recognising faces or tracking objects). *Computer vision* is thus a subfield of AI concerned with developing systems that obtain, analyse and understand information from images and other visual data.

Computer vision applications often make use of artificial neural networks. Usually, these programs know precisely what they are looking for.

Boden (2016) writes that Google built a huge artificial neural network in 2012 with over 1 billion connections. The system was presented with more than 10 million random images obtained from YouTube videos. The artificial neural network, equipped with deep learning, was not told what to look for, but after only three days, one artificial neuron unit had learned to respond to images of a cat and another one to human faces.

Computer vision consists of different elements to deal with visual stimuli: image acquisition and transformation, image analysis and image understanding (Warwick, 2012). Other processes are happening within this, such as converting pixels into bits, and finding edges and lines. Computer vision techniques have been further developed as the technology behind facial recognition, object recognition and movement tracking, and other applications. Object recognition is a computational system that can quickly detect what we see in a photo, (e.g., discerning people, animals or vehicles in a landscape photo). An object movement tracking system focuses on an object in a specific frame of a video, compares this to subsequent frames, and tracks the changes and conditions of this frame.

While much progress has been made with computer vision applications, which are successfully used in many professional contexts (e.g., the analysis of X-ray images), they are still systems with fundamental flaws, such as racial bias in AI/data systems and how facial recognition makes (terrible) mistakes. Beyond this, the deep learning behind computer vision faces difficulties (e.g., dealing with three dimensions). As a result, human visual achievements still surpass most contemporary AI (Boden, 2016). Several hurdles must be overcome before human-level computer vision is possible.

Speech Recognition

In the same way that computer vision allows machines to *see*, these systems have also developed the ability to *listen*. Speech recognition is an interdisciplinary sub-field of computer science, linguistics and AI that develops methodologies and technologies to recognise and translate spoken language into text. The main benefit of this translation is to make the spoken language searchable so that specific commands can be detected, which can put in motion other actions (Alpaydin, 2016). Speech recognition can be confused with voice recognition; the latter focuses on identifying an individual user's voice. *Speech recognition* is a subfield of AI that develops methods by which computational systems recognise spoken language and translate it into text.

Speech recognition technologies are evaluated on their accuracy rate and speed. Human language is complex, which makes speech recognition challenging. Advancements in deep learning have created new possibilities in speech recognition, improving the speed and reducing the error rate of detecting language and its translation into text (Boden, 2016). Nowadays, we use this technology in many daily activities. Beyond this, there are specific speech recognition applications in health care, the military, education or helping people with disabilities. Speech recognition entails three aspects: the synthesis, recognition and understanding of speech. Deep learning and artificial neural networks, in particular, are crucial for extracting the meaning of speech.

The complexity of human language remains one of the biggest challenges in advancing speech recognition (Alpaydin, 2016). One particular element is different languages and the accents within them. Speech recognition systems are trained on large datasets, and the more data is available, the more accurate these AI systems are. This benefits dominant languages and is a disadvantage for less commonly used languages (and their native speakers). Accents play a critical role, too: if the same word can be pronounced in different ways, the syllables and phonetics of the same word tend to vary, making it harder for a machine to process. Beyond challenges at the input level, there are also risks related to its output. Security is a significant challenge in the further development of this AI subfield.

There is some overlap between speech recognition and natural language processing because the latter focuses on the interaction between humans and machines through speech and text. Whereas speech recognition focuses on translating human language into text, natural language processing plays a role in how to interpret this text.

Natural Language Processing/Generation

Natural language processing relates to computational systems that analyse large amounts of natural language and can *read* and *understand* this. Natural language processing is also a subfield of AI, combining computer science and linguistics.

The main goal of understanding the content of documents is to extract information and insights from them accurately and to categorise and organise the documents themselves. *Natural language processing* is thus a subfield of AI that helps computational systems understand, interpret and manipulate human language, often on a large scale.

Natural language processing combines computational linguistics (rule-based modelling of human language) with statistical, machine learning and deep learning models. The power of deep learning is that, given sufficient examples, it can be applied in many contexts for a broad range of applications (Boden, 2016). For example, natural language processing is used for machine translation and information retrieval, including data mining of extensive collections of natural language texts (e.g., sifting through medical encyclopaedias or legal case decisions). It can also be used for dialogue systems that process human language through text. In understanding meanings, natural language processing systems can interpret and analyse the speaker or writer's intent and sentiment, a popular application of big data research.

Natural language processing is to be distinguished from *natural language generation*, a software process and AI application domain that produces natural language output. Much scholarly work (and recent controversy) focuses on *large language models*.

Large language models are a statistical representation of a language which tells us the likelihood that a given sequence of words, phrases or sentences can occur in this language (Luitse and Denkena, 2021). These models can be used to predict how sentences might continue, and, as such, a large language model can generate text. Powerful artificial neural network-based large language models – a famous example is Open AI's GPT4 – have become so sophisticated that it is difficult to distinguish their output from human language. This causes controversy as these large language models – like other machine learning/deep learning applications – have an enormous ecological footprint, produce biases, and pose substantial societal challenges (Bender et al., 2021). Discrimination is significant here, which is why Timnit Gebru, a Google AI ethics team co-leader who wrote about large language models and their biased outputs, was famously fired. It also sparks other controversies, such as AI's role in the production and circulation of disinformation.

The Case of the Self-Driving Car

The *DARPA Grand Challenge* is one of the pivotal moments in developing the current AI hype. The generous funding of DARPA accelerated the interest in developing technologies behind one of the most iconic contemporary AI applications: self-driving vehicles. Google/Alphabet (with *Waymo*, their autonomous driving technology development company) has clocked up millions of self-driving miles on public roads in the USA. Most vehicles produced by Tesla are equipped with hardware for (some kind of) autonomous driving, and the company continues to release software updates that move towards this goal. In China, new cities are built and equipped with sensors and other technologies enabling new types of AI-driven mobility. The progress in autonomous vehicles is thanks to significant developments in AI techniques, such as computer vision, motion planning and reinforcement learning.

Although highly complex, we can deconstruct the operation of self-driving vehicles into a combination of AI operations, which can be simplified as input–output relationships. A self-driving car can be seen as a super sophisticated *AI pipeline*, an interconnected and streamlined collection of machine learning/deep learning operations. AI pipelines are composed of *workflows*, which are interactive paths through which data moves through a machine learning/deep learning platform. Within this, the relationship between data and a model is as follows:

- *Input data* is used to develop the model. This data is fed to the algorithm and used to produce a prediction.
- The training model is improved using *training data*.
- The model is then deployed, and a central role exists for *feedback data*. Feedback data is used to improve the algorithm's performance with experience.

The AI pipeline for self-driving vehicles consists of six steps:

- The car has to orient itself in space and uses GPS and a detailed three-dimensional map of its environment. These high-resolution maps are generated by repeatedly driving through a specific neighbourhood to collect data and capture any changes in road conditions.
- When the car moves, it constantly collects data from cameras and sensors that provide 360-degree vision, ultrasonic and radar sensors and *lidar*.[1]
- The collected data about the location and immediate environment is combined to determine the car's route. Computer vision is used to characterise the car's environment and other objects: pedestrians, cyclists, other vehicles and their features.
- Because these components are moving on the road, AI needs to forecast the direction and speed of the movement. It uses motion planning to predict the actions of objects on the road and how the car can proceed in its environment.
- The fifth step is for the self-driving vehicle to determine how to respond intelligently to the changing environment. For example, it needs to decide how to deal with changes in the driving lane and detect traffic lights and other obstacles.
- Finally, search and planning is the AI subfield that teaches machines to compute and choose the correct sequence of resections to solve a given problem.

---

[1] Lidar (light detection and ranging) is a remote sensing technology that uses laser impulses to survey the environment and collects measurements to create models and maps of it.

There is still a lot of controversy about self-driving vehicles, and trust in them often plummets when crashes are reported (Siegel and Pappas, 2023). The media have widely reported accidents with Tesla or Waymo self-driving vehicles. Nevertheless, we need to balance this with the number of people killed and injured in traffic, often because of human errors. Despite the crashes, overall safety statistics for self-driving vehicles are pretty impressive, and it has been suggested that introducing them could save millions of lives.

AI Challenges and Controversies

Despite the hype about AI and the rapid proliferation of algorithmic systems in everyday life, these technologies are far from perfect. There are problems and limitations with regard to how AI is produced, how AI systems cause harm and how the use of AI can be problematic.

Imperfect Technologies

A significant challenge exists in the data used to train algorithms, which are the basis of machine learning/deep learning models (Andrejevic, 2019b; Daly et al., 2018). Today's AI systems often generate faulty results that cannot explain their decision-making process, so AI researchers investigate the potential of *explainable AI* (XAI; Arrieta et al., 2020). In essence, XAI refers to AI systems in which the proposed solution can be understood by humans, thereby providing more accountability. Beyond this, there are also technical problems with AI applications, particularly their difficulty adapting to new situations. These systems must learn how to deal with new problems based on limited examples (Alpaydin, 2016; Boden, 2016).

AI-driven systems cause harm. Harm can vary from discrimination to accidents: sometimes, people get injured or even killed when dealing with automated systems. The previous section discussed self-driving vehicles. Despite their ability to reduce the number of people being killed in traffic incidents, there are also casualties from deploying them. Crashes are widely reported in the media, raising questions about how to program AI systems to better deal with human drivers, other obstacles, or changes in the surrounding environment (Stilgoe, 2018). These crashes also undermine trust in self-driving vehicles, leading to safety concerns around the lack of control over AI (Russell, 2019).

We must also consider the problematic use of AI. A particular concern exists around autonomous weapons and so-called *killer robots*. Countries worldwide are looking at AI and other types of automation to equip their armed forces (Asaro, 2019). The US military, for example, uses machine learning to help analysts identify patterns in large amounts of surveillance data or to pilot autonomous drones. The latter are uncrewed aerial vehicles that have some degree of understanding of the intent and direction of their human operator. *Stop Killer Robots*, a global coalition of researchers and activists, campaigns for more humanity and less autonomy in automated systems and advocates a worldwide ban on fully automated weapons.

Transparency and Trust

A significant challenge of AI is its limited ability to explain its right or wrong decisions, even to its creators (Russell, 2019). These systems are highly complex, often built by large teams who are each responsible for a tiny facet of the application. The lack of transparency is so severe that AI and algorithmic applications are often described as *black box* systems (Burrell, 2016; Ananny and Crawford, 2018). A *black box* refers to a situation where nobody knows what algorithms are inside the systems, who was involved in their development, what data they have been trained on, etc. (Pasquale, 2015).

Inscrutability is a significant limitation of algorithms and a powerful deterrent to public trust in AI (Russell, 2019). In general, people tend to be hesitant when confronted with new technologies. One of the specific issues is whether these innovations are highly visible/tangible or are operating in the background. Many algorithmic/AI systems are already here, making decisions for us that we are unaware of. This creates additional challenges for gaining public trust.

A major challenge in AI research is finding ways to make algorithms and AI systems more understandable and accountable (Brevini and Pasquale, 2020), leading to XAI (see above). In this context, we must consider balancing AI developers' interests with society's. Indeed, more accountability in AI systems can come with a particular cost for their developers, while more transparency about them can also be misused by others, such as hackers (Ananny and Crawford, 2018). A complication in this is that human decision-making often contains elements of intuition, guided by instinct and experience. The problem for AI researchers is how much they can make their creations rationally explain themselves.

Bias and Injustice

In some cases, AI systems use algorithms that produce nonsensical decisions that are wrong but not harmful; their mistakes can (often) be easily caught and dealt with. A more problematic outcome, however, is that AI and algorithmic systems subtly but systematically discriminate against certain groups in society based on ethnicity, gender or class (Eubanks, 2018; Noble, 2018; Perez, 2019). Typical examples are:

- The *racial bias* in facial detection software. These systems often do not work correctly for non-white people as they are trained on biased datasets.
- *Gender stereotypes* in online search results. For example, searches for *doctor* or *engineer* predominantly yield images of men, while searches for *nurse* or *secretary* predominantly yield photos of women.

- Putting *marginalised people/groups at risk.* Algorithmic systems already (subtly or not) distort medical care or insurance rates that people receive, altering how they are treated in the criminal justice system.

AI tends to reproduce inequalities, leading to an intensification of discrimination (McQuillan, 2022). This is because the datasets based on which AI systems are trained are biased or the AI developers themselves – who tend to be more white, male and middle-class than average – are not representative of society and thus are contributing to new levels of exclusion and unfair treatment (Broussard, 2018).

Bias and injustice erode the trust between humans and AI systems. For this reason, we need to establish human control and create machines that benefit humans and align with society's objectives (Russell, 2019). Rather than being an equaliser, AI may not be better than humans at making life-changing decisions from a neutral viewpoint. If so, why would we – as a society – accept automated systems as fairer replacements for bankers, recruiters, law enforcement or judges?

Environmental Impact

AI's environmental impact is another big concern besides the problems and challenges already discussed. The work of Crawford (2021) helps us see the bigger picture of AI and the exploitation and extraction that are at the core of the global AI ecosystem. 'Anatomy of an AI System' (Crawford and Joler, 2018) dismantles the complex relationship of planetary resources, data and human labour behind AI. It opens up the debate on the cost of producing and deploying AI- and data-driven systems. This contradicts how companies and governments portray AI as a solution to global challenges such as climate change (Coeckelbergh, 2020). Google/Alphabet famously talks about how its AI subsidiary DeepMind uses machine learning to help optimise the energy use of Google's data centres. However, there is less openness about the actual energy cost of AI and machine learning applications by these companies.

This inspired media scholar and activist Benedetta Brevini (2021) to ask whether AI is *good for the planet.* She provides a detailed and critical analysis of the planetary costs of AI. Despite being pitched as a solution to help mitigate climate change, she argues that AI is worsening the situation. Using more AI services contributes to an accelerated extraction of raw materials and an intensification of unnecessary products, product obsolescence and waste of computational devices. Beyond this, there is the energy cost of AI: the computational power needed to process data and train algorithms massively increases energy consumption. Data centres continually demand electricity and water for their cooling systems. Brevini (2021) details how training a fairly basic algorithmic model emits more than 284 tonnes of carbon dioxide, equivalent to 1213 return flights between London and Rome. Rather than following the AI hype, we thus need to be aware of and think critically about its impact on our planet and climate.

Singularity and Superintelligence

The concept of *singularity* (Kurzweil, 2005) refers to a (hypothetical) point in history where technological development becomes radically faster and more uncontrollable, drastically impacting relationships between humans and machines. Kurzweil, a futurist employed by Google/Alphabet, predicts when AI reaches human-level intelligence. This achievement would then rapidly trigger the rise of *superintelligent AI* (Bostrom, 2014). While there is disagreement about whether it is technically achievable and when this moment is to come (see, for example, Boden 206), it sparks moral panic about (dystopian) technological futures. This is helped by science fiction movies, TV series and literature. For example, Wilson's (2011) novel *Robopocalypse*, written in the present tense, portrays AI in a dystopian context and explores the capacity of robots to take over control of humans.

This feeds into debates about what it is to be human and has advanced movements such as *posthumanism* and *transhumanism*. Posthumanism is a contemporary field of study (in philosophy, art and culture) dedicated to exploring what comes after humanism. This framework invites us to think about and clarify the future relations between biological humans and *hybrid posthumans* (Nath and Manna, 2023). Transhumanism is a philosophical and intellectual movement that advocates enhancing the human condition by using technology to improve cognition and longevity (More, 2013). These movements and the questions they ask become more relevant in an era where we increasingly use automated systems, and these technologies have become more advanced.

In 2022, a Google/Alphabet engineer was put on leave (and later fired) after saying that an AI chatbot using natural language processing and large language models had become sentient. It sparked much controversy and fed into debates about whether artificial general intelligence is possible and when it will come. But for an AI to become genuinely sentient, it would need to be able to think, perceive and feel, and scientists are divided on whether this is achievable. However, a debate like this makes it crucial to think about who controls the development of AI and what is at stake here. Leading AI company OpenAI, which received a large amount of funding for further developing services such as ChatGPT and DALL-E, sees it as its mission to establish artificial general intelligence and contributes to the hype around it. We will need to wait and see what happens with this in the following years.

Power, Inequalities and Injustices

Ultimately, how contemporary technologies look, and their impact (positive or negative) on society is determined by who is in charge of developing and deploying them. This comes down to the question of power. In social theory, *power* is a contested concept. Power is 'the capacity of actors to accomplish things in the world' (Wright, 2010: 111). In the context of AI, power decides who can and will benefit from new technologies and applications (Verdegem, 2021). A concentration of power in the hands of a small number of stakeholders (whether corporate or from government) increases the possibility of adverse outcomes, such as inequalities and injustice. Power is used to control society, and for AI and data-driven systems this means the power to decide how the world is categorised and how data commodification and extraction happen (Sadowski, 2019). Studying AI and its impact critically, avoiding inequalities and injustice, and ensuring that new technologies benefit society demand that we put power at the centre of our analysis (Verdegem, 2022). This also means diversifying and being inclusive in who is involved in the debates about the present and future of AI.

Learning Takeaways

- Despite the recent hype around ChatGPT and other generative AI services, AI has existed for over 60 years.
- A combination of breakthroughs in machine/deep learning techniques, a growth in resources with which algorithms can be trained and more computing power is behind the current period of AI hype.
- The AI we have is artificial narrow intelligence. It is unclear whether artificial general intelligence, the 'Hollywood AI', will ever become a reality.
- AI systems cannot *really* see, listen or write, despite breakthroughs in AI applications, such as computer vision, speech recognition or natural language processing/generation.
- Although powerful, AI technologies are imperfect and face challenges around transparency, bias, and their environmental impact.

Recommended Reading

Bartoletti, I. (2020). *An Artificial Revolution: On Power, Politics and AI*. London: The Indigo Press.

Broussard, M. (2018). *Artificial Unintelligence. How Computers Misunderstand the World*. Cambridge, MA: MIT Press.

Crawford, K. (2021). *Atlas of AI: Power, Politics, and the Planetary Costs of Artificial Intelligence*. New Haven, CT: Yale University Press.

Lee, K.-F. (2018). *AI Superpowers*. Boston: Houghton Mifflin.

Mitchell, M. (2019). *Artificial Intelligence: A Guide for Thinking Humans*. New York: Farrar, Straus and Giroux.

Recommended Listening

Radical AI, a podcast series centring marginalised and otherwise radical voices in the industry and academy for dialogue, collaboration and debate regarding AI ethics and the relationship between the humanities and machine learning. https://www. radicalai.org/

Part III

Applications and Controversies

7   Data, Industries and Globalisation   113
8   Data, Tech and Inequalities   135
9   Data, Journalism and Disinformation   157
10 Data, Automation and Work   175

7

Data, Industries and Globalisation

Learning Goals

- Learn what globalisation is in the twenty-first century and why it is relevant to understanding both media and data industries.
- Uncover the power battle in the rise of Silicon Valley and its tech corporations and compare that to recent developments In China.
- Deconstruct the economic imperatives and cultural impacts of the world's biggest tech companies, from Amazon to Alibaba, from Google/Alphabet to Baidu.
- What are the world's dominant data companies, and how can we study their power?
- Explore whether globalising the data industries is creating a new phase of colonialism.

Globalisation or Cold War 2.0?

The *cold war*, a period of geopolitical tension between the United States and the Soviet Union, ended in the early 1990s with the fall of communism. In the last decade, we have witnessed growing tensions between the United States and China, sometimes called a new *cold war*. While the first *cold war* was mainly a hegemonic struggle between capitalism and communism, *cold war 2.0* is focused on global economic leadership. The USA has been the world's largest economy since the twentieth century, but it is under threat by the emergence of China as a superpower. Tensions have been rising, ranging from trade and tariffs to alleged spying and tech rivalry. With Xi Jinping becoming the president of China in 2013 and the election of Trump in 2016, tensions intensified, and there has been the looming threat of a trade war between the two countries. The growing importance of digital technologies plays a significant role in this. While America's Silicon Valley still dominates the tech world, it feels pressure from China, especially since the announcement that China wants to become the global leader in AI by 2030. Chinese tech companies also aim to enlarge their global market share and sphere of influence across the globe. This power battle invites us to examine how globalisation plays out in the data industries.

How to Understand Globalisation in the World of Data

Globalisation is a buzzword and a complex concept that can refer to different things. Before discussing global media companies and data industries, we must understand *globalisation*. It was first used in the twentieth century, replacing the term *mondialisation*, a (French) reference to more interaction among people, governments, companies and other institutions worldwide. While one position is that globalisation is nothing new and has always existed (e.g., Flew, 2007), it gained in importance in the second half of the twentieth century with events such as the oil crisis in the 1970s, the fall of communism and the resulting global dominance of capitalism, the emergence of the internet, etc. (Beck, 1999). In essence, *globalisation* is used to describe an extension of the nation-state and, as a result, an increasing and unprecedented international interconnectedness between countries, economies and populations in the period since the cold war. New developments in communication technology played a massive role in facilitating the flow of information through networks (Castells, 1996).

What Is Globalisation Today?

While global military cooperation is an integral part of globalisation too, I discuss here the impact of globalisation at the level of economy, politics and culture (Ritzer, 2007):

- *Economic globalisation* refers to the growing interdependence of national economies across the globe through a massive increase in cross-border movement of capital, goods, services, technology, etc. In this sense, economic globalisation is the product of an increasing integration of national markets, leading to the development of a global marketplace. It results in worldwide trade and open markets (including the removal of trade barriers), global production, distribution and consumption, and the rise of *multinationals* (multinational corporations).
- *Political globalisation* situates the impact of global cooperation (on issues such as trade, security and the environment) and integration in developing a worldwide political system. Political globalisation coincided with the rise of intergovernmental organisations (such as the *United Nations* and the *World*

Health Organization) and government-independent elements of a global civil society, such as international non-governmental organisations (e.g., *Amnesty International* and *Greenpeace*). Political globalisation is linked to the (real or perceived) diminishing importance of nation-states and the realisation that specific challenges need global cooperation and cannot be dealt with by one or a few countries alone (the Covid-19 pandemic and climate change are good examples here).

- *Cultural globalisation* refers to the transmission of ideas, meanings and values across the world in a way that extends and intensifies (global) social relations. In particular, globalisation at this level is characterised by the emergence of global cultures – such as fashion, language, media, music and travel (Appadurai, 1996). The internet played a crucial role in the diffusion of global cultural consumption, adding a new layer to existing commodity exchange and colonisation processes, which have a more extended history of carrying cultural meanings worldwide. Cultural globalisation is critical in forming shared norms and how people associate their (collective and individual) cultural identities.

While advocates of globalisation talk about the opportunities it (supposedly) delivers – such as increased productivity, lower prices (in theory), innovation, and stimulation of growth and development – there is also a shadow side of globalisation which includes the rise of inequalities, cultural appropriation and homogenisation, (colonial) ethnocentrism and environmental degradation (Beck, 1999). Particularly around the end of the twentieth century, the anti- (or counter-)globalisation movement argued that human rights and dignity, the preservation of the natural environment and democratic institutions are under pressure by globalisation. While this criticism is mainly situated on the political left, a wave of nationalist (and therefore often anti-global) and populist political leaders have taken control in many countries.

Global Media and Communication

Media are crucial in the process of globalisation. Some scholars even include them in their very definition of globalisation: 'Globalisation is a process in which world-wide economic, political, cultural and social relations have become increasingly mediated across time and space' (Rantanen, 2005: 8). Beyond acknowledging this centrality, it is essential to look into how media and communication industries have approached globalisation. In many cases, *going global* is a central part of a business strategy: it opens up the opportunity to increase the market share of companies when their national market is saturated (Flew, 2018). Media and communication products and services are very suitable as they can easily be reused and repackaged, thanks to digitalisation and convergence. While their initial production costs may be high, their reproduction costs are marginal (in a digital environment) (Doyle, 2013).

Media corporations can use different strategies in their pursuit of going global:

- Developing international media products, with global TV series such as *Game of Thrones* and *Squid Game*.
- Using *economies of scale* and *scope* to increase market share and realise product diversification, such as redeveloping the movie *The Matrix* as a game alongside other merchandising products.
- Exploring opportunities and new markets, for example, the most successful reality TV shows like *Big Brother* have been franchised and broadcast in many countries beyond the original country.

A *transnational media corporation* is a corporation active in two or more countries, whereby the strategic decisions and allocation of resources happen based on economic goals and efficiency beyond the national market (and where the primary commodities are information and entertainment) (Doyle, 2013). These transnational media corporations tend to pursue an oligopoly, whereby they use strategies of acquisition and competition to establish their control and increase their dominance over the global market. In transforming themselves into transnational media corporations, media companies can follow different steps/phases: often, the starting point is establishing a dominant (national) market, and when that is realised (and the local market is saturated), they can extend their presence to an international market. After this, the next goal will be to consolidate their global position.

Globalisation and the Digital (Data) Revolution

The internet was a significant catalyst in the globalisation of media and communication. It meant the start of a new wave of *going global*. Before leading tech companies were even founded, the US government – notably Vice-President Al Gore – was championing the idea of the internet as a worldwide digital communication network, referred to as the *information superhighway* (Mosco, 2005). Although the US policy was, in the first instance, focused on establishing a national fibre-optic network, the combination of technology and politics created a new phase of globalisation in the sphere of communication. Even though Margaret Thatcher in the UK and Ronald Reagan in the USA introduced neoliberal politics in the 1980s, the Clinton administration in the 1990s (further) implemented neoliberalism and liberalisation: its central policies were focused on economic deregulation and a *laissez-faire* state oversight policy. Political economy scholar Dan Schiller (2000) refers to this as a new phase in the development of capitalism – which he framed as *digital capitalism* – whereby the internet is the backbone not only for globalisation but also for advancing the global capitalist system. In this analysis, *going global* refers to the neoliberal project in transnational communication: it is a process of colonisation of cyberspace, which happens at an unprecedented speed but is also characterised by the growing influence of advertising and the commodification of everyday life (Schiller, 2000).

What is the difference between the earlier waves of globalisation in media and communication and the current digital/data revolution? After all, radio, for example, was a global media platform before it became national/regional (Flew, 2007). We notice that most *big tech* companies were founded in the 1990s and rapidly became among the most valuable countries in the world. Companies such as Alibaba, Amazon, Apple, Baidu, Facebook/Meta, Google/Alphabet, Microsoft and Tencent have established themselves as leading internet companies before dominating the social media and mobile media markets and, more recently, also taking the lead in the AI and data industries (Verdegem, 2022). We are witnessing the emergence of two power blocks, one from the USA and one from China, involved in an intense battle for global dominance. This will be further discussed in the following sections.

A final thought before moving into the analysis of the global data industries involves the *chicken or egg* question: is it technology (e.g., internet, social/mobile media) that pushed for a new wave of globalisation (which is a *techno-centric* approach), or is it instead the other way round: should we see globalisation as the engine that has used digital technology to establish a new phase of global digital capitalism (which can be seen as a *political-economic* approach)? Answering this question is difficult, but we must look into these developments and analyse globalisation in the context of the data industries.

Silicon Valley and its Dominance over the (Western) World

Before looking into the so-called *big tech*, we must examine what ideas (or ideologies) are behind the tech companies dominating the Western world.

The Californian Ideology

In a seminal essay, 'The Californian Ideology' *(*written long before the current hype around data, AI and related technologies*)*, Barbrook and Cameron (1996) analyse the roots and ideas of the entrepreneurs/companies who would start to conquer the world from the US west coast. Barbrook and Cameron (1996: 1) contend that this ideology draws on a specific combination of 'the free-wheeling spirit of the hippies and the entrepreneurial zeal of the yuppies'. The techno-utopian and solutionist visions about the unlimited possibilities of technology – facilitated by the convergence of media, computing and telecommunications – brought together a 'loose alliance of writers, hackers, capitalists and artists' who are simultaneously optimistic and bohemian but also libertarian and embracing the free market doctrine.

In essence, the *Californian ideology* is based on three central tenets:

- *Technological determinism*: the belief that technology is the driving force in history and ultimately creates a more egalitarian and democratic society.
- *Cyber-libertarianism*: the idea that the internet develops a new world where individuals can be free from government and corporate control constraints.
- *New Left counterculture*: the belief in the importance of individual freedom, creativity and self-expression.

The common belief in the emancipatory potential of digital technologies inspired a generation of computer scientists and entrepreneurs to set up companies that colonise everyday lives (Larson, 2020; Couldry and Mejias, 2019a). From Silicon Valley, they started to export ideas about digital technology to Europe and the rest of the world, arguing that technology is *the* engine behind innovation. Anyone daring to question or critique some of their ideas would automatically be put in the camp of *Luddism* or anti-progress (Mueller, 2021). The problem with this Californian ideology is that it propagates only one vision for the future, negating the imagining of alternative ideas and neglecting some of the adverse outcomes of digital technologies (Liu, 2020).

GAFAM: American Big Tech

In his book *The Digital Economy*, Jordan (2020) writes that the digital economy is simultaneously an object of fear, fascination and hope. Those aspects feed into hype, leading to the rise of the so-called *big tech*. *Big tech* refers to a small number of companies that have an enormous impact on society and are hugely financially successful. Alongside their centrality in daily life and economic valuation, big tech is also associated with establishing global corporate monopolies (Dencik, 2022a). In this section, I discuss big tech in the Western world, while the following section looks into big tech in China.

The acronym GAFAM is often used to describe the size and power of big tech. It was first used in 2014 by television host Jim Cramer (of CNBC's show *Mad Money*) to refer to the Western world's five most prominent technology companies: Google/Alphabet, Amazon, Facebook/Meta, Apple and Microsoft. Even though the acronym was criticised for not being accurate (e.g., not including companies such as Netflix or Tesla), it is still widely used.

GAFAM companies have become the most valuable companies in the world. Table 7.1 illustrates how much the value of big tech companies has increased in the last decade. The Covid-19 pandemic – with lockdowns and reliance on digital technologies – massively contributed to this increase in value, alongside the current hype around AI. The rise in value has slowed down in 2022–2023 because of the tech layoffs (big tech companies in the USA organised rounds of redundancies) and ill-judged investments (e.g., Facebook/Meta's failed strategy to transform itself from a social media company into a *metaverse* platform).

Table 7.1   Value* of the world's leading data companies (GAFAM), in billions of US dollars

Company	Year founded	2010	2020	2023
Google/Alphabet	1998/2015	318	971	1570
Amazon	1994	56	1377	1297
Facebook/Meta	2004/2021		616	700
Apple	1976	250	1508	2893
Microsoft	1975	233	1485	2508

Source: macrotrends.net (2023)

*Expressed as market capitalisation – the value determined by the stock market.

In their book *Digital Dominance*, Moore and Tambini (2018) argue that big tech companies became so powerful for structural reasons, such as data collection and use, control over content, and market dominance. They explain this power concentration by arguing that digital markets are *winner-takes-all markets:* their access to data and use of machine learning algorithms, economies of scale, important user and employee branding, and network effects have given big tech companies the ability to control their market, especially by using strategies of *switching cost* and *lock-in*.

While *switching cost* refers to the human capital needed to learn how to use unfamiliar systems and software, resulting in a higher cost of switching to a different platform, *lock-in* has to do with user functionality, accumulated content and networks connected to one platform, which keeps users locked into existing platforms. The combined mechanism of high switching costs and lock-in makes it very challenging for new rivals to enter the market, as they need to provide a better user experience, better value for money, etc., to convince users to consider switching to a new platform. Hence, we witnessed the emergence of global corporate big tech monopolies.

Google/Alphabet: Organising the World's Information

Larry Page and Sergey Brin founded Google in 1998 and transformed it into a public company in August 2004. Google's original mission was 'to organize the world's information and make it universally accessible and useful', and its main product for doing so was an online search engine. Since then, Google has acquired many other companies, which has helped to diversify its activities. Essential acquisitions include:

- YouTube (video-sharing platform, 2006)
- DoubleClick (online advertising, 2008)
- Motorola Mobility (mobile devices, 2012 – later sold to Lenovo)
- DeepMind (AI startup, 2014).

In 2015, Alphabet was set up as a holding company. Its main segment is Google, which includes internet products such as search, advertising, maps, YouTube, apps, cloud, the mobile platform Android, Chrome, and Google Play, but also hardware products such as Chromecast, Chrome/Pixel laptops, tablets and phones. Other segments of Alphabet are X Development, Fiber, Nest, CapitalG, and DeepMind. As Table 7.1 shows, Google/Alphabet is a highly profitable company.

An essential element of the critique of the political economy of Google/Alphabet is its market dominance. The company dominates key digital markets, including online search, advertising and mobile operating systems (Lee, 2017). This dominance gives the company significant power to shape how people access information, influence how people spend their money, and control people through their devices. In addition to market dominance, Google/Alphabet can be criticised for its role in circulating disinformation (e.g., in the context of elections or the Covid-19 pandemic). The company also collects vast user data, including search history, browsing habits and location data. This data is the input for targeted advertising and the source for building user profiles that can be deployed for other purposes, including surveillance. Google/Alphabet also has been criticised because of its close relationship with the US government and has come under increasing scrutiny from other governments across the globe. The company has been accused of market power abuse, data protection violation and censorship.

Amazon: The Everything Store

Amazon was founded by Jeff Bezos in 1994 as an online book retail company. Since then, it has expanded its activities into e-commerce, providing services to four primary customers: consumers, sellers, enterprises and content creators. In addition, it provides marketing and promotional services, content production and other digital services. Amazon's strategy has been to develop a dominant brand and market share, driving competitors out of the market and reinvesting to optimise customers' experience and keep them within the Amazon ecosystem. While still growing its user base and control, Amazon is now most profitable through its activities in cloud computing. It launched *Amazon Web Services* (AWS) in 2006 to offer IT infrastructure services to other businesses. This enables these businesses to rely on Amazon's global network of servers to store and process data rather than invest in their own server infrastructure. AWS is now the leading supplier of cloud services (Calabrese and Rollins, 2017). In addition to being highly profitable (see also Table 7.1), it gives Amazon a strategic competitive advantage by having access to and control over immense datasets. With business models becoming increasingly data-driven, this requires a performant computing infrastructure, and Amazon is a world leader in this market.

A critical analysis of Amazon's political economy can be centred around several issues (Calabrese and Rollins, 2017):

- Its dominance and market power in several sectors (including e-commerce, cloud computing, and streaming) have raised concerns about anti-competitive behaviour. Amazon pushes not only traditional retailers and businesses out of the market, but also online competitors.
- A significant concern is Amazon's labour practices. Several investigations have shed light on exploiting workers, including productivity expectations (long hours and insufficient breaks) and workplace safety. In addition, Amazon has resisted the unionisation efforts of its workers.
- Taxation and government subsidies are also significant concerns. Amazon faced criticism for utilising complex tax structures and exploring tax loopholes to minimise its tax obligations. It also exploits incentives and government subsidies to open warehouses and distribution centres, creating competition among countries and regions.
- Amazon can also be criticised because of its role in establishing an ideology of convenience (Huberman, 2022). This refers to shopping experiences such as *Amazon Go* shops where customers no longer have to pay. Amazon establishes this convenience through ideological strategies such as *naturalisation* (making it all natural and self-evident), *obfuscation* (e.g., making the constant surveillance – and the power that it brings – invisible), and *promotion* (promoting beliefs and values related to convenience).

Facebook/Meta: The World's Largest Digital Advertising Agency

Mark Zuckerberg founded Facebook in 2004 with a couple of fellow students and roommates. Since then, Facebook has become the world's most important social media company. Originally a social network site, Facebook became a giant communication platform and one of the world's largest advertising agencies. It used an aggressive acquisition strategy to take over potential competitors and increase control over its platform, services and users:

- *Instagram* (acquired in 2012)
- *WhatsApp* (2014)
- *Oculus VR* (2014)
- Facial recognition company *Face.com* (2012)
- Advertising technology company *Atlas* (2013).

In October 2021, Facebook rebranded itself and changed the name of its parent company to Meta (Platforms), signalling its focus on developing the *metaverse*. However, this transition cannot be seen as a success. Since early 2022, Meta has reported a lack of growth in monthly users and a decline in profits, resulting in a substantive reduction in the company's share price. This also contributed to massive staff layoffs in November 2022 and April 2023.

Several aspects contribute to the critique of Facebook/Meta's political economy:

- Its business model focuses on targeted advertising, for which the company needs to collect and analyse massive amounts of data, contributing to corporate surveillance.
- Fuchs (2017c) argues that Facebook/Meta's capital accumulation strategy is based on exploiting users' digital labour. Facebook's users can be considered a *prosumer commodity*, actively engaged in producing and circulating content.
- Facebook/Meta uses its dominant position in the social media market for anti-competitive behaviour. For example, its control over user data and advertising revenue allows it to dominate the market and limit consumer choice. The company uses its international expansion into international markets following a global business model, thereby (negatively) impacting local economies, media landscapes and (the dependence on Facebook/Meta by) small businesses.
- There are also significant concerns about user privacy, data breaches and unauthorised access to user information. As a result, Facebook/Meta has faced scrutiny and regulatory action for its data practices.
- Another element of critique is based on Facebook/Meta's role in circulating disinformation and, as a result, its impact on democracy. The company has faced criticism for its algorithms prioritising engagement and amplifying divisive, misleading or even harmful content. The latter aspect is also linked to content moderation. Facebook/Meta is challenged with balancing freedom of speech and content moderation. However, the company has been criticised for its content moderation practices being opaque and prone to bias, in addition to the fact that people engaged in content moderation are exploited (Roberts, 2019).

Apple: Brand Above All

Apple is a technology company founded in 1976 by Steve Jobs and Stephen Wozniak. While Apple started as a hardware company, it has since evolved into one that focuses on designing, manufacturing and marketing personal computers, digital devices, mobile communication and portable music players. In addition to hardware, it also launched *iTunes* and later *App Store*, which helped Apple develop an ecosystem that brings together consumers and app developers. It also allows Apple to control its brand and its products and features. Apple has revolutionised the communication industry with eye-catching products such as the *iPod*, *iPhone* and *iPad*. While still dominating the mobile device market, the company – under pressure from other hardware producers – has increasingly shifted its attention to services to drive profits. Apple has been successful in this and has consistently been one of the world's most valuable companies (see Table 7.1).

The critique of Apple's political economy is centred around several elements:

- Given its position as one of the world's leading technology companies, concerns exist about the power its ecosystem (which includes hardware, software and services) possesses (Miller and Maxwell, 2017). Its control over the App Store and its policies on app developers have been the subject of criticism and concerns about fair competition, antitrust and the balance between platform control and developer freedom.

- There are questions about Apple's global manufacturing practices. Qiu (2016) scrutinises its manufacturing in China (particularly by the Taiwanese company Foxconn) and discusses concerns about labour conditions, worker rights, and health and safety standards. While Apple launched initiatives to address these issues through supplier responsibility programmes, it still faces challenges in ensuring fair and safe working conditions.
- Apple's success is built on its ability to develop innovative products and protect its intellectual property. However, the company has legal battles with competitors over copy infringement and patents. While intellectual property protection is critical for Apple's profitability, it also has implications for the broader innovation ecosystem.
- Given the centrality of data in its business model, Apple has tried to position itself as a leader in privacy and security by implementing end-to-end encryption and restricted access to user data. In this context, it has sometimes clashed with governments when they are asking for backdoor access to encrypted devices and data.
- Finally, Apple's tax practices have been scrutinised, mainly how it uses offshore tax havens and profit shifting to minimise its tax obligations. Apple has been accused of exploiting loopholes and engaging in aggressive tax planning strategies. Given its enormous wealth, there are questions about fair taxation and the need for international tax reforms.

Microsoft: The Master Operating System

Microsoft is the oldest company among GAFAM, founded in 1975 by Bill Gates and Paul Allen. It developed its business around personal computer (PC) operating systems (MS-DOS and Windows) and other software products, of which the *Office* package is the most famous. From this initial focus on PC software, Microsoft has since diversified its activities, providing multiple hardware and software services. In addition to PC operating systems, Microsoft also offers operating systems for servers, phones, games consoles and intelligent devices. Microsoft has increasingly invested in distributed computing environments, productivity applications, business solutions, video games (*Xbox*) and online advertising. In this context, it acquired other companies, such as *Skype* (2011) and *LinkedIn* (2016), to name but two. More recently, Microsoft obtained an exclusive licence to use OpenAI's GPT (*Generative Pre-trained Transformer*) software, announcing in 2023 a multi-billion-dollar investment to integrate *ChatGPT* into its services. As Table 7.1 indicates, Microsoft is a highly valuable company.

Analysing the critique of its political economy, it is clear that Microsoft uses its power to shape the tech environment (Birkinbine, 2017):

- Microsoft has faced criticism (and legal intervention) for its historical monopoly power in the software industry. The company has been accused of engaging in anti-competitive behaviour, such as bundling its software and limiting interoperability with competing software. The *browser wars* (between Netscape Navigator and Internet Explorer) are a typical example of this.
- Linked to using monopoly power, Microsoft has been involved in disputes over intellectual property and has used aggressive patent strategies to maintain its dominant position.
- Given the widespread use of its services, there are questions about privacy and data protection. Microsoft's products and services handle vast amounts of data, and concerns exist about data collection, retention, and potential government access to user information.
- This is linked to another contentious issue: Microsoft's close relationship with governments and its involvement in surveillance. Microsoft has secured significant government contracts for data services and cloud computing. Its role in providing technology and services has sparked debate about civil liberties and the ethics of technology companies involved in government surveillance.

Summary GAFAM

The analysis of big tech shows that there are common strategies these companies use to establish and maintain their dominance over the market: they use their position for anti-competitive behaviour (monopoly power); they maximise their profits by exploiting tax loopholes; some of the companies have questionable labour practices (in-house and via outsourcing) and they all are data-centred, which makes them critical players in corporate surveillance. Going back to ideas about the Californian ideology, US big tech companies still embrace technological determinism. An assessment of their libertarianism is mixed, as they profit from government contracts while simultaneously trying to escape their tax duties. Finally, one has difficulties seeing how New Left counterculture ideas are still present, especially at the company level.

The Rise of China as a (Tech) Superpower

It is an understatement to say that China has become an economic superpower. While industrial development was centred in western Europe in the nineteenth century and in the USA and Japan for much of the twentieth century, China had become the world's manufacturing powerhouse by the end of the century.

From Manufacturing Powerhouse to Tech Superpower

Although network-based information and communication became a new technological paradigm in the 1970s, it is thanks to globalisation that we have witnessed its expansion into a global communication network in the 1990s. The rise of the internet in China happened in the early twenty-first century. Due to its population size and increasing economic power, China became home to the world's largest number of mobile phone users in 2007, and its internet population became the largest in the world in 2008 (Qiu, 2009).

China's high-tech superpower development started in the 1980s (Tang, 2020; Zhao, 2008). After the Cultural Revolution under Mao Zedong, the Chinese government established universities and research institutes focused on technological development. This resulted in the development of new companies in the late 1980s, such as Huawei and Lenovo. Many companies began to export their products to other countries, and China increasingly became known as the *workshop of the world* (Qiu, 2015). The mid 1990s, with the development of the internet – as an infrastructure – was a second stage of industrial reform in China. Around the turn of the century, the Chinese tech industry grew, including new companies such as Alibaba, Baidu, and Tencent. These companies helped to drive the growth of e-commerce and the mobile internet in China. Especially after 2011, the government prioritised the internet industry, which has increasingly become the backbone of the economy (Tang, 2020).

In 2015, the Chinese Communist Party launched a national strategic plan, *Made in China 2025*. This plan aimed to move away from being the *world's factory* (a producer of low-tech goods facilitated by cheap labour costs and supply chain advantages). The goal was to upgrade its manufacturing capabilities and transform China into a *technology*-intensive (instead of *labour*-intensive) powerhouse. Not much later, the Chinese government launched a new vision centred on AI. In July 2017, the Chinese State Council published its *Development Plan for a New Generation of Artificial Intelligence* (K.-F. Lee, 2018). This plan outlines how China aims to achieve significant breakthroughs by 2025 and become the global AI leader in 2030. The Taiwanese AI researcher, ex-president of Google China and Chinese tech investor Kai-Fu Lee (2018) explains in his book *AI Superpowers* how China is well-placed to become a global AI leader for different reasons:

- The amount of funding it invests in AI (including science and education).
- Its ability to collect data (needed to train AI models, with fewer data protection regulations than other regions).
- Its tech start-up culture and entrepreneurial spirit (with fewer intellectual property restrictions and barriers to vertical integration).
- Its central government put AI development central in its policy-making.

BAT: The Chinese Internet Giants

Like GAFAM, the acronym BAT refers to China's most powerful tech companies. The BAT companies, which include Baidu, Alibaba and Tencent, are world-renowned internet companies that have an impact beyond the domestic market (Su and Flew, 2021; Yeo, 2023). Each of them dominates specific digital markets:

- Baidu is a leader in online search and AI (and therefore is sometimes called the *Google of China*).
- Alibaba mainly focuses on e-commerce and cloud computing (and can be seen as the Chinese equivalent of Amazon).
- Tencent dominates the social media and gaming markets (which has some equivalence to Facebook/Meta).

Picturing these Chinese companies through a comparison with their US counterparts illustrates the need to de-Westernise platform theory, as Western-centric platform studies do not consider the cultural and entrepreneurial context in which these platforms have been developed (Davis and Xiao, 2021). Having said this, the rise of the BAT companies is to be studied in terms of both their impact on nation-states and the global economic order (Zhao, 2008). Despite their similarities and differences, these companies compete for domestic and international market share, user base, access to and possession of data, profitability and technological innovation. Like their US counterparts, they are involved in large-scale acquisitions and mergers that empower their platforms and services (Su and Flew, 2021; Jia and Winseck, 2018).

In the same vein as with GAFAM, there is discussion of whether the BAT designation is comprehensive enough to include the major Chinese technology companies. Others include *Huawei* (telecommunications equipment and consumer electronics), *Xiaomi* (consumer electronics), *JD.com* (e-commerce), *Meituan* (food delivery and local services), *Didi Chuxing* (ride-hailing and mobility services) and *ByteDance* (the social media company behind *TikTok/Douyin* and news aggregator *Toutiao*).

The rise of the market valuation of the BAT companies is illustrated in Table 7.2. The market capitalisation data shows how much these companies – particularly Alibaba and Tencent – have grown in the last decade (similarly to some of the growth of Silicon Valley companies).

Table 7.2 Value* of the world's leading data companies (BAT), in billions of US dollars

Company	Year founded	2010	2020	2021
Baidu	2000	22	33	73
Alibaba	1999		540	626
Tencent	1998	37	510	764

Source: ycharts.com (2023)
*Expressed as market capitalisation – the value determined by the stock market.

While the US companies experienced a wave of lay-offs in 2022 and 2023, some-thing else impacted the BAT companies. In late 2020, the Chinese government initiated a series of regulatory actions to curb the power of Chinese technology companies. The crackdown on *big tech* includes an intervention on three levels:

- *Antitrust*: The Chinese government had been concerned about the growing power of *big tech*, including concerns that these companies could use their market power to stifle competition. These antitrust investigations led to fines, divestitures and other restrictions on their business practices.
- *Data privacy*: The government also enacted new data privacy regulations that require tech companies to obtain user consent before collecting and using their data. The measures are intended to give users more control over their data and allow them to request data be deleted.
- *Online content*: The Chinese government also implemented new regulations on online content designed to prevent the circulation of disinformation and protect national security. These regulations led to the (additional) censorship of certain types of content in China.

The combined impact of these regulatory measures impacted leading Chinese tech companies: their value on the stock market has fallen significantly, and some compa-nies have been forced to change their business practices. In 2023, it was reported that the crackdown on tech giants was ending. China's economy is expected to be back on track for economic growth, in which big tech is expected to play a significant role. The following subsections give a more detailed picture of the BAT companies.

Baidu: More than Just Online Search

Baidu is a technology company specialising in internet-related services and AI. It was set up in 2000 by Robin Li and Eric Xu (both educated in the USA). The devel-opment of Baidu as a major internet player occurred when the information and communication technologies (ICT) sector was driving *economic coupling* between the USA and China (Yeo, 2023). Baidu has been supported by transnational and, particularly, US capital since its inception. The Chinese online search market evolved within China's expanding market economy. Initially, Baidu's leading service was internet search, using an algorithm that ranked results based on the number of incoming links. In the early 2000s, the Chinese internet was dominated by portals such as *Sina* and *Sohu*. Baidu's services rapidly gained importance as they allowed users to search for text, images, news and even music. Like Google, its increased popularity and dominance as a search engine allowed Baidu to let advertisers com-pete and pay maximally to get ad exposure. Baidu became a public company in 2005 and invested heavily in additional services, including transaction services, maps, *Baidu Baike* (an online encyclopaedia), and related services. Because of the fierce competition in online search (e.g., competitors launched by Alibaba and Tencent), Baidu has expanded and diversified its business into AI, smart devices, cloud computing, etc.

Baidu's growth challenges the common perception that the Chinese internet market was cultivated solely behind the *Great Fire Wall*, managed by the Chinese state (Yeo, 2023). Instead, it is essential to see that China's internet sector has become a significant part of global capitalism. The current debates on *economic decoupling* (started under the Trump administration and continued/accelerated under Biden) need to be understood within the context of a battle over global dominance between the USA and China. However, it is crucial to comprehend Baidu's political economy within its specific context: adjusting its business to Chinese government policies while operating within a global capital market. Some of the recent regulatory interventions of the Chinese government were focused on market dominance, data governance (including data collection and use), and preventing the circulation of disinformation and undermining of national security, which impacted Baidu's business position (Yeo, 2023).

Alibaba: Leading the Globalisation of Internet Infrastructure

Alibaba is a Chinese conglomerate holding company founded in 1999 by Jack Ma (who stepped down as CEO in 2019), specialising in internet infrastructure, e-commerce, online finance, and content services. Alibaba's main activities initially were in online retail, operating three leading platforms:

- *Alibaba.com* is the largest business-to-business platform
- *Taobao* is China's biggest consumer-to-consumer platform
- *Tmall* is one of the most powerful business-to-consumer sites in China.

These platforms offer Alibaba a robust network of (third-party) providers for packaging, logistics, delivery and customer service. Alibaba is a leader in China's increasingly globalising internet and serves as a basic infrastructure for other Chinese companies to go global (Shen, 2021). It became a public company, listed on the New York Stock Exchange, in 2014. Alibaba is also known for the app *Alipay*, an online payment service facilitating digital transactions. Similar to *PayPal*, it only processes payments once products have been delivered as advertised, helping to boost trust in purchasing goods online in China. Like Amazon, Alibaba developed and diversified its services to make corporate and residential customers dependent on its infrastructure, giving it a competitive advantage over other platforms. Alibaba has also pursued a strategy of global development, investing in developing markets such as Latin America and Africa.

In analysing the political economy of Alibaba, it is crucial to highlight its role – as an infrastructure – in supporting the rise of the Chinese tech sector. However, this role needs to be balanced with Alibaba being deeply interlocked with the transformation of China itself, particularly around state–capital relationships that encompass conflict and cooperation (Shen, 2021). Alibaba's increase in value (see Table 7.2) has attracted criticism from the Chinese government. In 2020, the $37 billion initial public offering (IPO) of *Ant Group* (Alibaba's financial services affiliated company) was cancelled, and Jack Ma disappeared from public life for a while. Popular media interpret this as a confrontation between Ma (considered too entrepreneurial and critical about China's regulatory crackdown on big tech) and the Chinese government. Despite its ties with the Chinese government, Alibaba has attracted more regulatory scrutiny and has been the subject of antitrust investigations and fines. This had strategic implications for its global influence and relationships with international governments and businesses.

Tencent: Online Lifestyles and Gaming

Tencent (Holdings) is a multimedia conglomerate founded in 1998 by Ma Huateng, Zeng Living, Zhang Zhidong, Chen Yiran and Xu Chenye. Tencent provides internet and mobile services, video games, online advertising, and e-commerce transactions through its subsidiaries. Its most popular digital products are:

- *QQ* (instant messaging client and news platform)
- *Qzone* (social network)
- *QQ Games* (gaming platform)
- *WeChat* (mobile instant messaging (IM) service)
- *Tenpay* (an online payment competitor to Alipay).

QQ was launched in 1999 and is one of the most popular IM services; its user base contributed to the successful launch of Qzone in 2005. Tencent launched an IPO in June 2004. It identified itself as an *online lifestyle services provider* (Tang, 2020). Since then, it has developed into the most valuable publicly traded Chinese company, being the first Asian company to reach a valuation of $500 million in 2018 and $1 billion in 2021 before its valuation plummeted following the government tech crackdown (see Table 7.2). While sometimes compared to Facebook/Meta, Tencent differentiates itself by having online gaming as its most significant source of revenue: Tencent is the world's largest video game company. WeChat, nowadays the most influential Chinese social network service and called a *super-app* (Chen et al., 2018), was launched in 2011. Monetisation on WeChat happens via advertising but much more via other services, such as animated stickers used in text messages, in-game upgrades and online payments through Tenpay.

A critique of the political economy of Tencent can be focused on different levels:

- Its development into the most prominent Asian tech company can be explained through its use of network effects (building on QQ and gradually connecting more users while offering different services to them) and a strategy of expanding its business through (both domestic and international) horizontal and vertical integration (Tang, 2020).

- It also engaged in strategic partnerships. For example, Tencent was late on the e-commerce market but began collaborating with JD.com in 2014. A diversification strategy was pursued in banking, media, film production, etc.
- Similar to Baidu and Alibaba, Tencent's political economy needs to consider both the involvement and support of the Chinese government in its development and the crucial role of transnational financial capital. Jia and Winseck (2018) stress the importance of financialisation, concentration and capitalisation in this context. For example, Tencent's largest institutional stakeholder is the South Africa-based multinational media conglomerate Naspers.
- The crackdown on big tech by the Chinese government since 2020 has specifically targeted Tencent. Its dominance in the social media and gaming industries has been investigated in the antitrust context. In addition, the Chinese government has developed policies and regulations for the gaming sector, aiming to decrease the amount of time people younger than 18 spend on gaming platforms.
- Finally, given its essential role in social networking, Tencent is pressured to cooperate with government agencies to ensure its compliance with content control, censorship and data security regulations.

Summary BAT

The Chinese *big tech* companies have existed only for two decades but have rapidly become global players. Like their Silicon Valley counterparts, all these companies have actively pursued a strategy of occupying market share and diversifying their activities. Unlike their American counterparts, the BAT companies have been challenged by their government, mainly to curb their power. Another aspect that the above analysis reveals is the close integration of Chinese tech companies into global capital, an aspect often overlooked in this context.

Global Data Industries and Data Colonialism

Beyond the USA and China, how global are the data industries? There is much more to the world than just these two countries, no matter how powerful they may be.

How Global Are the Data Industries?

Sociologist and historian Immanuel Wallerstein's *world-systems theory* helps in answering these questions. According to Wallerstein (2004), the global capitalist economy can be seen as one single system divided into three parts:

- The *core* countries are the world's wealthiest and most powerful countries. High levels of industrialisation and technological development characterise them.
- The *periphery* countries are the world's poorest and least developed countries. They have limited industrial development and depend on the core countries for trade and investment.
- The *semi-periphery* countries are situated between the core and the periphery.

According to Wallerstein (2004), the world system is hierarchical and dynamic: it is hierarchical because the core countries exploit the (semi-)periphery, seeking cheap labour/nature (e.g., natural resources) and asserting control. But it is also dynamic because it constantly changes, and some countries can move from one group of nations to another.

Why is this relevant to the world of data? One relevant aspect is China's role in the digital/data economy. The USA, Europe, and Australia/New Zealand have traditionally been the core countries. In contrast, the BRICS countries (Brazil, Russia, India, China and South Africa) are considered semi-periphery, and most Latin America, Africa and Asia are periphery countries. While the USA is still the largest economy in the world, there is some expectation that China will overtake it. On the other hand, the hierarchies of the world system are also interesting when looking at data industries and how companies from the USA and China are looking at the *majority world* (Amrute et al., 2022; Ricaurte, 2022) to bring them under their sphere of influence. The following subsections discuss this.

Are We Entering a Phase of Data Colonialism?

In *The Costs of Connection*, Couldry and Mejias (2019a) argue that we live in a new social order in which our social interactions and daily life are transformed into a data stream. This happens through what they call *data relations*: a new type of human relations which enable the capture, extraction and processing of social data for commodification. The appropriation of human life through today's infrastructures of connection (digital platforms) provides, according to Couldry and Mejias (2019b: 337), the preconditions for a new stage of capitalism. They label this *data colonialism*: 'a new form of colonialism distinctive of the twenty-first century'. Couldry and Mejias (2019a, b) are not the first or only scholars to centralise the notion of *colonialism* in the data sphere. Arora (2016) and Mann and Daly (2019), among others, also use the colonialism framework to analyse data capitalism. Before this, van Dijck (2014) described the processes of exploitation and subjectification through notions such as *data extractivism/exploitation* or *dataveillance*. In any case, let us look deeper into how data colonialism offers a lens to examine contemporary appropriation and extraction practices.

Couldry and Mejias (2019a, b) explain that we have entered a new phase of colonialism, which prepares the ground for a new mode of capitalist production.

Data colonialism is 'an emerging order for the appropriation of human life so that data can be continuously extracted from it for profit' (Couldry and Mejias 2019a: xii). The scale and scope of data extraction need to be considered here: resource extraction has always been central in capitalism, but data is a new form of resource extraction. In terms of scope, data extraction is a critical element of surveillance, how the workplace is managed, how the gig economy is organised, etc. According to Couldry and Mejias (2019a, b), it is essential to acknowledge that data colonialism happens externally and internally: it creates new inequalities between the coloniser and colonised societies and *within* coloniser/colonised societies. The *data colonisers* are not states but *big tech* companies (although this happens sometimes in collaboration with/on behalf of the state).

Data colonialism is simultaneously a new social order for the appropriation of human life, with emerging forms of dependency and rule based on convenience, customisation and personalisation. But it is *also* a continuation of the Western (*core*) world's long-term attempt to impose a single version of rationality on the (rest of the) world. Unlike previous phases of colonialism, tech giants in the USA (GAFAM) and China (BAT) are at the forefront of establishing new data relations.

While it is essential to look at new practices of appropriation and extraction, the concept of *data colonialism* is not free of criticism. Couldry and Mejias (2019a) themselves stress they are not using it in a metaphorical sense. Still, Segura and Waisbord (2019) argue that data colonialism muddles the analysis of colonialism, as it diminishes the centralism of violence in colonialism. Calzati (2021) writes that the concept overlooks the historical-materialist roots of datafication and colonialism. Mumford (2022: 1512) states that the very idea of data colonialism has non-decolonial implications because it is primarily focused on explaining datafication as resource extraction and 'seems less concerned with the key decolonial insight that Europe convinced itself and others that it has a privileged objective position from which it may make universal assertions and claims'. Finally, Paola Ricaurte (2019) argues that data colonialism should be considered systemic oppression, which must be tackled by a multi-dimensional approach of decolonial, intersectional and feminist analysis.

Finally, how can we move from here, and what ideas are out there to start the process of decolonising data? While this is part of a more extensive debate, including the role and responsibility of knowledge and education institutes in the Global North, Couldry and Mejias (2019a) offer some thoughts on this. As they warn that racial, class, gender and economic inequalities are reproduced through data relations (but in a more opaque and effective way than before), colonised space and time must be reclaimed. This can happen by learning from decolonisation struggles. Ricaurte (2019) makes the same argument and stresses how important it is to involve and listen to people and communities who have been fighting against oppression and violence for centuries. She calls for centralising and being inspired by these people and their communities when considering alternative imaginaries.

Data and AI Industries: Towards a New Cold War?

We need to remember from the analysis of globalisation and whether tech giants are contributing to *data colonialism* that corporate entities dominate data collection and extraction. Big tech companies colonise our social lives in the pursuit of profit. But it would be wrong to assume that only private entities drive the global data industries; they do this from within a specific context, which governments determine. While the GAFAM companies are based in the USA and inspired by the Californian ideology, the BAT companies are based in China and have close connections with the Chinese state *and* transnational capital. Even though these two power blocks seem pretty different at first instance (the USA as an example of market capitalism, while China characterises state capitalism), they share their connection to transnational (financial) capital, and they benefit from a political climate of neoliberalism, which manifestly determines how our datafied societies look like.

While a world exists beyond the USA and China, other countries and continents are increasingly impacted by the dominance of GAFAM and BAT. Especially as AI becomes more central to our lives and economies, access to and control over data – a vital resource for AI development – becomes the subject of a modern arms race. In this context, we see the emergence of AI as the driver behind a new wave of colonialism and a new cold war. Investigative journalist Karen Hao (2022) has published stories documenting how AI creates a new colonial world order. The concept of the *AI cold war* first appeared in an article in *Wired* magazine (Thompson and Bremmer, 2018) and has since been discussed in various contexts. From our analysis here, it must be clear that data plays a crucial role in determining who has power over whom.

Learning Takeaways

- Globalisation in the context of media and data industries mainly refers to advancing the global capitalist system.
- The global tech, data and AI industries are dominated by two power blocks: GAFAM (Google/Alphabet, Amazon, Facebook/Meta, Apple and Microsoft) in the USA and BAT (Baidu, Alibaba and Tencent) in China.
- GAFAM companies aim to dominate their markets by various strategies, especially using their monopoly power.
- BAT companies are more interlinked to global capital than we might expect. The Chinese government has recently launched a regulatory crackdown to curb their power.
- The global power grab by big tech companies has been called *data colonialism*, although the comparison to colonialism is not free of criticism.

Recommended Reading

Birkinbine, B. J., Gomez, R. and Wasko, J. (2017). *Global Media Giants*. New York: Routledge.

Chen, Y., Mao, Z. and Qiu, J. L. (2018). *Super-Sticky WeChat and Chinese Society*. Bingley: Emerald Publishing.

Couldry, N. and Mejias, U. (2019). *The Costs of Connection: How Data Is Colonizing Human Life and Appropriating It for Capitalism*. Stanford, CA: Stanford University Press.

Huberman, J. (2022). *The Spirit of Digital Capitalism*. Cambridge: Polity.

Liu, W. (2020). *Abolish Silicon Valley: How to Liberate Technology from Capitalism*. London: Repeater Books.

Recommended Listening

Big Tech is a podcast series about big tech, inviting leading thinkers about how the world is transformed by technology, hosted by Taylor Owen and supported by the Centre for International Governance Innovation. https://www.cigionline.org/big-tech/

8

Data, Tech and Inequalities

Learning Goals

- Understand how inequalities play out in the world of data and tech.
- Identify how specific inequalities exist around data and class, gender and race/ethnicity and explore how to spot them in your own data life.
- Connect the debates on class, gender and race/ethnicity inequalities with social challenges explored earlier in the book.
- Reflect on how data divides resulted from and created lasting inequalities during the Covid-19 pandemic.

From Inequalities to Discrimination

The *Black Lives Matter* (BLM) movement started in 2013 in response to police brutality and racially motivated violence against Black people in the USA. In the following years, the hashtag #BlackLivesMatter gained prominence after new acts of violence, particularly in 2020 after the killing of George Floyd by police officer Derek Chauvin. This led to worldwide protests and renewed attention to countries' colonial history. In the UK, the statue of slave trader Edward Colston in Bristol was toppled. Beyond social movements and protests in the street, increased attention has been given to the role of data and digital technologies concerning inequalities. Books have been published about Black software (McIlwain, 2019), Blackness and surveillance culture (Browne, 2015), racist algorithms used by search engines (Noble, 2018) and Black cyber-cultures (Brock, 2020). Yet, there is so much more work to be done about inequalities and technologies along the lines of race/ethnicity, gender and class.

As data-driven applications are increasingly deployed, we need to be aware of the patterns of discrimination that exist around them (e.g., in access to and use of technology) or caused by them (e.g., computer vision for facial recognition or algorithms for predictive policing). This chapter helps you understand inequalities in the digital sphere and how they exist around social class, gender and race/ethnicity.

Digital Inequalities New and Old

Before discussing inequalities related to data and digital technologies, we must revisit the debates around the rise of the internet in the 1990s. I refer here to the concept of the *digital divide*. This concept was high on the policy agenda in the USA and Europe. In the mid-1990s, the US *National Telecommunications and Information Administration* (NTIA) was not only tasked to develop the *information superhighway*. It also needed to document the uptake of the internet. In their *Falling Through the Net* studies, the *digital divide* was first used to refer to the gap between those with access to new technologies and those without (NTIA, 1999). The digital divide had become a container concept for the divide between so-called haves and have-nots.

Although the metaphor of the digital divide successfully puts digital inequalities on the policy agenda (mostly in Western countries), it is a simplification of reality and thus entails several misunderstandings (van Dijk and Hacker, 2003; Selwyn, 2004). The dichotomous portrayal of haves versus have-nots was not tenable as this conceptualisation was too limited and rudimentary in analysis (Warschauer, 2003). Beyond the digital divide, research into ICT has comprehensively documented the traditional parameters of digital inequalities in North America and Europe: different levels of engagement with ICT were associated with income, gender, age, education and family structure (Verdegem and Verhoest, 2009).

The following subsections deal with the literature on digital inequalities and discuss them on three levels: access and infrastructure, skills and usage, and participation and inclusion.

First-Level Divides: Access and Infrastructure Inequalities

Van Dijk (2005, 2020) has spent his academic career documenting the digital divide and the use of ICT. He proposes the *multiple access model* for researching different levels of engagement with ICT (Courtois and Verdegem, 2016). In short, he distinguishes four kinds of barriers to access:

- *Mental access* refers to a lack of interest, computer anxiety or the unattractiveness of ICT.
- *Material access* has to do with the fact that people do not possess computers or network connections.
- *Skills access* is the lack of digital skills caused by insufficient user-friendliness of the technology and inadequate education or social support.
- *Usage access* refers to the lack of significant usage opportunities.

In his earlier work, van Dijk (2005) suggested a hierarchical relationship between these different access levels. More recently, the links between motivation/attitude, physical access, digital skills and usage are considered part of circular logic, meaning positive attitudes towards technology can also impact skills and use (van Dijk, 2020).

Supported by extensive empirical evidence (albeit mainly in North America and Europe), van Dijk (2020) has theorised digital inequalities and come up with different personal and positional categories that influence the resources individuals have at their disposal, whereby these resources have an impact on the levels of access. *Personal* categories include gender, race/ethnicity, intelligence, personality and health. *Positional* categories operate on a personal and societal level, including the labour position, education, household, network and nation/region. These categories thus determine the available resources, including temporal, material, mental, social and cultural resources.

In his book *The Digital Divide*, van Dijk (2020) also argues that there are three levels of digital divide(s):

- The *first-level* divide mainly focuses on physical access to ICT infrastructure and gained much attention between 1995 and 2003.
- The *second-level* divide focuses on skills and usage and has become more prominent since 2004.
- The *third-level* divide pays more attention to outcomes of ICT usage and gained increased attention starting in 2012.

Ellen Helsper (2021), in her book *The Digital Disconnect*, follows a similar line of thinking. However, she is also interested in the causes and consequences of the relationship between digital and social inequalities.

While access to and diffusion of ICT has always been a focal point in innovation studies (e.g., Rogers, 1995), nowadays we assume that access has become less relevant. However, a thorough analysis of worldwide internet penetration (e.g., Internet World Stats) reveals that different levels of access to ICT infrastructure persist. In 2023, almost 94% of North America's population was online, while in Africa it was 43% (Internet World Stats 2021). Another important nuance is that the access type can vary in different parts of the world. In the non-Western world, the internet is mainly accessed through digital mobile devices, thereby (partly) skipping the desktop and laptop internet era that the Western world went through, and this also impacts the skills, use and outcomes inequalities.

Second-Level Divides: Skills and Use Inequalities

Eszter Hargittai (2002) was among the group of scholars criticising the exclusive attention to access to ICT, and she, together with Paul DiMaggio, popularised the term *second-level digital divide*. They pointed out that what is essential is not so much *who* has access to the internet but *what* they can do with it. The second-level digital divide thus refers to the extent to which people can use ICT efficiently and effectively. This depends on skills, knowledge and support networks (Courtois and Verdegem, 2016). While some experts and policy-makers declared that the digital divide was overcome in the early twenty-first century, researchers and other policy-makers documented that more should be considered than physical access alone. New attention was given to what skills people need to use applications that can support the economy, society and culture. This resulted in projects investigating digital skills and differences in terms of ICT use.

Van Dijk and van Deursen were involved in research on operationalising and measuring digital skills. They notably contributed with their distinction between medium-related skills and content-related internet skills (van Deursen and van Dijk, 2011):

- *Medium-related skills* are people's operational skills to use the internet and its services (e.g., navigating the internet).
- *Content-related skills* include both information and strategic skills. The former refers to locating information (e.g., choosing search terms), whereas the latter is about taking advantage of the internet (e.g., making the right decision to reach a specific goal).

Van Deursen and van Dijk (2011, 2014) have operationalised and measured digital skills and their determinants in several projects. This type of research fed into a broader debate about literacy. Media and digital literacy is broader than skills and includes the ability to create content, critically evaluate content and understand the interests of content producers (Livingstone, 2004).

The scales for measuring internet skills were used in surveys investigating internet use and policy discussions about what literacy initiatives to undertake. Beyond this, these studies also observed different patterns of internet use. Different engagement with ICT was also considered an aspect of the second-level digital divide (Warschauer, 2003; van Dijk, 2020). More specifically, digital divide scholars became interested in how people use the internet and how this can be substantially different in terms of frequency and time spent online, as well as the type of internet use and for what purposes it is used. Another usage gap was identified. Inspired by the so-called *knowledge gap theory* (Tichenor et al., 1970), positing that highly educated people get more out of their media use, scholars observed a gap between people using primarily information, education and career-oriented online applications and others who were mainly using commercial and communication applications for entertainment (van Deursen and van Dijk, 2014; Zillien and Hargittai, 2009). Thus, attention shifted from who has access to what they do with it and what they (can) achieve with ICT. And yet another level of digital divide emerged, one focused on outcomes.

Third-Level Divides: Outcome Inequalities

This *third-level digital divide* goes beyond access, use, and skill levels. The focus here is on the difference in outcomes that users achieve by their internet use, even if access and use are relatively similar (van Deursen and Helsper, 2015). Outcomes can play out in different spheres, including economic, social, political, cultural and personal development. Research has shown, for example, that people with higher education, jobs and younger generations benefit much more from the internet than those with lower education jobs and older people (e.g., paying lower prices for products or better health information) (van Dijk, 2020). An important nuance here is how society values specific outcomes differently; productivity in the workforce is considered more important than personal well-being or creative expression (Helsper, 2021). Another question is whether the outcomes extend traditional inequality patterns or include new forms of social exclusion (Ragnedda, 2017).

In addition, a broader discussion exists around the relationship between access to ICT and participation in society. This deals with whether access and use of digital technology are necessary and sufficient conditions for full participation, online or offline. Carpentier (2011) investigates participation in political terms and asks how participation is linked to power and the ability to participate in decision-making. He considers participation as part of a process of co-decision. This co-decision is essential so that people can be involved in the production and use of technology and the content circulated via digital platforms. This brings us to discussions beyond digital inequalities and how technology, social exclusion and discrimination are linked.

The Role of Technology in Reproducing Social Inequalities

Helsper (2021) prefers discussing *socio-digital inequalities* instead of digital ones. She is interested in the causes and consequences of inequalities. She takes a holistic approach and brings (economic) systems and structures, capabilities and agency, socialisation and context, and nature and nurture into the analysis of inequalities. She links different types of socio-economic resources to digital resources, analyses what drivers and causes exist between them, and theorises how these relationships result in different outcomes and consequences:

- For *socio-economic* resources she looks at economic (class), social (social capital), cultural (socialisation) and personal (literacy) resources.
- Regarding *digital* resources, she analyses infrastructure and access, digital skills and learning, literacy and digital engagement.

Extensive empirical data supports these theoretical assumptions and relationships, which helps consider the bigger picture of socio-digital inequalities.

One of the contributions of Helsper (2021) is that she provides insights into how to think about opportunities versus outcomes. Inequalities in digital *opportunities* can be caused by access, literacy or engagement. These elements, however, are also impacted by personal dispositions and different types of resources. On the other hand, there is an interplay between inequalities in opportunities and inequalities in *outcomes*. The latter can manifest in economic, social, cultural and personal well-being outcomes. This analysis is vital for investigating the relationship between data, tech and inequalities.

Technochauvinism and Technosolutionism

Technochauvinism is a set of ideologies surrounding tech culture with the over-arching belief that technology is always the solution, introduced by Meredith Broussard (2018) in her sharply titled book *Artificial Unintelligence: How Computers Misunderstand the World*. This concept is accompanied by a range of other values such as techno-libertarian beliefs, neoliberal meritocracy, the conviction that computers and tech are always *objective* and *unbiased*, the belief in free speech without the recognition of the problem of online harassment, but also 'an unwavering faith that if the world just used more computers, and used them properly, social problems would disappear and we'd create a digitally enabled utopia' (Broussard, 2018: 8). One of the risks of technochauvinism is that it entails a particular world-view leading into a reinforcement of socio-economic inequalities, but also raises questions whether technology is the driver behind creating a better world.

Broussard's critique of technochauvinism is highly relevant, particularly in a world where technology companies are among the most valuable companies, and these companies' political power is larger than that of some countries. Broussard is not the first to be critical of technological ideologies. Evgeny Morozov (2013) also provides a critical account of *technological solutionism* in his book *To Save Everything, Click Here*. In this work, Morozov analyses some of the values and world-views prominent in and around Silicon Valley. Technological solutionism is a more extreme version of *technological determinism*. The latter is a term associated with (among others) Thorstein Veblen, a well-known critic of capitalism, and refers to the belief that technologies are the driving force in a society and determine the development of its social structures and cultural values (Wyatt, 2008).

By critiquing *technosolutionism*, Morozov (2013) is warning us of the dark side to the utopianism surrounding big data/tech. He talks about the widespread use of technology for surveillance and a potential *dictatorship of data*, where algorithms used for data mining and automated recommendations are inscrutable and unaccountable *black boxes*. In response, there should be more efforts for *algorithmic auditing*, an approach to detect potential bias in data systems (Mittelstadt, 2016).

Black Boxes and the Production of Science and Technology

What are black boxes? A *black box* is a concept used in *science and technology studies* to refer to how the social production of science and technology is often obfuscated. There is secrecy on how specific industries are organised, particularly those heavily relying on digital technologies. The social implications of certain decisions made by invisible practices of governments cannot be scrutinised. Frank Pasquale (2015) argues that the black box is a useful metaphor because it has a double meaning:

- It is a recording device, for example, the system monitoring data (or movements) in planes or trains.
- It can refer to 'a system whose workings are mysterious; we can observe its inputs and outputs, but we cannot tell how one becomes the other' (Pasquale, 2015: 3). Some of this is kept hidden because knowledge is power: the ability to scrutinise specific individuals or practices, without being scrutinised yourself, is one of the most important forms of power.

Deconstructing black boxes, particularly in a data context, is not easy. There is not only the challenge of secrecy, but also the difficulty of complexity. Some systems are secret because one cannot access certain content or how something works. But Pasquale (2015) also criticises how the law is used to prevent scrutinising secret algorithms because commercial secrecy is prioritised over the right of citizens to privacy. In addition, some algorithmic systems can be so complex that it is hard to understand how inputs are linked to outputs and what decisions are made. Tech engineers in Silicon Valley often work on specific aspects of the platform, and few people have a complete overview of how these systems operate.

Researchers and activists are pushing for transparency to overcome secrecy and complexity. For example, the Association for Computing Machinery (ACM) organises the yearly FAT (since 2020, FAccT) conference. It is a conference that brings together researchers and practitioners – from computer science but also social sciences and humanities and legal scholarship – interested in fairness, accountability and transparency in socio-technical systems. This type of research aims to understand inequity in digital technology and offers solutions for fighting back.

Tech, Inequalities and Class

When we think about how our society is organised and to what groups people belong, we can consider several socio-demographic variables. Divisions exist around race and ethnicity, gender, sexuality, age and generational groups, and social class. Even though societal change and digital technologies have made the individual more important, the relevance of these classic socio-demographic variables has not diminished. Our societies are still characterised by social stratification, despite people arguing that in modernity, individuals have more agency to overcome divisions and stratification (Giddens, 1990). *Social stratification* refers to how people are grouped into a set of (often hierarchical) social categories. Examples are the upper, middle and lower classes. These categories have a material dimension in that they impact how many resources are available to people and their life opportunities.

What Is Social Class, and Why Does It Matter to Data?

Let us begin with social class, an aspect of identity and a basis for inequality that is sometimes less examined in the digital sphere. The late Marxist sociologist Erik Olin Wright (2015) argued that there are three main sociological approaches when it comes to class:

- *Marxian class analysis* starts from the premise that class is determined by the position people have with respect to the means of production: the ruling (capitalist) class owns and controls the means of production, whereas the working class has no other means of production than their labour.
- *Weberian class analysis* also departs from power relations and rules that give people control over resources; however, it offers a more complex picture. According to Weber (1924/1947), societal categories exist along the lines of economic class, social prestige and political power.
- *Stratification class analysis* considers various social background conditions in an individual's life, leading to different levels of economic well-being.

The difference between Marxian and Weberian class approaches is that the first sees different social positions in locations within the relation of domination and exploitation in production, where the central conflict is over *production*. The latter assumes different locations within market relations (e.g., jobs/occupations), and consequently, the conflict is mainly situated at the *distribution* level (Wright, 2015).

Class and Digital Capital

Sociologist Pierre Bourdieu (1986/2011) offered another perspective on class: he based his theory on consumption related to cultural practices, not on our possession of economic resources. In doing so, he distinguishes between different types of capital:

- *Economic capital* refers to the financial resources people have at their disposal.
- *Social capital* involves the social contacts and networks people can rely on.
- *Cultural capital* is linked to the skills and education people have acquired.
- *Symbolic capital* refers to the status and power gained from the other types of capital.

Ragnedda and Ruiu (2020) take a Bourdieusian perspective on digital inequalities and introduce the concept of *digital capital*. They argue for this position because digital capital should be conceived as a specific type of capital, and by dividing digital capital into subcomponents, it can be quantified and measured. What is digital capital? While some authors see it as something that is being incorporated into other types of capital, Ragnedda and Ruiu (2020: 30) define it as 'the accumulation of digital competencies (information, communication, safety, content-creation and problem-solving), and digital technology'. They argue that both the possession of digital technology and what we can do with it and how we can strategically use it need to be taken into account. Furthermore, they see this accumulation as a historical process that relies upon several economic, cultural, social and personal investments and social benefits.

The following subsections examine social class concerning digital technology's production, ownership and impact. We start by discussing class concerning the production of tech. We then look at how class and ownership of digital technologies are related. Finally, we reflect on the impact of tech on class divisions in society.

Working Class and ICT Production

Jack Linchuan Qiu (2009) proposes the concept of the *working-class network society*. This is a reflection on the development of China and how it has become the manufacturing powerhouse of the planet. Whereas western Europe initially dominated industrial production, and later the USA and Japan, China is now undoubtedly the industrial factory of the world (Gao, 2012). Because of globalisation, China's dominance in manufacturing is networked into the global economy. Unlike previous phases of industrial production, however, the production of goods is organised around incorporating information and knowledge into the labour process. At the same time, manufacturing in China is focused on ICT.

How is this related to class? Class divisions exist based on different levels of access to and control over information processing tasks. Consequently, this results in differential access to ICT, both at work and in real life. Qiu (2009) aims to understand whether ICT helps people experiencing poverty or promotes the ruling class's interests. He analyses the transformation towards a new working class, which is *informational* and centred on network labour. Based on extensive fieldwork, he documents the vulnerability and exploitation of workers and low-end users in China, but also the emergence of class differences through processes of social differentiation and networked connectivity. Qiu's analysis sheds light on class divisions *among* the producers of ICT and global consumers and class distinctions *within* China. For example, he talks about migrant labour, the importance of places and communities, and the growing polarisation between villages and cities. In later work, Qiu (2016) also talks about the potential for resistance and how networked and non-networked workers should organise to abolish what he calls *iSlavery*.

Boys and Their Toys

Moving on from the informational working class and the production of ICT, we need to consider class and the ownership of and control over tech. When discussing digital capitalism and participatory culture, we referred to Fuchs's (2017a: 70) comments about Silicon Valley, which he provocatively refers to as 'white boys with their "participatory" toys'. In this context, it is relevant to investigate who owns the leading global tech and data companies. The book *Global Media Giants*, edited by Birkinbine et al. (2017), has five chapters that discuss the political economy of Apple, Microsoft, Google/Alphabet, Amazon, and Facebook. These companies are not only among the most valuable companies in the world; their owners and founders are all white men who feature in the top 10 of the world's billionaires (Forbes, 2021):

- Jeff Bezos (no. 1, Amazon)
- Bill Gates (no. 4, Microsoft)
- Mark Zuckerberg (no. 5, Facebook/Meta)
- Larry Page (no. 8, Google/Alphabet)
- Sergey Brin (no. 9, Google/Alphabet)

These men are all American and had in 2021 a cumulative net worth of $578.5 billion (Forbes, 2021). In China, leading tech conglomerates are also in the hands of a small number of wealthy businessmen, even though there are signs that the Chinese government has started a crackdown on the power of the CEOs of companies such as Alibaba, Baidu, Didi and Tencent.

We are witnessing an increasing division between the owners of leading tech companies, whose power and wealth are growing, and the rest of us. We, the people and users of digital technology, increasingly depend on ICT products for our work and everyday life. At the same time, our wages have decreased or stabilised at best, and we are increasingly confronted with precarious labour. Whether you prefer a Marxian or Weberian approach to class, it must be clear there is a power imbalance when controlling the production and distribution of tech. And this has a clear impact on everyday life and our well-being.

The Digital Poorhouse

This is even more apparent when we look at the impact of big data and digital technology on people's lives. Virginia Eubanks (2018) writes about this in her book *Automating Inequality*. She analyses how digital technologies are increasingly used in social policies and service delivery for disadvantaged groups. Eubanks's analysis is based on ethnographic work and interviews. It aims to understand the use of algorithms and automation in human services, including welfare payments, homeless services and services around family/child support.

This is a different picture of data and tech's role in everyday life. Whereas the upper and middle classes embrace the possibilities offered by tech companies such as Google, Tencent, Didi and Uber, we are much less aware of how data is being used to implement new surveillance, profiling, punishment and exclusion regimes. Sara Wachter-Boettcher (2017) discusses the failures and biases of digital technologies in her book *Technically Wrong*. She coined the term *algorithmic inequity* to refer to the impact of algorithms trained on biased datasets and documents what goes wrong in the design and development of technology, excluding or alienating (often vulnerable and marginalised) groups in society. Cathy O'Neil (2016) writes about how big data increases inequalities in her book *Weapons of Math Destruction*.

Eubanks (2018: 38) uses the term *digital poorhouse* to talk about how data and automation are used 'to rationalise and streamline benefits, but the real goal is what is has always been: to profile, police, and punish the poor'. So, we have moved from inequalities in access, skills and use of ICT over class divisions in the production and ownership of digital technologies to how data and automation are used against certain groups in society, particularly the disadvantaged ones.

Tech, Inequalities and Gender

While class is an essential variable in terms of digital inequalities, whether as *cause* or *effect*, it often interacts with other socio-demographics such as gender and race/ethnicity. This section focuses on gender inequalities concerning digital technology and data, while the following section looks at the relationship between race and inequalities.

Computer Boys and Programmed Inequality

The history of computing has some excellent, although often underappreciated, accounts of how there has been a shift in culture in tech regarding gender equality (Ensmenger, 2010). In the late 1960s, there were a large number of women working in computer programming. At the time, there was a shortage of programmers. The combination of low entry barriers and subsidised technical education made programming appealing to many women who would otherwise be trapped in traditionally female occupations. A 1967 article in *Cosmopolitan* magazine referred to the first generations of female computing workers as *the computer girls*. Female participation in computer science programmes, however, started to decline in the mid-1980s, and only in the 1990s did historians of computing begin to recognise the crucial contributions women made to the development of computing.

Computer science was a field initially welcoming for women but has transformed into one that was 'made masculine', writes Ensmenger (2010: 240). With this phrase, it is not suggested that the discipline and its practitioners are all male, but rather that its ideals have shifted to masculine ideals. In his book *The Computer Boys Take Over*, Nathan Ensmenger (2010) explains how this shift happened and how the *bad boys of programming* took over control. Making computer programming more professional coincided with making it more masculine. Instead of computer girls, computing began associating with *whizz-kid computer boys*. This is still very present in the mythology of male (also white) computer nerds, often represented as essential to building successful tech start-ups.

Mar Hicks (2017), in their book *Programmed Inequality: How Britain Discarded Women Technologists and Lost Its Edge in Computing*, provides a comprehensive account of the history of computing and illustrates how women operated the first computers in the 1930s until after the Second World War. After that, data processing evolved into a feminised machine underclass. Hicks (2017: 364) argues that gender is 'a classed category as much as class is a gendered category: women occupy fundamentally different social levels than even their nearest male peers simply by virtue of being women'. This is a bold statement but – unfortunately – a sad reality. It also shows how class and gender are closely interconnected. Hicks states that this technocracy (dominated by men) had a high economic toll on the United Kingdom, as it lost its leading role in computing and programming.

Technofeminism and the Digital Housewife

Feminism has long been conflicted over the impact of digital technologies on women, torn between utopian and dystopian visions of what the future might hold. Data and digital technologies, such as automation and robots, are central to two opposing visions:

- The digital world creates new possibilities for liberating conventional gender roles and imagining gender-free futures.
- A concentration of economic power, masculine domination, and control of women and nature characterises the technoscience project.

Wajcman (2004) aims to overcome this polarisation in the framework she calls *technofeminism*. Drawing on social constructivist studies, also known as *science and technology studies*, Wajcman combines ideas of social shaping and feminism. *Social shaping* means that technical efficiency, socio-technical circumstances, and institutional interests determine the use of technologies. It also signifies that specific pre-programmed gender roles concerning technology can be challenged.

A radical application of *technofeminism* can be found in the work of Donna Haraway, the author of *A Cyborg Manifesto* (1985/2016). This work is an upbeat vision of cybernetic organisms (*cyborgs*), which points to a bright future for socialist feminism in the technological age. The cyborg is emblematic of a post-gender world.

Wajcman (2004) ultimately rejects the optimism of *A Cyborg Manifesto*, mainly because this vision does not address the mundane and controlling nature of many women's relationship with technology. Technofeminism itself, however, remains a valuable framework for studying technologies and subjectivities, and their ideas not only guide empirical work but can also be the source of inspiration for activism and policy-making in the sphere of gender and technologies.

Kylie Jarrett (2016) focuses on the domestic sphere and examines how free (digital) labour is gendered. She departs from a Marxist-feminist perspective and focuses on *reproductive labour*. This is what Marx referred to when talking about work in the domestic sphere. Jarrett (2016: 3) uses the metaphor of the *digital housewife* to refer to the free/consumer labour behind 'the seamless and engaging interfaces of popular digital media platforms'. The digital housewife clicks and shares, thus contributing to capital accumulation like the unpaid domestic worker. Unlike other perspectives that state that users are either empowered or exploited by their digital engagement, Jarrett (2016) argues that the exploitation of free labour on digital platforms does not necessarily lead to alienation but can also foster mutuality and reciprocity. The following subsections shift the attention to data and the roles of gender bias within it.

The Male/Data Gaze and How to Counter It

Let us return to David Beer's (2019) concept of the *data gaze*. He uses this concept in the context of how data sees us, how data judges us, and so on. We need to understand how those evaluations by data (as implemented in data analytics) are coming about. 'The data gaze is a concept that targets an understanding of the connections, structures and performances of power within analytics', writes Beer (2019: 7). Crucial about the data gaze is to scrutinise how the way of seeing something is linked to power. This is so because the people or organisations behind data analytics can decide what is seen and how it is evaluated. In a similar vein, scholars have written about the *male gaze*. In feminist theory, this refers to depicting the world in general and women in particular from a masculine, heterosexual perspective (Banet-Weiser, 2018). It is a way of portraying and looking at women that empowers men while sexualising and diminishing women.

How do we get from the data gaze to data bias? Caroline Criado Perez (2019) links gender inequalities to data bias and documents how the latter is manifested in different spheres, including daily life, the workplace, medical care, and public life. She documents how bias in data leads to a knowledge gap and is a source of systematic inequalities and discrimination against women. Perez demonstrates how scientific knowledge is biased: it is not gender-neutral because it represents the male half of the world, which she terms the *default male* (Perez, 2019). The other half often remains invisible in data. This has been exacerbated in digital technologies because those are often based on big data, algorithms and machine learning. Perez not only criticises the problems of tech and data bias but also points at some of the solutions to overcome this. More concretely, she argues that evidence-based approaches must be prioritised to counter assumptions from researchers and practitioners. These evidence-based solutions should focus on the underlying mechanisms of gender differences.

Data Feminism

Another way of tackling inequalities in data and tech is proposed by D'Ignazio and Klein (2020). In their book *Data Feminism*, they challenge the privileged positions that data hold and the existing hierarchies and biases they reproduce. The authors use an intersectional feminist lens to examine unequal power structures in data and discuss attempts to rectify them. Their approach is inclusive in the sense that they analyse structural oppression faced by women, immigrants, people of colour, indigenous communities and LGBTQ+ people. They propose focusing on *data justice* rather than *ethics*. The latter is commendable for addressing biases and the need for fairness, accountability and transparency but falls short of addressing unequal power relations. Still, here it suffices to say this concept is grounded in a commitment to working towards social justice, particularly how this is changing in the context of datafication (Dencik et al., 2016, 2019).

D'Ignazio and Klein (2020) are not against tech and data systems; they argue that data science needs a feminist approach to advocate for justice. In doing so, they propose seven fundamental principles: examine power, challenge power, elevate emotion and embodiment, rethink binaries and hierarchies, embrace pluralism, consider context and make labour visible. *Data feminism* discusses and provides an overview of related theories and practices of these principles and offers methodologies, examples and guidelines as part of a call for action to reimagine data, tech and their problems in terms of inequalities and power imbalances.

This work also highlights how intertwined the forces of power, such as class, gender and race, are. The following section goes deeper into data, tech and race.

Tech, Inequalities and Race/Ethnicity

#CodedGaze

The hashtag *#CodedGaze* was popularised by Joy Buolamwini, a (then) graduate student at the MIT Media Lab. This is another use of the term *gaze* when discussing data, tech and inequalities. Buolamwini (2016) uses this concept to refer to the 'embedded views that are propagated by those who have the power to code systems'. Being a Black computer science student, originally from Zambia and then studying at Georgia Tech, Oxford and later MIT, she discovered that some of the tech projects she was researching – particularly on computer vision – did not work well for people of colour. Through her own experience, she became more interested in the need for diversity in coding. She calls this *InCoding* – inclusive coding – helping to build technology that reflects the diversity of its users and creators (Buolamwini, 2016).

Diversity and inclusivity in tech are needed to counter algorithmic bias. Buolamwini is one of the people behind a movement of scholars and activists who have observed and documented that particular data and AI technologies work better for some groups in society (e.g., *computer vision*, to the benefit of white people) and are more effective when used to target other groups in society (e.g., *predictive policing*, at the expense of people of colour). This is caused by who develops these applications and what data is used. A lack of diversity in the companies and organisations developing tech products contributes to this. Wachter-Boettcher's (2017) term *algorithmic inequity* (discussed in the previous section) is relevant here. Algorithmic systems are not neutral or objective: if they rely on biased inputs, they will also generate biased outputs, and this illustrates the importance of good data (Daly et al., 2018).

Computer vision for facial recognition is based on *machine learning* techniques, and its accuracy is determined by training datasets with pictures of faces. If those training datasets are not diverse, this has consequences. Wachter-Boettcher (2017) describes how Google Photos' automatic image tagging service classified people with dark skin as gorillas simply because the algorithm was trained on datasets with predominantly white people. Algorithmic bias leads to discriminatory practices. In addition to being trained on non-inclusive/diverse datasets, many of these systems are also not audited for accuracy, which can have devastating consequences. As a result, these systems are discriminatory because they can lead to misidentification and the loss of civil liberties.

Buolamwini went on to set up the Algorithmic Justice League to advocate inclusive practices in coding and create awareness about algorithmic bias and its impact. The 2020 Netflix documentary *Coded Bias* tells Buolamwini's story and her important work in tech. The following subsections further investigate race and technology and help us to understand the risks of exclusion and discrimination and the need for inclusivity in tech.

Race, Ethnicity, Identity and the Internet

Lisa Nakamura is one of the leading scholars researching the ethnic assumptions embedded in the representations of race in digital media. In her book *Cybertypes* (Nakamura, 2002), she counters the portrayal of the internet as an online utopia with fluid identities and infinite possibilities. Instead, she insists that race matters on the internet and argues that racial stereotypes – what she calls *cybertypes* – are hardwired in our online interactions. There is, for example, the cybertype of Asian technology workers (all very tech savvy). In contrast, African Americans were cybertyped as *have-nots* (not having access or skills when it comes to ICT). In *Digitizing Race*, Nakamura (2008) further documents how the internet, particularly social media, is central to developing ethnic and gender-identified visual cultures. She argues that diversity is articulated through digital racial formation. The latter refers to how 'race is formed online using visual images as part of the communication and dialogues between users' (Nakamura, 2008: 11). Cultural production and reception complicate racial formation as an ongoing process. Through multiple case studies, Nakamura demonstrates that digital media are a space of re-embodiment rather than disembodiment and colourblindness.

In the context of police brutality and anti-racism activism (e.g., the Black Lives Matter movement), more attention is given to *Blackness*, particularly profiling and discrimination. Simone Browne (2015) theorises Blackness through the lens of surveillance. She powerfully proves how Blackness played a central role in structuring institutions and practices of security, from the slave trade and the modern prison (built to reflect the panopticon design) to contemporary biometric technologies. Her book *Dark Matters* (Browne 2015) argues how surveillance studies consider race fundamentally in accounting for monitoring and control technologies. Furthermore, this research also provides a historical accounting of the technologies being used to monitor blackness and subjugate people of colour in the USA and other places.

André Brock's (2020) book *Distributed Blackness* is also critical in researching race/ethnicity and technology. He manages to merge internet/computational studies with linguistic work through the lens of *critical techno-cultural discourse analysis*. The latter is a methodological approach that interrogates ideological influences within the technological artefact. Brock argues that Black identity should not only be studied in the context of racism; instead, it is also vital to investigate sociality and identity online, for example, how Black Twitter can be a 'satellite counter-public sphere' (Brock, 2020: 86). Counter-publics occupy and reclaim public spaces and use them strategically, for example for arguing against stereotypes and describing particular group interests.

Both works on Blackness demonstrate the need to embed these projects in the context of racial capitalism.

Racial Capitalism

Racial capitalism is a term coined by Cedric Robinson (2020) in his book *Black Marxism: The Making of the Black Radical Tradition*. This book is a response to the (then) failure of Marxist studies to account for the racial character of capitalism. Robinson argues that *racialism* – the belief that different groups in society possess different behavioural traits, which are based on the superiority of one race over another – inevitably permeates social structures. *Racial capitalism* forces us to acknowledge that capitalism *is* racial capitalism: capital can only be capital when it engages in a process of accumulation based on producing and moving through relations of inequality among different human groups. Racial capitalism has received renewed attention in the context of social inequalities, particularly around environmental justice but also disparities related to the Covid-19 pandemic.

In his recent book *World Computer*, Jonathan Beller (2021) also studies racial capitalism. His analysis is focused on how computational technologies not only support the logic of capital accumulation but also facilitate types of identity-related oppression such as racism or sexism. Beller (2021: 4) argues that the algorithmic optimisation of society for profit allows us to see computation as 'a fifth estate [in addition to the press as the fourth estate] that has, in fact, absorbed all the others for its calculus'. This work helps explain how everyday datafication functions as an engine for differentiation through codifying human differences. *Computational racial capital* is the term Beller (2021) uses to refer to how capital accumulation relies on social differentiation processes that make data about class, gender or race/ethnicity computable through abstraction. Linked to this are what Beller calls *derivative conditions*: datafication and computation about social differences result in packets of information that can be bundled into financialised assets. The following subsection further investigates the role of technology as a racial formation.

Race as Technology

We now move on to how this is applied to data and technology. Wendy Chun (2009) elaborates on what *race as technology* means: she talks about *racial formation*, which refers to 'the process by which social, economic and political forces determine the content and importance of racial categories, and by which they are in turn shaped by racial meanings' (Omi and Winant, 1986: 61–62). Technologies are thus used to make distinctions regarding race, even though those might not necessarily exist in society. Beth Coleman (2009) writes about race as technology, too. Her analysis aims to move race away from the biological and genetic systems that have historically dominated its understanding. This means that it moves race from an object to a technique. Coleman (2009: 178) sees race as 'a disruptive technology that changes the terms of engagement with an all-too-familiar system of representation and power'. Race is then used as a mechanism, a tool, by the powerful and with lasting impact on modern society and its structures.

The activist-academic Ruha Benjamin, whose work analyses the relationship between innovation and equity, follows a similar line of thinking. In her seminal book *Race After Technology*, Benjamin (2019) investigates how new technologies perpetuate racial discrimination. She repurposes the term *Black box* – the obfuscation of the social production in tech – to refer to the racism that is inherent in a lot of tech development. Benjamin (2019) introduces the notion of the *New Jim Code*, which references Michelle Alexander's work *The New Jim Crow* – how the US carceral system produced a new racial caste system. She refers to this as the *anti-Black box* to demonstrate how seemingly race-neutral technologies, such as algorithms and other applications – which are often promoted as progressive and superior in comparison to old discriminatory systems – not only replicate or worsen racial bias but also encode inequity. Benjamin (2019) argues that the anti-Black box, together with race-neutral policies and laws, are powerful tools that can be and are used for white supremacy.

Algorithms of Oppression

Safiya Noble's (2018) book *Algorithms of Oppression* is yet another pioneering work at the intersection of what Benjamin (2019) calls *race-critical code studies*. Noble draws on Black feminist theory and critical race studies to investigate the social effects of algorithms and particularly how specific groups and communities are the victims of gender and race-based oppression. She analyses the inequalities in the presentation of engagement with certain groups in society outside the *preferred* (i.e., white and heteropatriarchal) norms. From a personal experience of seeing what search results Google delivered when using terms such as *Black girls*, *professor*, or *criminal*, Noble (2018) demonstrates the biased nature of search engines and the algorithms active in the background to produce them. Her work convincingly rebukes the claim that technology is neutral.

She calls *algorithmic oppression* the structural racism and sexism that happens online, which is based on 'algorithmically driven data failures that are specific to people of colour and women' (Noble, 2018: 4). She argues that part of the challenge of understanding algorithmic oppression is to understand the mathematical formulations that drive automated decision-making, but also being aware that humans make the decisions; they are not objective decisions. Noble combines the intersectional framework with information science and political economy perspectives, as this socio-technical research needs to understand the commercial interests that drive how algorithms are used and the corporate power of big tech's oligopoly that is at the basis of data discrimination. And the latter is particularly impacting already marginalised groups in society.

From Digital Inequalities to Data Divide(s)

Having started this chapter by discussing the traditional digital divide, we now need to consider if and how this plays out in the big data era. Since the beginning of the twenty-first century, the digital inequalities debate has shifted from access to technology to use and impact. With the rise of big data, there has also been discussion about whether a big data divide exists. Of course, the shortcomings of referring to a divide/gap, two separate groups, and suggesting that it can easily be overcome must also be acknowledged here. The reality is more complex than this.

Conceptualising the Big Data Divide

How can we conceptualise (*big*) *data divide(s)*? Depending on the perspective or stakeholders involved, this concept has different meanings and understandings. One of the people associated with coining this notion is the late Michael Gurstein, best known for his work on developing and defining community informatics. Gurstein (2011) wrote about an emerging *data divide* in the context of open data. The open data movement campaigns for making different types of data available for multiple purposes, most notably for public and non-profit initiatives, so that society can benefit from this. In this sense, the data divide refers to a distinction 'between those who have access to data which could have significance in their daily lives and those who don't' (Gurstein 2011). This definition is pretty straightforward, but let us not forget the problem of this dichotomous portrayal.

danah boyd and Kate Crawford (2012) elaborate on the data divide in their article 'Critical Questions for Big Data'. According to them, limited access to big data creates new inequalities. Their argument is similar to that of Gurstein, and they raise particular concerns about some organisations (companies and universities) having access to big datasets and being able to research while others do not. boyd and Crawford (2012: 674) argue that 'the current ecosystem around Big Data creates a new kind of digital divide: the Big Data rich and the Big Data poor'. In this context, we – as a society – are losing out as it means that some research teams can conduct specific research projects, which cannot be replicated because other – independent – researchers/teams do not have access to the same amount of data.

The latter aspect points towards another critical dimension of the data divide, which relates to distinctions in terms of what people or organisations can do with data. Lev Manovich (2012) writes that there are roughly three groups involved in the *big data divide* debate:

- There are the people who *create* data (whether consciously or not).
- Another group are those who have the means to *collect* data.
- Another group is those with the expertise to *analyse* the data.

This is an important nuance as it challenges the assumption that people or organisations with access to data are also – automatically – able to make sense of it. This is not always the case, so there is a privileged position for those with the knowledge and expertise to gather insights from data.

However, Mark Andrejevic (2014) adds a critical twist to these different conceptualisations. According to him, the *big data divide* is helpful to describe the asymmetric relationship between:

- *Data collectors* (those who collect, store and mine large quantities of data)
- Those whom data collection targets.

In essence, Andrejevic (2014: 1676) adds *power* to this discussion, as there is one group who is in the position to collect data and make sense of it: 'Putting the data to use requires access to and control over costly technological infrastructures, expensive data sets, and the software, processing power, and expertise to analyse them.' Few organisations simultaneously have access and resources to do this, which gives them power over the people, groups and organisations who are the target of data collection and analysis. This results in a sense of powerlessness, where individuals operate within structured power relations they dislike but feel unable to challenge.

These different positions illustrate the tensions around having access to (big) data and the ability to generate insights from it. It also explains why (large and small) companies are involved in the open data movement, arguing that making data available creates opportunities for collaboration and realising benefits for everyone. They say that some companies are on the losing end of the *data divide* if they cannot access data and generate profit. We must be careful about stakeholders' positions in this debate and what drives their arguments. Given the increasing omnipresence of data and its economic value, competition over access to data is intensifying and creating monopolies. There is, however, one dimension of data inequalities that has not been discussed yet: putting the origins of data in a global perspective. I will discuss this in the following subsection.

The Global Data Divide

With more research focused on big data, the inequalities around them and their impact, there is growing awareness that many studies depart from a Western perspective, ignoring other parts of the world and how this new wave of innovation is implemented in different contexts. Payal Arora (2016: 1681) addresses this with research on what she calls 'the bottom of the data pyramid'. She refers to the people of the Global South, who experience the impact of an increasing datafication of their everyday lives. Arora (2016) argues there is a (Western) bias in framing big data as an instrument of empowerment. She looks at how democracies, identities and geographies in the South are datafied, but not with the positive connotation many would expect. For example, rather than empowering citizens in the Global South, data-driven systems often lead to an intensification of surveillance, which has its roots in colonial identification practices. Marginalised and vulnerable people at the bottom of the data pyramid are having databased identities, characterised by stereotypes of racism and sexism, forced upon them. Finally, the database geography of development projects does not consider local contexts and is characterised by a strong historical bias for socio-economic factors.

Stefania Milan and Emiliano Treré (2019) have been working on this, too and founded the *Big Data from the South(s)* project. This initiative calls for a de-Westernisation of critical data studies and a more nuanced understanding of what *the South* means. As such, their Big Data from the South(s) agenda includes five conceptual operations:

- Milan and Treré (2019: 324) argue we need to move beyond data universalism, which they define as 'the tendency to assimilate the cultural diversity of technological developments in the Global South to Silicon Valley's principles'. They call for a move away from Western normalisations and generalisations towards an agenda that analyses epistemic justice and promotes the formation of alternatives.
- The South must be reconsidered as a plurality that embraces the dynamism and diversity of interpretations beyond the geopolitical denomination.
- Data-driven systems and practices need to be analysed through a decolonial lens, acknowledging the historical processes of domination, extraction, exploitation and oppression that characterise the Souths.
- Milan and Treré propose to put agency at the centre of our analysis, meaning that socially engaged scholarship should focus on data activism/data justice rather than datafication.
- Finally, they plead for unleashing novel data imaginaries. With this, they call for a new alliance between activists and people on the ground working together with academic observers to develop a 'thorough "Southern" theory of change for the datafied society' (Milan and Treré, 2019: 329).

These principles become more relevant when considering the context of the Covid-19 pandemic.

A Deeper Look into Data Divides in the Context of a Pandemic

The UK-based *Ada Lovelace Institute* conducted a study in 2021 on the data divide during Covid-19, analysing public attitudes on data divides. During the pandemic, digital inequalities had an effect on who can be represented and who has the agency to shape data-driven technologies at a time of the acceleration of digital tech (e.g., tracking devices and vaccine passports) and its adoption and use.

Milan and Treré (2020) also write about the data divide(s) in the context of the pandemic. They conceptualise these divides as *data poverty*, which manifests itself in two different ways:

- Data gaps or poverty exist in low-income countries, where there is less data availability and statistical capacity to handle the counting and processing.
- Data poverty also exists as a form of invisibility whereby some groups in society (e.g., foreign nationals, homeless people, gig workers) – whether in the Western world or the Global South – are ignored or not included in official measurements and reporting.

Milan and Treré (2020) argue that *solidarity from below* should be central in countering this. This includes helping to reveal alternative narratives about vulnerable groups, thus allowing them to reclaim their visibility. Overcoming data inequalities means we need more representative, inclusive, proportionate and effective data governance.

Learning Takeaways

- Digital inequalities exist at three levels: access and infrastructure, skills and use, outcomes.
- Social class is linked to digital inequalities as tech companies are led by a small number of very rich (white) men, whereas data and algorithms are used to target vulnerable groups in society.
- Computer science was made masculine, resulting in a tech industry dominated by (white privileged) men. Technofeminism aims to counter this male domination.
- Data and algorithmic systems are biased and result in racism and oppression.
- Data divides refer to asymmetric relationships between data collectors and people and communities who are the target of this data collection.

Recommended Reading

Arora, P. (2019). *The Next Billion Users: Digital Life Beyond the West*. Cambridge, MA: Harvard University Press.

Bhattacharyya, G. (2018). *Rethinking Racial Capitalism: Questions of Reproduction and Survival*. London: Rowman and Littlefield.

Buolamwini, J. (2023). *Unmaking AI: My Mission to Protect What is Human in a World of Machines*. New York: Random House.

D'Ignazio, C. and Klein, L.F. (2020). *Data Feminism*. Cambridge, MA: MIT Press.

Mullaney, T.S., Peters, B., Hicks, M. and Philips, K. (2021). *Your Computer Is on Fire*. Cambridge, MA: MIT Press.

Recommended Listening

The Good Robot, a podcast series in which Elenear Drage and Kerry McInerney ask experts: 'What is good technology?', 'Is good technology even possible?', 'How can feminism help us work towards it?' https://www.thegoodrobot.co.uk/

9

Data, Journalism and Disinformation

Learning Goals

- Establish the role that data and AI applications play in changing how we produce and consume media, especially journalism.
- Understand the factors that are feeding a crisis of journalism and news production.
- Trace the connection between algorithms, personalisation of news and political polarisation.
- Understand the opportunities and challenges of data and automated journalism.
- Define the differences between fake news, disinformation and misinformation.
- Assess the risks emerging from disinformation and deepfakes on democracy.

How Polarisation Feeds Disinformation and Challenges Journalism

The combination of political polarisation, a pandemic, war and a cost-of-living crisis poses severe challenges for our society. Digital technologies offer opportunities and challenges for journalism. They can simultaneously be a force for good and accelerate a falling trust in media and democracy. Algorithms and data can enable a more personalised news experience, customised to your interests and needs. However, this also feeds into more polarisation as we are confirmed in our beliefs and no longer exposed to diverse opinions and perspectives. In the aftermath of the Covid-19 pandemic, with multiple wars happening far and near and with a looming environmental crisis, this is the ideal breeding ground for conspiracy theories and information wars. The emergence of *deepfakes*, a type of visual disinformation based on AI applications that use deep learning, which can generate images or videos based on large datasets and make it sometimes challenging to conclude whether something is real or fake, can be a powerful weapon in this polarised information landscape. If deepfakes do not manage to deceive people, at least they have the potential to further reduce the trust in media and politics, with potentially severe consequences for our democracies.

Changes in News Production and Consumption

How we produce and consume news has changed with the introduction of new technologies, from the radio to television and social and mobile media. But with the advent of big data and AI applications, we are seeing accelerated change and unprecedented shifts to not just news but also how we engage in politics. Many observers and scholars are warning of fundamental challenges to our democracy. This section discusses the transformations to how data and journalism have collided.

Information and News Paradox

When we talk about news and journalism in the age of data, we need to clarify the concepts of *news* and *journalism* and how they change over time. Journalism produces news, but it is less clear what is precisely understood by *news*. The concept seems so basic that we do not often think about how to define it. One of the most influential studies, which proposed a taxonomy of news values, was written by Galtung and Ruge (1965). In their work, they were explicitly concerned with when events become news. This landmark paper included 12 news factors (frequency, meaningfulness, reference to elites, etc.). Harcup and O'Neill (2001, 2017) have twice revisited the original Galtung and Ruge taxonomy based on empirical research and offered more contemporary versions. Table 9.1 gives an overview of the findings of these two studies.

Table 9.1   Overview of news values (Harcup and O'Neill, 2001, 2017)

Harcup and O'Neill (2001)	Harcup and O'Neill (2017)
1. The power elite	1. Exclusivity
2. Celebrity	2. Bad news
3. Entertainment	3. Conflict
4. Surprise	4. Surprise
5. Bad news	5. Audio-visuals
6. Good news	6. Shareability
7. Magnitude	7. Entertainment
8. Relevance	8. Drama
9. Follow-up	9. Follow-up

Harcup and O'Neill (2001)	Harcup and O'Neill (2017)
10. Newspaper agenda	10. The power elite
	11. Relevance
	12. Magnitude
	13. Celebrity
	14. Good news
	15. News organisation's agenda

Like these news values, Mark Deuze (2019) defines *journalism* based on values that can be attributed to it (breaking news, uncovering the truth, providing public services, etc.). Jürgen Habermas (1962/1989) famously wrote *The Structural Transformation of the Public Sphere*, in which he discusses different shifts in journalism and criticised the decay of the public sphere, whereby the dependence on selling advertisements and the growth of commercial media resulted in an invasion of the public sphere by private interests and turned the critical public into a passive consumer public.

In a different, although complementary critique, Neil Postman (1986) reflected on the changes in media too, particularly news. He argued that technology can never substitute human values and observed a so-called *information paradox*: we have never been surrounded by more information and news, yet we are not better informed. Postman (1986) mainly discussed the potentiality of *information overload*. He was more concerned about the public being oppressed by their addiction to amusement (cf. Aldous Huxley's *Brave New World*) than about oppression by state control (cf. George Orwell's *Nineteen Eighty-Four*). Journalism scholar Michael Schudson (1998) also engaged with these questions and proposed the notion of *monitorial citizens*. He argued that the days of informed citizens are over and that the world has become so complex and changes so quickly that one can never (hope to) be fully informed. We can, however, hope to *monitor* our interests. He stresses this is a collective endeavour: together, we can know more (differently) than we ever can as individuals.

This analysis also points to what can be called the *crisis of journalism*. There is as much talk about the crisis of journalism as democracy itself (Barnett, 2002). Scholars have come up with different analyses of the roots of this crisis. James Curran (2019), for example, talks about:

- Government censorship
- Elite sourcing
- Economic decline.

The Reuters Institute for the Study of Journalism has published a yearly *Digital News Report* since 2012. These reports are based on a large-scale survey which covers (online) news consumers in 46 markets (representing about half of the world's population). The reports provide a wealth of information about the state of news and highlight some aspects that contribute to the crisis of journalism. In addition to what has already been mentioned, the decline of trust in media and journalism, polarisation and fragmentation, and the circulation of dis/misinformation are also considered main concerns, thus contributing to the crisis of journalism.

The rise of social and mobile media has manifestly impacted how we consume news and, as a result, how it is produced, packaged and circulated. As such, their combined influence has confronted journalism with new opportunities and challenges. Social media have changed users' participation in news: audiences actively share content, impacting how news is gathered and reported. This brings about ethical and editorial challenges. On the other hand, mobile media have forced news organisations to adjust their reporting to cross-media portfolios that use several platforms to publish. Mobile devices create new opportunities for reporting, including citizen journalism. In the remainder of this section, we discuss the change in journalism focused on three distinctive levels:

- Commercial pressures
- Changing news consumption
- Technological change.

Commercial Pressures Versus News Values

News organisations are confronted with declining income because of the fall in circulation and readership, a decline in advertising income and a fragmentation of attention (Franklin, 2014). The internet and social media, in particular, play an essential role in this. In the Western world, tech giants Facebook/Meta and Google/Alphabet are nowadays the largest advertising companies in the world – taking away advertising spending that used to go to traditional media companies – and they also disrupt the distribution of content to audiences and their attention. As a result, news organisations are under pressure to develop new business models to adjust to innovation, new platforms and audiences (Pavlik, 2013). Therefore, media organisations feel increased commercial pressure, ultimately influencing editorial decisions (Curran and Seaton, 2018).

Traditional print journalism has undergone a wave of *tabloidisation*, which refers to the influence of tabloid newspapers on the simplification of journalistic content (by preferring entertainment, scandals and sports), depoliticisation of the public, and lowering journalistic standards (Wasserman, 2009). A crucial impact of social media on journalism is the aspect of sharing. Sharing is an essential characteristic of social media (Meikle, 2016) and also popped up in the most recent study of Harcup and O'Neill (2017) about news values. Sharing is as much part of engagement on social media platforms as posting content and commenting on other people's posts.

Sharing means a shift in media audience behaviour made possible by convergence. Jenkins et al. (2013) see sharing as an essential part of what they call *spreadable media*. They position *spreadability* against *stickiness* in media, which refers to content designed to attract and hold audiences' attention. Spreadability, however, refers to content intended to be shared, remixed and distributed by audiences.

Shareability is also connected to content that can *go viral*. Viral news can be defined as news stories that spread in an online networked media environment, primarily through social media, much faster and more broadly than other news stories. Not all content or news is the same. Because of economic pressures, media organisations seek to publish content that is remarkable but also has the potential to go viral. Denisova (2022) refers to *viral content* as communication that spreads like wildfire: it suddenly spreads quickly and cannot be stopped. While shareable content that can go viral was initially attributed to *Buzzfeed* and other similar online platforms, which focus heavily on personalisation, visualisation and trivialisation and use strategies of *clickbait* (headlines that are designed to make readers click on them) and *listicles* (articles that are written in a list-based format), traditional media organisations are under pressure to adopt some of these new strategies, and use them in how they present and distribute news content, which ultimately leads to tensions between commercial goals and editorial choices (Denisova, 2022). As discussed in the final part of this section, media organisations also use big data analytics and AI to predict the shareability of media content.

Changing News Consumption

Having discussed the economic pressures that led to changes in the business models of media organisations and new ways of packaging and circulating news content, let us now shift attention to the users and look into how news consumption patterns are transforming. Of course, this is connected to the aspects discussed above, and news organisations can argue – in their defence of putting shareability more central as a news value – that they are responding to changes in usage patterns and new habits and demands from their audiences.

Longitudinal research by Costera Meijer and Groot Kormelink (2015) studied patterns of news use between 2004 and 2014. They argue that while social and mobile media might not have unleashed a revolution in news consumption, they changed how people consume news. Their study distinguishes 16 user practices in engaging with news: reading, watching, viewing, listening, checking, snacking, monitoring, scanning, searching, clicking, linking, sharing, liking, recommending, commenting and voting. The list of user practices provides a more nuanced understanding of how new platforms allow for new types of news consumption.

Research by the Pew Research Center and the Reuters Institute also documented how online news consumption via social and mobile media has increased. This was accompanied by the growing importance of pictures and videos, complementing (or sometimes replacing) textual content. As a result, people might check in more often on the news, but the average time spent on news has decreased. When looking at news consumption in the last few years (see, for example, the Reuters Institute reports), we notice a couple of striking observations which need to be considered in the context of the Covid-19 pandemic and lockdowns across the globe:

- While news consumption had increased (particularly online) in 2020, the pandemic also brought about economic worries for news organisations and audiences concerned about the circulation of disinformation, particularly on social media.
- The year 2021 saw a peak in interest in the news. Still, the bleak nature of the news (first about the pandemic, later about the war in Ukraine, climate change and economic hardship) resulted in an increasing group of news consumers who started to avoid the news.
- In 2022, trust in news decreased in several countries, often fed by political fragmentation.
- In the same year, the influence of social media platforms Facebook/Meta (even more so in 2023 because Facebook started to pull back from the news) and Twitter (because of the uncertainty after its takeover by Elon Musk) began to decline, while the platform TikTok gained prominence, particularly among younger audiences.

News avoidance and declining trust in the news are persisting issues now in news consumption research.

Data and Technology as a Gatekeeper

Finally, much change in the news sector can be linked to technology. The rise of social media and mobile applications meant that news organisations had to play according to the rules of platform companies. News is also increasingly consumed and engaged with via mobile news apps. In both cases, technology is determining how news is distributed and consumed. In this final subsection, we discuss:

- How digital technology creates more data about audiences and what can be done.
- How has digital technology become a news gatekeeper, and what are the challenges of this?

First, with the increased digitalisation and datafication of news, more opportunities become available for data collection and analysis about users and their engagement with content, other users, advertisers and the platform(s). We have already discussed how *social media logic* is based on programmability, popularity, connectivity and datafication (van Dijck and Poell, 2013). This new logic not only determines how platforms are run and how other organisations that offer content via them are subject to this, too; it also means that more data about audiences and their behaviour can be collected and fed into metrics and analytics (Christin, 2020). This audience knowledge can be collected through basic Google/Alphabet or Facebook/Meta analytics, and news companies have developed in-house data collection infrastructures. In this context, tensions might exist over data collection and resource exchanges between news and third-party apps. In any case, the digital news industry provides more possibilities for collecting data and, therefore, feeding into the audience and big data analytics to predict the shareability of news (Tandoc, 2014).

Second, the role of algorithms as gatekeepers also needs to be discussed. We have already explained the *filter bubble* (Pariser, 2011) and the challenges that exist around this. When discussing the news crisis, the concept of an *echo chamber* is also essential. Sunstein (2001) wrote about this in his book Republic.com. Let us define these concepts and then review the empirical studies examining their impact. Pariser (2011) proposed the concept of a filter bubble to capture his concern about the increasing use of personalisation in ranking internet search results and social media feeds. Jamieson and Cappella (2008: 76) an *echo chamber* as 'a bounded, enclosed media space that has the potential to both magnify the messages delivered within it and insulate them from rebuttal'. An echo chamber can thus be seen as a bubble with like-minded ideas and opinions in which some people actively choose to live. A filter bubble is an echo chamber, but this is primarily produced by ranking algorithms, which engage in personalisation that we – users – have no say in. Societal concerns exist around filter bubbles and echo chambers, specifically in the context of polarisation in the political sphere. However, empirical research on this matter found that echo chambers are much less widespread than is commonly assumed, while there is no empirical support for the filter bubble hypothesis (Bruns, 2019; Dubois and Blank, 2018). In other words, while we think we can blame technology for polarisation, we might have to blame ourselves or have to come up with different metaphors.

Data and Automated Journalism

Let us start with a definition. What is data journalism, and is it more than just *journalism* that's done with *data*? Another take is that it is journalism's response to the datafication of society. But these are not super helpful definitions. *Data journalism* is 'a deeply contested and simultaneously diffuse term', Fink and Anderson (2015: 468) write. There is no universally accepted definition, as disagreement exists over how central data should be, what is included under data, and what is not. For example, is reporting about election polls data journalism? The fluidity of defining data journalism depends not only on data but also on technology, which is rapidly changing. A good, operational definition of *data journalism* is offered by data journalist Simon Rogers (2016): 'Using data to tell stories in the best possible way,

combining the best techniques of journalism: including visualisations, concise explanation and the latest technology. It should be open, accessible and enlightening.'

The Rise of Data in Journalism

The history of data journalism started in the 1950s and was then called *computer-
assisted reporting*. It was the first organised and systematic approach using
computers to collect and analyse data to improve the news (Gray et al., 2012). From
the 1960s, media organisations started using it for investigative journalism, independently monitoring power by analysing public records databases with scientific
methods (Anderson, 2018). Data journalism became more prominent and institutionalised in the first decade of the twenty-first century (Bounegru and Gray, 2021). At
the same time, however, it became much more contested as governments, companies and other influential organisations started to push back. The latter must be seen
in the context of losing faith in public institutions and expert knowledge and the
rise in manipulation and disinformation (see the following section in this chapter).
Precisely for this reason, Bounegru and Gray (2021) chose *Towards a Critical Data
Practice* as the subtitle of their (edited) book: with this, they stress that neither data
nor data journalism can be taken for granted; what is necessary is to reflect on how
critical engagements with data might modify data practices, thereby making space
for public imagination and interventions around data politics. Above all, they argue
that data journalism refers to a diverse plurality of practices rather than a single,
unified set of practices.

So what does data journalism do exactly? Loosen et al. (2020) explain that the
majority of data-driven journalism initiatives contain the following elements:

> Projects build on (large) datasets – often digital and, in most cases,
> quantitative – which serve as the raw material to conduct some form of
> (statistical) analysis and enable the identification and telling of (news)
> stories.

> Projects include (data) visualisation elements in that their presentation
> includes graphics such as maps and bar charts.

> Projects are characterised by *participatory openness* and *crowdsourcing*,
> meaning that users are involved in the data collection, analysis and
> interpretation.

> Projects often embrace an open data/source approach and celebrate the
> ideas of openness and transparency.

One of the most prolific cases of data journalism is the *Panama Papers*, a massive
leak of 11.5 million documents published in 2016 by the International Consortium
of Investigative Journalists (Diakopoulos, 2019). The leaked documents exposed
widespread offshore financial activities and tax evasion among politicians, wealthy

individuals and public figures worldwide. Whistleblower Edward Snowden called this the most significant leak in the history of data journalism.

Automating the Newsroom

Data journalism must be distinguished from using artificial intelligence or algorithms in journalism. While *computational journalism* (Anderson, 2013) is used as a broad term in this context, other authors have proposed different labels: *algorithmic journalism* (Dörr, 2016), *automated journalism* (Graefe, 2016), *machine-written news* (van Daelen, 2012) and *robot journalism* (Carlson, 2015). An operational definition of computational journalism is 'finding, telling, and disseminating news stories with, by, or about algorithms' (Diakopoulos and Koliska, 2017: 809). Surprisingly, this definition is quite close to the one about *data journalism*, whereby algorithms replace data. Given the problematic nature of defining AI and its application in the newsroom (see Chapter 6 and Broussard, 2018), it makes more sense to talk about automating the news or computational journalism rather than call it *AI journalism*.

In an overview article about the history of automation in journalism, Linden (2017: 123) asks the question, 'Why are there still so many jobs in journalism?' thereby echoing Autor (2015) in his historical account of workplace automation. Automation in the newsroom is not new. Since the 1960s, there have been experiments with automatic content production, for example, for weather forecasts. Since the 1990s, some automation has been implemented in sports, medical and financial reporting. Associated Press, for instance, hired the services of the technology company Automated Insights to cover sports games. In 2006, Thomson Reuters announced the use of automation to generate financial news stories. More famously, when in March 2014 an earthquake hit southern California, the *Los Angeles Times* was the first newspaper to publish the story, three minutes after it happened. It was able to do this because it had invested in *Quakebot*, an algorithmic generator that turns data into a news narrative without human input (Carlson, 2015). This is one of the first iconic examples of automated journalism, and since then news outlets across the globe have developed or made use of automated news content services.

It is essential, however, to distinguish different types of automated journalism:

- *Automated content production.* This is the most controversial application of automated journalism (Montal and Reich, 2017). It refers to algorithms and software that can develop news stories independently (Diakopoulos, 2019). This application uses *natural language generation* (see Chapter 6).
- *Data mining.* This application of automated journalism can be seen as a process that is used for discovering new and valuable knowledge from data – 'finding the news in data' (Diakopoulos, 2019: 45). It happens through the extraction of useful information from a more significant subset of data. The Quakebot case is an example of data mining.

- *News dissemination.* While the first two applications focus on news production, this application deals with news distribution. Digital news reaches the consumer via search engines, social media, news aggregators, etc. Algorithms and automated systems are used to distribute content to their users. Controversy exists here about ethical considerations over *algorithmic transparency* (Diakopoulos and Koliska, 2017).
- *Content optimisation.* Finally, this type of automated journalism refers to using data and audience analytics (including data mining algorithms) for news personalisation. This can happen via customised newsfeeds or chatbots. Automated bots can provide a personalised news experience (Jones and Jones, 2019).

Opportunities for Automated Journalism

Having conceptualised automated journalism and explained the role of data and algorithms in different applications, we now look at their impact. This subsection reviews the opportunities that automating the newsroom can bring (Graefe, 2016), while the next goes deeper into some of the challenges:

- *Increased efficiency and speed.* News can be produced in nearly real-time, or at least when the data becomes available. It should reduce the time it takes to deliver news (including updates) to audiences, and this efficiency should – in theory – help journalists so that they can focus on in-depth reporting and investigative work. The Quakebot report of the earthquake by the *Los Angeles Times* serves as a good example here.
- *Scale.* Automation expands news production by producing news that could previously not be covered due to limited resources. News such as sports, weather forecasts, financial and economic information can easily be automated without losing quality.
- *Accuracy.* Unlike humans, algorithms do not get tired and do not need breaks. Automated reporting thus allows us to avoid errors and overlooking facts. However, an essential condition here is that automated systems are correctly programmed and use accurate data – which is often not the case (Diakopoulos and Koliska, 2017).
- *Objectivity.* In principle, automated systems are based on algorithms, which follow predefined rules for analysing data and producing news stories. As such, we are told that automated journalism should increase objectivity. However, we should be cautious about claims of unbiased systems and data (Montal and Reich, 2017).
- *Personalisation.* Automation can help create personalised news feeds for specific users, groups and communities, tailored to their interests and preferences. This level of news personalisation can enhance user engagement and create a more satisfying news consumption experience.

- *News on demand.* The ability to personalise news stories and analyse data from different angles also provides opportunities for offering news on demand. Algorithms can be used to answer specific questions or to look into particular scenarios and perspectives.

Challenges Presented by Automated Journalism

Some of the listed opportunities of automated journalism can only deliver on the condition that the algorithmic systems on which it is based use accurate and unbiased data. Beyond this, we must look at other challenges to judge the usefulness of automated journalism. Challenges exist at the level of individual journalists, the newsroom and journalism in general.

At the level of individual journalists, questions arise around employment and authorship. Among the most significant concerns about automated journalism is the loss of employment if more news organisations use automated systems instead of humans. In theory, automation would free up time for in-depth reporting, but often it ends up in a cost-cutting operation (Cohen, 2015). A related aspect is authorship: is it a piece of content written by a human or software, and can we talk about *algorithmic authorship* (Montal and Reich, 2017)?

Challenges also exist at the level of newsrooms. News organisations depend on platforms and tech companies not only for news distribution but also for the provision of automated systems, and this opens up questions about autonomy (Simon, 2022). In addition, there are issues with transparency and accountability when automated systems produce news content. Algorithmic systems can provide an account of *what* is happening but cannot explain *why* things are happening (Graefe, 2016).

Finally, for automated journalism in general, there are also challenges about credibility and quality. Concerns about the perceived quality of automated news are not that different from concerns about the perceived credibility of news in general. However, there are questions about fairness, accuracy, error, etc. (Waddell, 2018). The success of automated journalism is dependent on data availability and quality, which is a precondition for running these systems. Of course, the writing quality is an issue, as algorithmic systems cannot understand what human language is (Graefe, 2016).

When evaluating the potential and limits of automated journalism, Diakopoulos (2019) reminds us that it is crucial to reflect on the human values that are embedded in the design and use of these technologies, as well as the changes in journalist practices that emerge from blending in algorithms into news routines. Finally, reflection is needed on the contribution that algorithms and automation play in enhancing the sustainability of news production.

Disinformation and the Trust Crisis

Journalism is in a crisis. So is democracy. We are witnessing *epistemic* crises in our public sphere, threatening to undermine political agency (Dahlgren, 2018). Western democracies are threatened by populist revolt, and the digital media, once thought to contribute to a better democracy, have exacerbated the crisis (Pickard, 2019). The spread of *fake news* and *disinformation* further undermines the trust in the media, experts and institutions and contributes to a deepening trust crisis. What is the role of digital media and data-driven platforms in undermining news and democracy, and how we can fight back?

Conceptualising Disinformation

While *fake news* is often associated with the 2016 US presidential election contested by Donald Trump and Hillary Clinton and the dismissal of mainstream news as fake news by Trump afterwards, it would be wrong to assume this is a new phenomenon (Tandoc et al., 2018). Misleading or false information, presented as news, is as old as news itself and must be seen as part of a long-standing project of efforts in Western democracies to influence and persuade people through spin, propaganda and political marketing. People and organisations engaged in this can be motivated by the intent to make political or financial gains. According to Bakir and McStay (2018: 157), 'the digital media ecology has proliferated, democratised and intensified the scale of fake news'. *Fake news* is a popular but problematic term (Freelon and Wells, 2020), and researchers have instead proposed *information disorder* as a more neutral and informative concept (Wardle and Derakhshan, 2017). Others have proposed a plethora of alternative terms, such as *post-truth* (Waisbord, 2018; Farkas and Schou, 2020), *disinformation* (Bennett and Livingston, 2018), *mal-information* (Wardle and Derakhshan, 2017), *misinformation* (Valenzuela et al., 2019) and *junk news* (Howard, 2020).

While it would lead us too far to offer a detailed analysis of the benefits and downsides of each of these concepts, I prefer using *disinformation* as a subcategory of *misinformation*. *Fake news* is a problematic term as people frequently mix up different categories:

- News that is *invented* to make money or to discredit others
- News that has a basis in fact but is *spun* to suit a particular agenda
- News that people do not feel comfortable about or disagree with.

In a detailed analysis of the origins and use of *fake news*, Tandoc et al. (2018) developed a typology in which it has been deployed historically. Their typology includes news satire, parody, fabrication, manipulation, advertising and propaganda. The terms *media manipulation, information fabrication* and *propaganda* deserve some more elaboration:

- *Media manipulation* is a broad term for manipulating news frames, setting agendas and propagating specific ideas. Often, this includes *attention hacking*

through the strategic use of social media, memes and bots (Marwick and Lewis, 2017).
- *Information fabrication* refers to news with no factual basis but published in the style of news articles to create legitimacy.
- We talk about *propaganda* as news created by a political entity to influence public and political perceptions.

Finally, how can we distinguish between *misinformation, disinformation* and *mal-information*? *Misinformation* can be defined simply is the accidental statement of factually incorrect claims. *Disinformation* is a subcategory of misinformation, and while successful disinformation campaigns might contain accurate information, their crucial characteristic is that misleading information is spread to cause harm (Freelon and Wells, 2020). It is thus strategic or intentional. It is important to remember that misinformation and disinformation and their effects are complex and interwoven with countless socio-political and psychological issues. Finally, *mal-information*, a neologism seemingly borrowed from malware or malicious software, has been introduced to describe accurate information released for harassment, such as *doxing* – publishing private details about somebody without their permission (Wardle and Derakhshan, 2017).

Disinformation as a Part of Human Communication

Now that we have offered some conceptual clarification, let us look into the history of disinformation and what has been driving it. Misinformation, disinformation and propaganda have always been part of human communication. The invention of the Gutenberg printing press in 1493 revolutionised the possibilities for journalism and amplified the dissemination of disinformation. While propaganda played a huge role in the twentieth-century wars (including the cold war), the internet's arrival in the late twentieth century, followed by social media in the early twenty-first century, dramatically increased the circulation of misinformation and disinformation. The internet lowered entry costs for new competitors, which helped to undermine the business model of traditional news sources that enjoyed high levels of public trust and credibility (Lazer et al., 2018). The digitalisation of news also challenged conventional definitions of news: platforms give non-journalists a space to reach a mass audience. At the same time, the rise of citizen journalism made the link between news and journalists more complex (Tandoc et al., 2018).

Social media play a crucial role in the proliferation of disinformation. They are the platforms on which users produce, consume and exchange different types of information, including news. Social media bring together large networks of audiences, and as such they facilitate the exchange and spread of information, including misinformation. The campaigns around the Brexit referendum in the UK and the 2016 US elections are seen as pivotal moments in which the spread of disinformation on social media had substantial political consequences (Lazer et al., 2018). We look deeper into this in the next subsection.

When Disinformation Undermines Politics

Cambridge Analytica was an example of how data plays a role in political campaigning. In that context, social media functions as a tool to collect data about people, which feeds into the construction of user profiles that can then be deployed to offer customised political messages. Beyond this, it is also important to inquire about the precise role that social media plays in the circulation of disinformation. In a landmark study, Tucker et al. (2018) provide an extensive literature review of how the interplay of political polarisation and disinformation impacts democracy. They look into different aspects, including the producers of disinformation, strategies and tactics of spreading disinformation and how polarisation and disinformation are related:

- Different actors are involved in the modern media ecosystem, all playing overlapping and sometimes competing roles in producing and amplifying disinformation. They include trolls, bots, fake news websites, conspiracy theorists, politicians, highly partisan media outlets and particular governments.
- Different tactics and strategies are used for spreading disinformation online, from using bots and trolls to directly sharing information and manipulating search rankings to censorship, hacking and other tactics.
- Polarisation produces significant challenges for liberal democracies. Partisan division impacts political institutions, and hostility towards *other* groups encourages extreme tactics and undermines compromises. These developments increase the political system's vulnerability to partisan disinformation, accelerated by widespread social media use and distrust of the mainstream media.

From their literature review, Tucker et al. (2018) also identify research gaps, which include understanding the effects of exposure to disinformation (e.g., what are the causal mechanisms that may explain opinion change), the need to conduct cross-platform research (e.g., comparing the prevalence of behaviour and causal effects across different platforms) and the necessity of researching audiovisual content versus text. Later in this section, we look into synthetic media and deepfakes. Beyond this, it is clear that studies on disinformation, political participation and their impact on democracy should not just focus on the online information environments: aspects that need to be taken into account, too, are general levels of political engagement, traditional media use and the behaviour of politicians/political parties. Finally and most importantly, when analysing disinformation in the political context, it is crucial to broaden the focus beyond the US and Western contexts. As is often the case, most of the studies conducted and published focus on data collection and analysis in the Western world, which ignores an understanding of how disinformation impacts politics and democracy in the majority world.

When Disinformation Meets Pandemics and the Climate Crisis

While most of the research on disinformation has focused on the political sphere, we also need to look into how (knowingly or unwittingly) false information is produced and circulated in other contexts. Particularly important here is to look at information in the context of pandemics and climate change.

The term *infodemic*, a portmanteau of information and pandemic, was initially coined in 2003 by David Rothkopf (during the 2002-2004 SARS outbreak) but rose to prominence during the Covid-19 pandemic. The *World Health Organisation* (WHO) declared that besides the pandemic threat originating from the SARS-CoV-2 virus, we also had to be aware of the consequences of the *infodemic*. The latter refers to a situation where a large amount (or even overabundance) of information is available, which often includes false or misleading content and which spreads rapidly and widely through various communication channels, especially the internet and social media. Bruns et al. (2022) have researched this within the broader context of media coverage of the pandemic and how conspiracy theories have emerged.

When we talk about conspiracy theories, we also need to look at the circulation of disinformation about climate change. Disinformation is closely linked to climate change scepticism and denialism. Interestingly, climate change is highly politicised and subject to polarisation (Anderson and Huntington, 2017). Like disinformation in the political sphere, several actors are financing, producing and amplifying disinformation. Underlying belief systems, social norms, and psychological heuristics such as *confirmation bias* are considered essential factors contributing to the spread of disinformation. No single approach can address issues of climate change disinformation, and multidisciplinary and multifaceted approaches are necessary to combat this information crisis.

When Disinformation and Automation Create Deepfakes

One aspect that we still need to discuss is how AI and so-called *synthetic media* can automate and advance the development and circulation of disinformation. A subcategory that came to the fore in recent years is *deepfakes* (Meikle, 2022). Let us start with some conceptual clarification. *Synthetic media* is a collective term for media content, such as images, video, audio and text generated using AI algorithms. The term *synthetic* implies that the content is artificially generated. *Deepfakes* are a specific type of synthetic media that use AI (and, more specifically, *deep learning*) techniques to create or manipulate audio or video recordings of people. The term itself is a portmanteau of *deep* learning and *fake*. Deepfakes use a technique called *generative adversarial networks*, which are two neural networks that compete against each other. One network, the *generator*, generates new images or video, whereas the other, the *discriminator*, determines whether an image or video is real.

Ultimately, by analysing vast amounts of data, deep learning algorithms can learn to map the facial features of one person to another, thereby creating a seamless and often highly realistic image or video that appears to show a person in the video saying or doing things they never did. Deepfakes have gained significant attention for their potential use in creating celebrity pornographic videos, revenge porn, hoaxes, bullying and financial fraud (Meikle, 2022). In addition, concern about their impact on society also exists around their potential to deceive, manipulate and spread disinformation.

Vaccari and Chadwick (2020) have studied the use of political deepfakes as a distinctive form of visual disinformation. As a relatively new form of video-based disinformation, deepfakes can increase uncertainty, which – as a result – might contribute to a reduction of trust in news on social media. They can also compromise the trust in political news on social media. As a key finding of their research, Vaccari and Chadwick (2020) conclude that while political deepfakes might not always manage to deceive individuals, they can sow uncertainty, which in turn might also reduce trust in news, particularly on social media where deepfakes are often widely shared.

How Do We Fight Back to Protect Our Media?

A final note about disinformation is the question of how we counter false information and how we can fight back. In 'A Field Guide to "Fake News" and Other Information Disorders', Bounegru et al. (2018) offer some insights on how digital methods can be used to analyse disinformation, such as how to study political memes on Facebook or map troll-like practices on Twitter. The European Commission (2018), in a report on media literacy and how to tackle disinformation, proposes to work around four elements:

- *Transparency.* Create more awareness and transparency about the use and role of algorithms in news production and distribution processes.
- *Media diversity and pluralism.* A diversity of sources, opinions and owners of media outlets contributes to media pluralism.
- *Credibility for media institutions.* While this principle is valuable, it must be realised in the age of speed and competition.
- Tackling disinformation is *a shared responsibility* of platform, civil society and governments.

Learning Takeaways

- Journalism is in crisis. Commercial pressures, changing consumption patterns and habits, and technological change require news organisations to rethink how they produce and distribute news.
- Data and algorithms become new gatekeepers, but we need to be aware of the consequences of personalisation and how it feeds into polarisation.

- Data journalism embraces the possibilities of data to improve the news and investigative reporting.
- Automation in the newsroom creates new opportunities and challenges.
- Disinformation is the intentional spreading of misleading/incorrect information to cause harm. It contributes to polarisation, and new AI-based applications such as *deepfakes* can further reduce trust in news.

Recommended Reading

Bounegru, L. and Gray, J. (eds) (2021). *The Data Journalism Handbook: Towards a Critical Data Practice*. Amsterdam: Amsterdam University Press.

Christin, A. (2020). *Metrics at Work: Journalism and the Contested Meaning of Algorithms*. Princeton, NJ: Princeton University Press.

Farkas, J. and Schou, J. (2020). *Post-Truth, Fake News and Democracy: Mapping the Politics of Falsehood*. New York and Abingdon: Routledge.

Meikle, G. (2022). *Deepfakes*. Cambridge: Polity.

Pickard, V. (2019). *Democracy without Journalism? Confronting the Misinformation Society*. Oxford: Oxford University Press.

Recommended Listening

Power Corrupts is a podcast series about the hidden and often nefarious forces that shape our world, hosted by Brian Klaas. https://www.powercorruptspodcast.com/

10

Data, Automation and Work

Learning Goals

- Engage in critical thinking about work and labour in the sharing economy and gig work to see through the hype.
- Learn the realities of automation and data work in a global context.
- Envision the alternatives for workers and communities to organise and fight back.

From the Sharing Economy to Automation: Flexibility or Exploitation?

The launch of ChatGPT by OpenAI in 2022 accelerated the hype around so-called *generative AI*. In 2023, everyone started to use ChatGPT or other AI services that can generate text, images or even software code in response to a simple prompt. Soon it was reported that people working in communication, public relations, design or coding might see themselves becoming members of the precariat class, as their jobs could be at risk of automation. While generative AI services are powerful in what they can achieve, they also have severe limitations. For example, they do not understand what a language is, nor do they grasp the images and pictures they produce. However, what is less known is the hidden infrastructure in the background that is necessary to run (generative) AI services, such as the people (often based in the Global South) who are paid next to nothing to do content moderation for ChatGPT, an outsourced type of labour) or the fact that these services are trained on data (text or images) that you and I have produced and shared.

Generative AI seems to be the newest wave of hype promising us more freedom and flexibility as digital technologies will do some of our work. But just as is the case with the sharing economy, gig work and other new hypes, the proposed benefits do not come without caveats. While the sharing economy benefits people with assets, the gig economy means we no longer have to go to the shop ourselves or cook or collect our take-away meals. Automation produces winners and losers. The platforms make us more dependent on them, and the companies controlling AI services are seeing their value booming. But we need to know more about what this means for the workers in these new types of work.

What Is Work? What Is Labour?

Work and labour seem such mundane concepts that everyone knows what they mean. Especially in the Western world, work and labour are so connected to life itself, as is illustrated in the saying 'work to live' (or 'live to work'). However, as familiar as we are with these terms, various definitions and perspectives exist around them. For example, the context in which work is done can vary: from caring responsibilities in households and families, to being employed by a boss or working in your own business. Another important nuance is whether work is paid or not. In this particular dimension the monetisation of work comes into play. But then again, a large part of socially necessary work (e.g., raising children) is priceless (even if it is transformed into employment). Throughout history there has been a lot of forced, compulsory labour too (e.g., working for feudal lords or in slave contexts). This just illustrates that what is understood under work/labour depends on spatial and temporal contexts. It is important to acknowledge here the role that industrialisation has played in transforming the world of work and how Eurocentric perspectives on work have been forced upon other parts of the world, mainly through colonisation. In this sense, we must be aware of the limits of the Eurocentric narratives on work, particularly from a feminist and a global history perspective (Komlosy, 2018).

How can we understand work, and how is labour related to it? In simple terms, *work* is a broader concept common to all societies that refers to the application of human effort, skills, knowledge or technologies to produce goods and services that satisfy human needs (Fuchs and Sevignani, 2013). Work can take different forms: physical work, mental tasks or creative endeavours. It can be carried out to sustain oneself, contribute to society or express oneself. On the other hand, *labour* is a specific type of work usually seen in the context of employment or economic (re) production (Grint, 2005). Like work, it involves individuals' physical and mental efforts to produce goods or services. However, what is specific about labour is that it is done in exchange for a wage or other compensation. According to Marxist scholars Fuchs and Sevignani (2013: 240), 'labour is a necessarily alienated form of work, in which humans do not control and own the means and results of production'. Labour is a key factor of production in capitalism, alongside capital and natural resources (Fuchs, 2014a). Examples of labour are factory (e.g., assembling cars), agricultural (e.g., planting crops and harvesting vegetables and fruits) and construction (e.g., building houses) labour. For some examples of work, such as care work (e.g., raising children or caring for the elderly) and creative work (e.g., composing music or writing), it is less clear whether it is labour. It can exist outside and within economic (re)production and be done in exchange for a wage.

Labour as a Valorisation Process

We must remember the historical and socio-political aspects of defining work and labour (Komlosy, 2018). The perspective of political economy is thus well suited to help us understand how work and labour are connected, specifically in the digital context. Not only industrialisation but also digital technologies transform the world/future of work. Much scholarly attention has been given to *digital labour* (e.g., Fuchs, 2014a; Jarrett, 2022; Scholz, 2013). Before we go deeper into this concept, we must elaborate on our political economy perspective on work/labour. According to Marx (1867/1976: 284), the work process – in which humans use technologies to create goods and services from nature or culture – consists of three elements:

- Purposeful activity, that is, work itself
- The object on which that work is performed
- The instruments of that work.

Marx (1867/1976) calls this work process the *productive forces*. We must distinguish *labour power* (subject) and the *means of production* (object). The means of production – which are natural forces, technologies, infrastructures, and resources – have two dimensions (Fuchs, 2014a):

- The object of work
- The product of work.

Table 10.1 further explains what these elements entail in different modes of organisation of the productive forces.

Table 10.1   Object and product of work (based on Fuchs, 2020)

Type of economy	Object of work	Product of product
Agricultural economy	Nature	Basic products
Industrial economy	Basic industrial products	Industrial products
Information economy	Experience and ideas	Informational products

In a capitalist economy, the process of economic production contains two parts (Fuchs, 2020):

- The work/labour process (focused on creating *use values*)
- The valorisation process (creation of *surplus value*).

To understand this, we must return to the centrality of commodification in capitalism. Essentially, *commodification* refers to the transformation of use values into
exchange values. The former refers to the qualitative side of a product, the way it
satisfies human needs and wants, while the latter is the (quantitative) proportion at
which a commodity can be sold for a certain amount of money (or be exchanged
for other entities). According to Marx (1867/1976), the capitalist possesses goods and
services with use value at the end of the labour process. But they are not interested
in keeping them for their own use; they want them for their exchange value and,
in addition to this, they want a commodity that is greater in value than the sum of
the values of the commodities used to produce it (labour power and the means of
production). This is called *surplus value*. Creating surplus value (i.e., valorisation)
through workers' production is central to capital accumulation. Capital and profit
originate in the unpaid part of workers' labour conducted in class relations, which
Marx (1867/1976) calls *surplus labour*. Profit is the monetary expression of surplus (the amount of unpaid labour-time workers perform) over the invested sum of
money (Fuchs, 2020). This brief explanation of surplus value/labour is necessary for
conceptualising digital labour.

Let us look at an example before we discuss this concept. A furniture company
invests $100 to produce a wooden table: $50 for raw materials (e.g., wood), $20 for
labour cost (in wages) and $30 for overhead costs (rent, utilities, etc.). The company
wants to get back the invested $100 and make a surplus/profit beyond the invested
capital and chooses to sell the table for $150. The surplus value is thus $50, which
the company's owner makes.

When Labour Becomes Digital

How do the labour and valorisation process work in the digital sphere? This is what
digital labour deals with. It asks how internet platforms such as Facebook/Meta,
YouTube and Weibo make money. We already discussed the *audience commodity*
(Smythe, 1977) and its adaptation to the context of digital media, what Fuchs (2010)
calls a *prosumer commodity*. In essence, the business model of online platforms is
based on targeted advertising, monetisation of user data (personal data and user-
generated content), and predictive algorithms.

Digital labour emerged around the early 2000s as an essential theoretical concept
in the Marxist critique of the political economy of digital media. It has been used to
critically analyse how capital accumulation happens on corporate internet platforms
(Fuchs and Sevignani, 2013). The Marxist critique states that users create value,
which is central to generating profit, but are not remunerated (Fuchs, 2014a). As
such, the surplus value created by users' unpaid labour is appropriated by the
capitalist owner of the platform. In addition, the debate about digital labour exists
beyond what happens on the platform in the informational sphere. Fuchs (2014a)
documents extensively how exploitation is present in the overall value chain of

digital media/technology: in addition to what happens on platforms, value is also created and appropriated in industrial labour (e.g., the workers from Foxconn and other companies who are working extremely long days in unhealthy circumstances to assemble our IT devices) (Qiu, 2016) and even in agricultural labour (e.g., the people who work in exploitative circumstances – most often in the Global South – to harvest minerals, which are essential for the production of IT devices) (Fuchs, 2014a).

Despite its contribution to raising awareness about the different processes behind platforms and in the global IT value chain, the (Marxist) *digital labour* concept has also received criticism. For example, there are questions about whether user participation on social media platforms can be categorised as *labour* (Jarrett, 2022), while others argue whether something can be called *exploitation* when people are having fun engaging with it (Scholz, 2013). Other critiques focus on where exactly value is created. For example, Arvidsson and Colleoni (2012) posit that the realisation of the value accumulated by social media companies occurs on the stock market rather than in direct commodity exchange (on the platform). Finally, and more fundamentally, Gandini (2021) writes that digital labour has become an empty signifier because the concept has evolved into an umbrella term used to describe different practices and instances around labour and digital technology which have no relation to the original theory. For example, according to Gandini (2021), *platform labour* does not fit the label *digital labour* as it has some specific characteristics, differentiating it from what happens on social media. Nevertheless, I agree with Jarrett (2022) that users are engaged in value-generating labour, and as such, it remains an important framework to analyse and discuss precisely how this happens in the context of data, automation and AI.

Labour and Class

Class is a central element in debates about work/labour that we have not discussed explicitly yet. Of course, we have already talked about how value is appropriated by the owners of (social media) platforms. There is a group that benefits from this user engagement, and when one group benefits from something, there is a likelihood that another is disadvantaged. So it is essential to reflect on what *class* means and how this notion has evolved in the digital sphere. As a critical concept in sociology, *social class* is a grouping characterised by shared socio-economic circumstances (Wright, 2015). One could argue that the members of the grouping have a common social status, typically determined by factors such as wealth, income, education, occupation and social networks.

Karl Marx offers a critical approach to class. In the *Communist Manifesto*, Marx and Engels (1848/1976) argue that capitalism is characterised by a social antagonism between the capitalist class (what they call the *bourgeoisie*) and the working class. In this sense, class is related to the concept of *modes of production*. This refers to:

- How a society produces its essential material goods (*labour power* and the *means of production*)
- The social relationships of members of society to those means of production (*relations of production*).

Essentially, one class (the capitalist class – a relatively small group) owns and controls the means of production. They are the class that owns capital and uses this to buy labour power. The other, much larger group, whom Marx calls the *proletariat* (the working class), neither owns nor controls the means of production. The working class owns nothing and can only survive by selling its labour power (Fuchs, 2020).

Erik Olin Wright (2015) has written extensively about class and argued that beyond the capitalist and working classes, there is a third group in between, the middle class. According to him, the *middle class* are those social groups that have elements from the other two groups. For example, middle managers have some power similar to capitalists in that they exercise power over workers, but like workers themselves, they (most often) have no absolute control over investment decisions. As such, Wright (2015) concluded that the middle class occupies contradictory positions within the class structure: this class is pulled towards capital and labour in both directions. Around the antagonism between different classes exist neighbouring concepts such as *class position* (which is determined by a group's role in the production process and its relation to the means of production) and *class conflict* (the conflicting interests given different roles in the economic systems and relation to the means of production) (Fuchs, 2020).

How relevant is the class concept in the contemporary era? While it might be the case that class boundaries are becoming more blurred, the ubiquitous nature of digital media – dominating our working and private lives – and growing levels of inequality are essential reasons to investigate and reflect on people's relation to the modes of production in society. Given that inequalities are increasing and the extraction of value from labour is still an essential characteristic of contemporary capitalism, it becomes only more relevant to understand how social class evolves in the era of datafication and automation.

A New Precariat Class

One of the criticisms of the social class concept is whether the antagonism between the capitalist and working classes (even with the inclusion of the middle class) is still valid for our contemporary society. Given multiple crises, the middle class is being squeezed, and the working class is under pressure across the globe. So it is essential to reflect on what class means in the twenty-first century, especially in a world governed by platforms, datafication and automation.

Given the increase in economic insecurity and precariousness of employment, which started in the 1980s and 1990s but intensified after the 2007 financial crisis (and the implemented austerity to deal with this), Standing (2011) proposed a new conceptualisation of class, which includes the notion of the *precariat class*. This class analysis of contemporary capitalist societies identifies seven classes:

- *The elite or plutocracy*. This is the ruling class in the classical Marxist sense. This group's financial strength shapes political discourse and economic and social policies.
- *The salariat*. Members of this group have stable full-time employment and are concentrated at the top level of large corporations, government agencies and public administration.
- *The proficians*. This term merges traditional professionals and technicians and covers people earning high incomes on contract, as consultants or independent workers.
- *The old 'core' working class (proletariat)*. Members of this group rely on mass labour and wage income without control or ownership of the means of production.
- *The precariat*. Members of this group can be distinguished by three characteristics:

  o *Distinctive relations of production*. While they are being pressured to accept unstable labour, they have no occupational identity or narrative, which gives them existential insecurity.
  o *Distinctive relations of distribution*. They rely on money wages, without non-wage benefits, rights-based state benefits or informal community benefits – they live in debt and economic uncertainty, whereby mistaken decisions or illness can easily tip them over the edge into the underclass.
  o *Distinctive relations to the state*. They are the first class in history to be losing cultural, civil, social, economic and political rights – as such they are often dependent on charity.

- *The unemployed*. These are people with no access to wage income.
- The *lumpen-precariat* (or *underclass*). This is 'a detached group of socially ill misfits living off the dregs of society' (Standing, 2011: 8).

Standing's (2011) analysis is not so much about describing class composition; instead, he is concerned with differentiating the *precariat* from the rest of the class structure, especially the working class. While this conceptualisation can be criticised by more traditional class analyses (see, for example, Wright, 2015), it opens up the debate about new types of socio-economic positions and modes of production that simultaneously offer more flexibility but also more precariousness. Before we talk about this in the context of the sharing and gig economy, we need to discuss the notion of the *cybertariat* too. This is yet another concept aimed at scrutinising how labour is changing in the digital era, especially relevant to the context of our project.

Ursula Huws (2003) used the term *cybertariat* in the title of a collection of essays written over three decades, in which she examines the restructuring of employment and daily life from a feminist political economy perspective. In a book published about a decade later, Huws (2014) reflects on how a growing portion of the workforce has become involved in performing digital labour and producing intangible products. While jobs in information and digital technologies are considered *white-collar* jobs and not working class (unlike *blue-collar* jobs, which usually involve manual labour), Huws (2014) argues that many of these jobs are low-paid and menial. Similarly, Rosalind Gill (2007) also wonders whether people working in the digital media industries can best be labelled *techno bohemians* or the new *cyber-tariat*. Based on this research, there are questions to be asked about how much flexibility and liberation digital labour brings about. Despite being celebrated as the future of work, which benefits the people engaging in it, some of the downsides make digital labour unsustainable for many people.

From the Sharing Economy to Gig Work

Significant developments in the world of work in the past two decades have seen the rise of the sharing economy and gig work. Although they are different phenomena, they are related in that they both promise freedom and flexibility while bringing about precariousness.

What Is – or Was – the Sharing Economy?

Although the idea of an economy based on collaboration (and thus sharing) rather than competition is not new, the notion of a *sharing economy* became prominent in the aftermath of the 2007–2008 financial crisis. Harvard professor and founder of the Creative Commons Lawrence Lessig used the term in his book *Remix* (2008). While he mainly considered its potential in the cultural sphere, the idea of sharing and *collaborative consumption* also found its way into physical resources. The latter term was proposed by scholars who embraced the new potential of the sharing economy. Belk (2010) considered collaborative consumption as something that started as part of *Web 2.0*, in which people became more actively involved in distributing things to others. While this was mainly immaterial in the Web 2.0 era, this changed afterwards when sharing tangible assets became a widespread trend. Botsman and Rogers (2010) understand *collaborative consumption* as accessing underutilised resources (which can be goods and services but also information, skills, time or money) in innovative and creative ways, thereby reinventing traditional market behaviour. Maximising asset use through efficient redistribution and shared access models is the idea.

But what exactly is the sharing economy? Sundararajan (2017) considers it a new version of capitalism, which he frames as *crowd-based capitalism*. It has the following characteristics:

- The sharing economy creates new markets enabling the exchange of goods and services, which should result in higher levels of economic activity.

- The sharing economy opens up new opportunities for everyone so that resources and assets can be used to (almost) total capacity.
- Rather than being centrally organised through institutions and hierarchies, the sharing economy is based on crowd-based networks whereby capital and labour are supplied in a decentralised way through crowds and crowd-based marketplaces.
- The personal and professional level becomes increasingly blurred.
- Traditional full-time jobs are replaced by casual labour and contract work, whereby the boundaries between work and leisure become increasingly blurred.

While these are mainly values associated with it – creating new markets and opportunities for everyone and thereby blurring work and leisure – we also need to look at concrete applications of the sharing economy. Sociologist Juliet Schor (2016) writes that sharing economy activities fall into four broad categories, as shown in Table 10.2.

Table 10.2 Sharing economy categories and examples

Category	Example(s)
Recirculation of goods	Craigslist or eBay/Taobao
Increased utilisation of durable assets	Airbnb/Tujia or Uber/Didi
Exchange of services	TaskRabbit
Sharing productive assets	Cooperatives, communal offices/spaces or peer-to-peer services

While the conceptualisation of the sharing economy by Botsman and Rogers (2010) and Sundararajan (2017) is quite rosy, we need to review the promises critically and investigate the impact of the sharing economy. Frenken and Schor (2017) offer a nuanced evaluation here. While sharing economy enthusiasts argue that it offers environmental, social and economic benefits, we must look at the whole picture:

- Regarding *sustainability*, car sharing, for example, sounds good, but its long-term impact and how many cars it takes off the road remain to be seen.
- *Social benefits* can be seen as increased social capital and trust among participants. However, the act of sharing happens on corporate platforms. We have already discussed how platform behaviour is determined by datafication and commodification.
- Assessing the *economic benefits* of the sharing economy is more complex, as the question remains: who gains from what? For example, owners of second homes might be able to make money on their property when it is unused, but the impact of Airbnb (or equivalent platforms) can also harm hotel and other hospitality industries; it can contribute to negative experiences for neighbours

(noise and nuisance); and finally, the distribution of income and welfare is likely to be uneven (where it can, in an extreme case, drive residents out of the market and force them to leave their neighbourhood).

Tech critic Evgeny Morozov (2014) is straightforward in his assessment of the sharing economy. The label *sharing* suggests that ownership is no longer necessary and that we can satisfy our needs with products and services that are available to us. However, he is critical of the sharing economy because it only benefits people with assets they can make available in exchange for rent. Furthermore, he writes that the sharing economy masks a failing economy and argues that it is mainly a way of dealing with the consequences of a financial crisis while not engaging with its causes. Other disadvantages of the sharing economy are weakening labour conditions, erosion of workers' rights and increased precarious work. The leading sharing economy platforms such as Airbnb and Uber operate in regulatory grey areas, often leading to disputes and tensions with traditional industries and government authorities.

Moving to a Definition of Gig Work

The sharing economy and gig work are connected through the platforms on which they are both reliant. The *gig economy* fits many of the characteristics that are part of what Sundararajan (2017) calls *crowd-based capitalism*. The discourse about creating new opportunities for everyone and replacing full-time jobs with casual/contract labour is similar. Both concepts are surrounded by the hope of creating new possibilities regarding freedom and flexibility. However, there are essential differences between the concepts too: the main one is that the sharing economy is about participants sharing assets that they own, while gig work is about providing labour (which can also be done by owning assets, as both Uber drivers and Deliveroo riders own their cars and bikes). But let us provide a more comprehensive definition of the gig economy. Woodcock and Graham (2020) write that the *gig* in the term *gig economy* refers to something short-term, similar to a music performance. Artists might perform once or multiple times. They might get paid for it or not. The gig economy is defined as 'labour markets that are characterised by independent contracting that happens through, via, and on digital platforms' (Woodcock and Graham, 2020: 3). The work offered on these markets is casual and non-permanent.

Legal scholar Valerio De Stefano (2016) distinguishes two forms of *gig work*:

- *Crowd work.* This type of work implies completing a series of tasks through online platforms.
- *Work on demand via apps.* This refers to the execution of traditional work activities (e.g., transport, cleaning, running errands) that are channelled through apps, which are managed by firms that are involved in setting quality standards and the selection of the workforce.

In other words, the first type of gig work happens entirely online or on the platform, whereas, in the second type, the platform is the intermediary to put people carrying out traditional work in touch with clients or parties on whose behalf this work is being done. Other scholars, such as Vallas and Schor (2020), reserve the label *gig work* for jobs such as taxi, courier and cleaning services, tradespersons, performing artists and caregivers, whose labour is carried out locally. They distinguish this from *crowd working* (e.g., micro-tasking, creative projects, influencers and content creators) at the global level. As such, they use spatial dispersion as the criterion to separate the two types of work in the gig economy.

Beyond the exercise of classifying gig work, what is important here is the observation that the platform, as a digital infrastructure in conjunction with algorithms and apps, becomes central for managing work (Woodcock and Graham, 2020). The gig economy also changes work in itself. It has been heralded as a new type of work that offers much greater flexibility for workers, employers and customers (Lehdonvirta, 2018). At the surface level, it seems there are only benefits for everyone involved:

- Workers can choose the work they want to do, when, where, and for whom.
- Employers get more freedom to choose how and when they hire workers.
- Customers benefit from the ease of use of work being carried for them.

However, there is a shadow side to all of this, which is often less talked about: the transformation from traditional work and full-time jobs to gig work and crowd work also means there is a risk of weakening of workers' rights and employment protection, low or unpredictable pay, dangerous and stressful working conditions, and precarity in general (Wood et al., 2019). While employers and customers benefit from this new arrangement, it makes workers more vulnerable as a result of low pay and the lack of safety and health regulation, retirement income, health insurance, etc. (van Doorn, 2017). Even more worrying is that some of the principles of gig work are increasingly being applied in workplaces that used to be organised around full-time and stable employment, leading to what Scholz (2016) calls the *Uberisation* of work.

The Sharing Economy and Gig Work in Practice

Having provided a general picture of the sharing economy and the role of gig work, we now look at what this means in practice. In doing so, we look in particular at the role of algorithms in managing work. In recent years, some excellent ethnographic studies have been published about working in the sharing economy and engaging in gig work. For example, Alex Rosenblat (2018) published the book *Uberland: How Algorithms Are Rewriting the Rules of Work*. It is based on the author's experience riding over 5000 miles with Uber drivers, daily visits to online forums, and face-to-face discussions with senior Uber employees.

The company Uber was founded in 2010. Its mission was to revolutionise transportation, and by doing so, it promised to deliver entrepreneurship for the masses through its platform. Uber treats its workers (drivers) as *customers* of algorithmic technology and promotes them as *self-employed entrepreneurs*. By claiming to operate in a world of consumption rather than a world of labour, Uber excuses itself from a series of obligations that it finds inconvenient. It does so by relying on *technological exceptionalism*, the idea that the regulations and laws that apply to its industry competitors or predecessors (in the transport industries) do not apply to it because it is a technology company. Uber maintains it is not a taxi company but a tech company that uses *neutral* algorithms to facilitate connections between drivers and consumers. It also uses the myth of *glamorised millennial labour* by promoting the idea that working for Uber is working for a global tech company, not a taxi service. Uber deliberately confuses categories such as innovation and lawlessness, work and consumption, algorithms and management, neutrality and control, and sharing and employment. Uber seeks to standardise work for the masses through *algorithmic management* while simultaneously distancing itself from any responsibility towards its workers.

Some concepts in this example deserve further elaboration, particularly algorithmic management. Advancements in AI, machine learning and data infrastructure are transforming management. *Algorithmic management* can be seen as using computational algorithms to automate organisational functions traditionally carried out by human managers (M.K. Lee, 2018). One of the main drivers of using algorithms for decision-making and management is that they are efficient, optimised and driven by data. Using algorithmic management in the workplace contributes to what is called *Humans as a Service* (Prassi, 2018). Amazon initially used this phrase to use its Mechanical Turk services.

While algorithmic management benefits employers, there are serious downsides for the workers being subjected to it. In this sense, it is crucial to see algorithmic management as a system of control. Wood et al. (2019) have written about algorithmic control in the gig economy. Based on empirical data obtained in six countries in the Global South, the authors conclude that not only the long work hours, the lack of job security or formal employment protections are challenging; in addition, the centrality of algorithmic control also shapes the work on online platforms. While algorithmic management techniques are supposed to offer workers high levels of flexibility, autonomy, task variety, and so on, these control mechanisms also bring about low pay, social isolation, overwork, sleep deprivation and exhaustion. On top of this, as Rosenblat (2018) observes in her analysis of Uber, algorithmic management is certainly not neutral. There are biases in the rating system, and Uber uses algorithms to deal with price surges, etc. Algorithmic management and control are central to automation and the future of work.

Automation and Data Work

As already observed in Chapter 2, we are experiencing a *fourth industrial revolution* (Schwab, 2016). This term refers to how breakthroughs in fields such as robotics,

AI, quantum computing, nanotechnology, biotechnology, and so on will impact our society. AI, algorithms and data will play a key role, and there are predictions about what this means for the future of work.

Considering the Future of Work

Every week brings a new prediction – or dire warning – about what jobs will be automated and by when. While discussions about automation have been going on ever since the industrial revolution, they re-emerged recently in the context of the fourth industrial revolution and the hype around generative AI, which came to the fore in 2022–2023. Economists and futurists have always been investigating and speculating about automation and the future of work. One of the landmark papers here is a study conducted by Frey and Osborne (2017). Their article 'The Future of Employment: How Susceptible Are Jobs to Computerisation?' has been widely cited in academic papers. It has also resulted in much coverage in popular media, particularly generating gloomy headlines about machines taking over jobs, leading to mass unemployment. This section discusses automation, the role of data and algorithms, and the future of work.

But let us start by looking at what the Frey and Osborne (2017) study says and how it has been received in the scholarly community. They have implemented a novel methodology, using a typology of high-, medium- and low-risk occupations depending on the probability of computerisation (i.e., a classification of the likelihood these jobs will be automated). According to their analysis, 47% of the total US employment is in the high-risk category, meaning that those are jobs – according to the authors – that could be automated in the next two decades. They mainly include jobs in transportation, logistics, and administration. In the study, an algorithm predicts the susceptibility to automation. While the Frey and Osborne (2017) study has attracted a lot of citations, it has also been under criticism because of the methodology used. Let us look more in detail at perspectives on automation.

Critiques of the Hyperbole with Automation

In a critical review essay on automation, sociologist Judy Wajcman (2017) asks: 'Is it really different this time?'. She discusses high-profile books about the promise of digital technologies and robotics, such as *The Rise of the Robots: Technology and the Threat of a Jobless Future* (Ford, 2015), *The Future of Professions: How Technology Will Transform the Work of Human Experts* (Susskind and Susskind, 2015) and *The Second Machine Age: Work, Progress, and Prosperity in a Time of Brilliant Technologies* (Brynjolfsson and McAfee, 2014). Wajcman (2017) is critical of the hyperbole spirit manifested in these books, but also about the utopian/dystopian nature described in them. While the books are picked up by popular media and hyped in business circles, they eschew technological determinism and do not address the broader context in which these technologies are developed and implemented. For example, when claims are made about robots and machines taking over jobs from humans, there is no mention of the social character of skills and expertise, and there is no reflection on how professions traditionally have been structured around a gendered division of labour. What is needed is a critical analysis of the pros and cons of automation and its impact on the future of work.

Brynjolfsson and McAfee (2014) are ultimately optimistic about the outcome of automation. Also, in their follow-up book *Machine, Platform, Crowd* (McAfee and Brynjolfsson 2017), they argue that while jobs will be lost through automation, a bright future lies ahead if only the right policies are implemented. This is needed – so they claim – to avoid a polarisation in the labour market and a rise in inequality, on the one hand, and to achieve greater freedom and more creative work for everyone, on the other. The problem with these analyses is that the effects of technology are considered political but not their causes (Wajcman, 2017). Any critical analysis of automation should also look at the politics of how technologies are developed and implemented. And that means questioning power, as Urry (2016: 11) writes: 'The key question … is who or what owns the future – this capacity to own futures being central in how power works.'

Power and politics are vital topics in recent (critical) books about automation, such as *Automation and the Future of Work* (Benanav, 2020), *Work Without the Worker* (Jones ,2021), and *Automation is a Myth* (Munn, 2022). Benanav (2020) challenges the idea that rapid automation leads to the end of the work as we know it. He argues that most automation perspectives/theories are characterised by technological determinism and do not consider socio-economic and historical perspectives on labour. While critical about automation, the author does explore a positive vision for the future and suggests that social movements should be central in organising for a post-scarcity world. Jones (2021) is critical of AI and automation and stresses that while algorithms are often touted as the future of work, millions of workers in the Global South are behind data processing and automation. He calls for resistance and organisation against the *microwork* tendency. Finally, Munn (2022) challenges the fantasy of full automation as a labour-free utopia. He argues that machines are still dependent on human labour for support and maintenance and demonstrates that the myth of automation ignores the social, cultural and geographical forces that shape technologies at the local level. Instead, according to Munn (2022), we need a new reconfiguration around labour. This means that socially beneficial automation should be non-alienating, controlled by humans, ecologically sustainable, lead to liberation instead of damage, be based on cooperation instead of exploitation, and so on.

Automation as Ghost Work

What is common about these critical perspectives on automation is the acknowledgement of how much hidden (human) labour is happening (and necessary) in the invisible infrastructure of AI and data applications. So, let us look at what data work means and how it is organised. Often, it comes down to dividing up massive projects into tiny parts. In the previous subsection, the notion of *microwork* was mentioned. Let us look closer at what this means. Irani (2015) has extensively researched crowdsourcing systems based on microwork, mainly focused on Amazon Mechanical Turk (AMT). In a previous section, Mechanical Turk was already described as *Humans as a Service* (Prassl, 2018), referring to *software as a service*. *Microwork* is a type of work based on the remote completion of small information-processing tasks, such as classifying an image or categorising a sentiment expressed in a comment (Lehdonvirta, 2016). According to Irani (2015), AMT produces a division of labour between *innovative* and *menial* workers, intensifying divisions and tensions within new media production cultures. Microwork systems, such as AMT, not only use worker control systems, but also feed into concerns about worker fairness and alienation due to microwork in crowdsourcing systems.

This analysis of microwork in the context of crowdsourcing systems resonates with what Gray and Suri (2019) call *ghost work*. By this they mean the intentionally hidden work done by a vast, invisible human labour force. It is hidden beneath the surface of apps, websites and AI services where workers perform high-tech piecework (microwork), such as flagging X-rated content, proofreading, and designing engine parts. Automated services that we all use every day are dependent on this ghost work. Still, the people doing this are often paid less than the legal minimum compared to traditional work; they have no access to health benefits and can be fired at any time for any reason. Gray and Suri (2019) make a compelling case that digital platforms such as Amazon, Google/Alphabet and Uber (and their Chinese equivalents) cannot function smoothly without the work and exploitation of these ghost workers. One of the main problems is that there are no labour laws to govern this type of work, and this is also because these assembly lines of microwork are occupied by a surprisingly diverse range of workers, often geographically dispersed.

In the fascinating project 'Anatomy of an AI System', Crawford and Joler (2018) provide an anatomical map of the Amazon Echo service and explain thoroughly how the software components involve the collection and processing of large amounts of data, which is used to train and improve the AI algorithms that power the device. In the same way, investigative journalist Karen Hao (2023) documented in a podcast the hidden labour that is needed to filter violence and abuse out of the much-hyped ChatGPT. We need to remember from this that AI and data work primarily happen beneath the surface, are purposefully invisible, are based on exploiting workers, and are not subject to any labour law due to their specific organisation.

Technological Unemployment?

To conclude this section on automation and data work, we need to reflect on what promises are being made, what fears are being fuelled and what the reality will be for whom. The insights about microwork and ghost work already contradict the portrayal of automation as a liberating force, enabling freedom and space for creative work for everyone. Debates about the impact of digital technologies on work have always been here. John Maynard Keynes (1930/1963) wrote in 1930 about the potential impact of technology on employment. In the essay 'Economic Possibilities for Our Grandchildren', he speculated how technological advancement could progress to a point where machines and automation would drastically reduce the need for human labour. He coined the term *technological unemployment* to describe the situation whereby new technologies lead to mass job displacement. While often used as part of a project of scaremongering by economists and commentators, Keynes believed this to be a good thing, as it would free people to pursue other activities, such as arts, education and leisure. It seems clear that reality is not moving in that direction (yet), so the final section of this chapter looks into resistance and alternatives.

Alternatives and Resistance

When we think about (digital) labour, gig work, automation and the future of (data) work, we can see that profound changes are happening in the world of work. These changes are all connected to digital technologies. But it would be incorrect to assume that it all comes down to technology. That would be what we call a *technological determinism* approach. Societal structures and power dynamics also impact how work is organised and distributed in society.

Change and Reform in Digital Labour and the Future of Work

There is a power relation between labour and capital or between workers and those who control them. We have seen how the value chain of the digital economy is based on extraction and exploitation, from mine workers sourcing the minerals for IT devices and people doing invisible work behind platforms to workers rushing to get our meals or groceries delivered at home. The sharing economy, and particularly the rise of gig work, demonstrates that there is a growing discrepancy between discourses (or ideology, if you will) about increased freedom, opportunity and entrepreneurialism, on the one hand, and the reality of people and communities who can participate in reaping the benefits of this, on the other. Finally, a critical analysis of automation reveals that full automation as a labour-free utopia is a fantasy, as it is based on exploitation through microwork and ghost work. So, we cannot conclude that the promise of liberation is fulfilled.

The question is, how do we get on with this? Moving forward, we can choose between three scenarios:

- *No change.* This means we continue to observe rising inequalities and exploitation of workers.
- *Reformism.* We can aim to improve things on the ground while simultaneously working on alternatives.
- *Radical change.* In this scenario, we aim to pursue a radical agenda including changes in the ownership and control of the digital environments in which we are active.

We can all agree that no change is unsustainable for anybody. In the rapidly changing world of work, we need to think about improving the current situation, resisting inequalities and exploitation, and imagining alternatives. The following paragraphs look into some options.

Collective Action for Fair Work

As Kylie Jarrett (2022) writes, the opposition between the capitalist and working classes is at the heart of capitalism. While the capitalist class has more power, the working class has the advantage of numbers, and therefore an essential avenue for bringing about change is to organise collective action. Even though the labour movement has been weakened by decades of neoliberalism and a crackdown on labour power, we have seen shimmers of hope in recent years. For example, there have been attempts to organise gig workers in the UK, culminating in several waves of strike action among Deliveroo riders and Uber drivers (Cant, 2020). The Independent Workers of Great Britain labour union has become the UK's leading union for precarious workers, including workers in the gig economy. This is a significant breakthrough as one of the characteristics of gig workers is that their labour is individualised and geographically dispersed. Across the Atlantic, the Alphabet Workers Union was established in 2021 and is one of the outcomes of the 2018 Google walkouts. It is one of the first attempts at unionising workers in the (big) tech industry. In India, drivers on the Uber and Ola platforms have been collectively organising strikes over income and labour conditions. Sometimes strikes and other collective actions from gig workers include *algorithmic activism*. Chen (2018), for example, has documented how Didi Chuxing drivers counteracted the platform by using bot apps, which help to game the system (e.g., drivers avoiding punishment for not accepting rides that are not beneficial for them).

Workers' struggle can take on multiple forms, including unionising the work environment, hacking algorithmic management systems, setting up tactical collaborations, and organising strikes and resistance (Jarrett, 2022). The academic world can help, too, by writing about how the gig economy is organised, documenting the patterns of exploitation, informing policy-makers and civil society, and so on. An excellent example is the *Fairwork* project, a network of researchers and organisations aiming to set and measure fair standards for the future of work, who have published interesting reports about gig work globally.

Platform Cooperativism (or Socialism?)

When thinking about reformism, one of the popular examples is the *platform coop-erativism* movement. Scholz (2016) has been researching alternatives for challenging digital capitalism to create better working conditions for people working in the digital economy. According to Scholz (2016), workers should be at the centre of creating alternatives and advocating for decent digital work. Worker self-management includes three core elements:

- It aims to embrace digital technologies but reshape and transform its ownership model. For example, one option is 'cloning the technological heart of Uber, TaskRabbit, Airbnb or UpWork' (Scholz 2016: 8) and reforming it to work for the workers.
- It puts solidarity at its core, which should happen with platforms owned and governed by workers, unions, cities or cooperatives.
- It strives towards benefits for the many, not the few, and thus hopes to radically reframe concepts such as innovation and efficiency.

Platform cooperativism itself should be based on principles such as collective own-ership, decent pay and income security, transparency and data portability, appre-ciation and acknowledgement, co-determined work, a protective legal framework, worker protections and benefits, protection against arbitrary behaviour, rejection of excessive workplace surveillance, and the right to log off (Scholz 2016; see also https://platform.coop). Of course, cynics could say this all sounds good but is too romantic to work in reality. However, there are examples of successful cooperative platforms, such as Fairmondo and Loomio. Of course, this is not to say there are no challenges in establishing cooperatives. Sandoval (2020), for example, documented the challenge to cut loose from capitalism's exploitative and extractive dynamics, making her cooperatives an example of *entrepreneurial activism*. Finally, Muldoon (2022) finds inspiration in the *cooperativism* movement to develop a vision of what he calls *platform socialism*, which is an attempt to recode our digital future and think about developing civic platforms that work for the people, not profit. He makes sev-eral concrete proposals, at both the local and international level, on how grassroots communities and social movements can reclaim the emancipatory power of digital platforms.

Neo-Luddism

Finally, another route, in addition to aiming for reform and coming up with alterna-tives, is one of resistance. Platform cooperatives are also part of a resistance strategy, as they strive to create an alternative ownership and control regime. However, they do this within the existing digital economy. A more radical alternative of resistance, which has become more prevalent in recent years, is the *neo-Luddite movement*.

Critical scholars draw parallels between the Luddite movement of the early nineteenth century in England, when textile workers smashed machinery as a protest, and the modern-day resistance to technology in the workplace (Mueller, 2021; Munn, 2022). While people showing sympathy for the ideas of neo-Luddism are easily dismissed as technophobes or primitive people against innovation and progress, there is a misconception about what the Luddites were aiming for (Sadowski, 2021). The Luddites were not randomly smashing machines; they were explicitly targeting those machines owned by bosses known to exploit workers by keeping their pay low, disregarding their safety and speeding up the pace of work. The destruction of machines was a tactical response by workers, aware of how these tools make their labour conditions more exploitative. And finally, the Luddites were part of a social movement that wanted technology to be deployed to make work more humane and give workers more autonomy rather than increase productivity and drive down costs.

Mueller (2021) argues that workers' future stability and empowerment depend on subverting certain digital technologies and preventing their usage where possible. He uses examples of how hackers and other technologists challenge surveillance and control systems. Ultimately, the neo-Luddite movement can inspire us to learn from past struggles to drive back the excesses of big tech, the exploitation of (gig) workers, and the extraction of large amounts of user data on digital platforms (Sadowski, 2021). Above all, it is an invitation to think critically about digital technologies and their impact on our lives, including the future of work.

Learning Takeaways

- Labour is a valorisation process in which surplus value is created.
- The sharing economy and gig work promise freedom and flexibility, but we must be aware of the rise of precarious labour.
- Algorithmic management provides efficiency for platforms but is not neutral and serves as a system of control over workers.
- Automation generates headlines about massive job losses, while data and AI systems depend on ghost work and microwork.
- Workers can strike back by engaging in collective action and exploring options for reform and radical change.

Recommended Reading

Graham, M. and Ferrari, F. (2022). *Digital Work in the Planetary Market*. Cambridge, MA: MIT Press.
Gray, M. L. and Suri, S. (2019). *Ghost Work: How to Stop Silicon Valley from Building a New Global Underclass*. Boston: Houghton Mifflin Harcourt.
Jarrett, K. (2022). *Digital Labor*. Cambridge: Polity.

Munn, L. (2022). *Automation Is a Myth*. Stanford, CA: Stanford University Press.
Scholz, T. (2016). *Uberworked and Underpaid: How Workers Are Disrupting the Digital Economy*. Cambridge: Polity.

Recommended Listening

The Anti-Dystopians is a politics podcast about tech, hosted by Alina Utrata, https://www.alinautrata.com/podcast

Part IV
Conclusion

11   Data Justice, Activism and Resistance   197

11

Data Justice, Activism and Resistance

Learning Goals

- Understand how power works in the world of data.
- Learn about the subject and approach of critical data studies.
- Recognise the different types of data discrimination, harms and violence and how this invites us to think about how to resist and fight back.
- Consider the strengths and differences between data ethics, data justice and data activism.

Communities Strike Back Against Big Tech's Extraction of Resources

AI and data-driven systems depend on the extraction of resources. Minerals such as copper, lithium and cobalt are essential for the wires, circuits and batteries in the digital devices through which we use these systems. These minerals are mined in different parts of the world, often in the Global South. But the minerals in devices are only one part of the story; to let algorithms do their work of data processing, big tech companies have established massive data centres across the globe. These data centres are part of an essential infrastructure for running AI services, such as ChatGPT. However, in the context of global warming and climate degradation, there are increasing tensions between data centres and the surrounding local communities, particularly around the use of water and electricity. Both in the Global North and South, communities have started to organise around what is called *data (infrastructure/centre) activism* (Lehuedé, 2022). They engage in collective action to protest against big tech's problematic community and environmental record. This type of data activism, rooted in local communities in different contexts, mobilises people to protest against excessive water usage, electricity usage, water pollution, etc. While grassroots activism should be combined with influencing policy and bringing about regulatory change, it is hopeful to see people and communities coming together to stand up, resist and demand different futures.

When Data and Politics Collide

Although (big) data is often considered a relatively new phenomenon, its collection, analysis and storage are hardly new and, therefore, should be considered in their historical context (Hacking, 1983/2015). From public records in the nineteenth century, large-scale data processing machines in the European World Wars in the twentieth century and the personal computer in the 1980s and 1990s to always on/connected devices in the twenty-first century, there is a constant in having protocols for collecting, representing and sharing data (Bigo et al., 2019). What is new is the amount, speed and variety of data being collected, analysed and stored (boyd and Crawford 2012). We have to remember, however, that data is present in and manifests itself through three elements (Ruppert et al., 2017):

- *Things*. An essential understanding of data is that they are (material) things, such as content being distributed via devices, servers and cables.
- *Language*. While we often think about data in terms of 0s and 1s, there exists a more complex and elaborate language around it, such as code, algorithms and programming.
- *People*. While both (material) things and language are important, data would not exist without the people generating it and those behind its collection, analysis, storage, etc. Here, we think about scientists, engineers, information technologists, designers, entrepreneurs, etc.

Combining these three elements invites us to reflect on what Bigo et al. (2019) call the worlds, subjects and rights of data. Their *Data Politics* book considers these three aspects as essential domains of data politics.

First, when thinking about *data worlds*, knowing the elaborate infrastructure on which data is dependent is crucial. There is a profound technological materiality about data, which consists of objects, equipment, routers, cables, servers, switches and other devices. What is new about the *data revolution* (Mayer-Schoenberger and Cukier, 2013) – compared to its industrial and postindustrial predecessors – is that most communication infrastructures are invisible/operating in the background. Therefore, we are hardly aware of them. The core elements of these infrastructures – data centres and data farms – are often based in remote, inaccessible locations, far away from where the communication is happening. This invites us to question how these data worlds are created and governed.

Second, while we often talk about governance by data/knowledge, we risk ignoring the emergence of *data subjects*. Data subjects are created through various digital interactions, determining how they are known and governed (Cheney-Lippold, 2017). Here, we need to ask how subjects are part of the work and the making of data through which they come to be known.

Finally, if data increasingly governs us and the accumulation of data also subjects us, it is essential to be concerned about *data rights*: who owns, uses, sells, accesses, distributes, and modifies that data? In this context, data becomes an object of conflict over and struggle for the rights to it. Therefore, we must question how subjects can exercise their rights, especially by communicating, sharing, expressing and engaging with digital devices and platforms. Considering these questions, power and politics are at the centre of everything.

How Power Connects Data and Politics

Thinking and asking questions about new worlds, subjects, and rights of data makes it clear that we need to reflect on data and politics. And when we talk about politics, we talk about *power*. According to Thompson (1995), we can distinguish coercive, economic, political and symbolic power. While these dimensions are equally important, let us focus now on *political power*. The latter is related to the authority to coordinate individuals and their interactions. In a pragmatic definition, Wright (2010: 111) refers to it as 'the capacity of actors to accomplish things in the world'. The question is then how data is connected to power and politics.

Tony Benn, the late UK Labour politician, famously listed five questions that are essential for inquiring about the functioning of a democracy and interrogating power:

- What power have you got?
- Where did you get it from?
- In whose interests do you use it?
- To whom are you accountable?
- How can we get rid of you?

These questions can and should also be asked in the context of (big) data. This means we must inquire about the actors and institutions that have power in data worlds and their relation to power and control, inequalities, voice, welfare, etc. Politics and power are fundamental in the realm of data. Discourses are used to justify the production and usage of data, and analysing them can reveal ideologies and interests. Data reflects the values and intent of those who produce it, and it is used to perform political work, which includes sustaining, undermining or transforming public values and social life. Who owns and controls the means of data production, circulation and usage holds tremendous political power (Cheney-Lippold, 2017; Kidd, 2019).

How can we understand *data politics*? Ruppert et al. (2017: 1) write that 'data politics asks questions about the ways in which data has become such an object of power and explores how to critically intervene in its deployment as an object of power'. But it is not only an object of power but also an object of knowledge. Let us unpack this a bit. When we talk about data as an object of power, we refer to the power that governments and corporations have in collecting data and doing things with it. We should look at the struggles around data collection, analysis and storage and how data brings about new forms of power relations and politics at scale. At the same time, data politics is also concerned with how data is being used in how we interpret the world (Cukier and Mayer-Schoenberger, 2013) and how, as such, it is central to knowledge production. Investigating data, politics, power and their relationships is the subject of *critical data studies*. Let us look at this concept in more detail.

Introducing Critical Data Studies

The emerging field of *critical data studies* is a reaction to data science approaches that treat (big) data only as a scientifically empirical and therefore largely neutral phenomenon (Iliadis and Russo, 2016). Critical data studies challenges the so-called *digital positivism* (Mosco, 2014) associated with big data and asks critical questions about the political, economic, ethical, cultural and social challenges data poses. This includes critically inquiring how data is generated and curated and how it has/holds power over everyday life in all its complexities. Geographers Dalton and Thatcher (2014) were among the first to ask what critical data studies should include. In a blog post for *Society and Space*, they listed several provocations that should be central in an approach to critically interrogating big data and its impact on society:

- Situating big data in time and space
- Rejecting the idea that technology is neutral
- Confronting *technological determinism* (and rejecting the claim that big data determines social forms)
- Demonstrating that data is never raw
- Critiquing claims about big data – that it speak for itself, replaces theory and will replace small data
- Countering data, in the sense that alternative, socially progressive data regimes are a possibility too
- Explaining what critical researchers can do to expose the power and impact of data and how we should engage with it.

Kitchin and Lauriault (2014) make a similar argument and propose that critical data studies should critically study *data assemblages*, which refers to the technological, political, social and economic apparatuses and elements that constitute the variety and complexity in how data are produced, circulated, shared, sold and utilised. In studying data assemblages, we must distinguish their technical and contextual aspects. The former refers to how data are collected, processed, stored, shared, analysed, etc., but also the infrastructure, hardware, software, databases and interfaces needed. On the other hand, contextual aspects refer to the discursive and material components linked to knowledge and philosophy, finance and politics, law and governance, actors and stakeholders, geography and markets, etc., surrounding data. Data assemblages are part of a *data ecosystem*, which is 'the wider data landscape comprising a number of data assemblages, where there are co-determinous relationships between them' (Kitchin, 2022: 25). The metaphor of an ecosystem is helpful as it consists of mutually interacting organisms (several stakeholders with their own goals, values and norms), which makes it complex and dynamic. Richterich (2018) adds to the conceptualisation of critical data studies that it can encompass both research *on* big data and research *with* big data. While there are examples of research groups that focus on the latter (e.g., the Digital Methods Initiative at the University of Amsterdam), critical data studies predominantly focuses on the critique of big data approaches. Finally, a central project of this field is to critically analyse the structures of *data power*.

Throughout this book, we have discussed power. But what is *data power* exactly? Going back to the definitions of *power* according to Thompson (1995) and Wright (2010), we can frame *data power* as the capacity of actors to make decisions, accomplish things and realise their will against the will of others *using data*. Kennedy et al. (2015) write about it as the capacity of data to influence and transform a particular set of relations and activities. In the introduction of their edited book *New Perspectives in Critical Data Studies*, Hepp et al. (2022) argue that there exist ambivalences in three areas around data power:

- *Global infrastructures and local invisibilities.* While the global data industries are dominated by behemoths such as GAFAM and BAT, the local aspects of these infrastructures are primarily invisible, such as the workers in the Global South who operate the data infrastructures or the local communities engaging in and behind *data activism*.
- *The state and data justice.* While the state is behind *surveillance capitalism* (as the Snowden revelations have demonstrated) and data colonialism, we also expect it to be a counterpart to the data power of big tech, by safeguarding the welfare, balancing interests, etc.
- *Individual everyday life practices and collective action.* The impact of datafication on everyday life is profound, and there is simultaneously emancipatory potential for people through data practices. Still, these very practices can also be appropriated by state authorities and companies, which creates challenges for *data activism*.

Datafication, Discrimination and Violence

There is an ambivalence at the heart of data power. This ambivalence exists around the three stakeholders in the world of data:

- (Global) corporate entities
- Governments
- Citizens (individuals and communities).

The central antagonism we are faced with is how, on the one hand, data (and digital technologies in general) can lead to empowerment and improvement of everyday life, and, on the other, it can lead to discrimination, harm and even violence. Or, framing it differently, we need to ask who benefits from datafication and who suffers from it? And do we need to accept this suffering?

This chapter focuses on questions about justice, activism and resistance in the realm of data, but it means we must also ask against what and whom we are fighting back. To answer this question means we elaborate on the discussion of *data colonialism* and the inequalities that surround class, gender, race and ethnicity and look at datafication concerning discrimination and violence.

Data and Discrimination

We first need to conceptualise what *data discrimination* means exactly. In the introduction to a collection of essays focusing on this topic, Seeta Gangadharan (2014: 2) writes about *data discrimination* as an umbrella term 'to refer to processes of algorithmically driven decision-making and their connection to injustice and unfairness in society'. This definition puts the role of algorithms central in dealing with data and suggests how their interaction can lead to adverse outcomes that bring about unfairness and injustice. Neighbouring concepts, in the context of AI, algorithms, data and machine learning, include accountability, bias, equity, ethics and inclusion. While it is hard to come up with a universally accepted definition of discrimination, it is crucial to distinguish direct and indirect discrimination (Favaretto et al., 2019):

- *Direct discrimination* refers to discrimination against minorities or disadvantaged groups based on sensitive discriminatory attributes related to group membership, such as race/ethnicity, gender or sexual orientation.
- *Indirect discrimination* refers to unintentional or accidental discriminative behaviour against a minority/disadvantaged group.

It is important to mention here that data discrimination often happens in a context characterised by asymmetrical power structures, which discriminate against already marginalised subjects (Leurs and Shepherd, 2017).

Data discrimination can be the result of the application of data analytics, using different digital techniques such as automated decision-making systems, data mining, deep learning, neural networks, profiling, and scoring systems, which are designed to analyse large datasets to reveal patterns, trends and associations concerning human behaviour (Favaretto et al., 2019). These systems and technologies are applied in a variety of contexts, including banking (e.g., being offered a mortgage or not), the carceral system (being granted or rejected parole), education (being offered a place at a university), health care (access to medical procedures), insurance (getting insurance or not), migration (border control) and occupation (having a job application accepted or rejected). What is common to these different applications is that algorithms or machines, rather than humans, increasingly take or influence decisions. Data- and algorithmic-driven technologies are becoming more entwined with people's sensitive personal characteristics and increasingly impact their daily actions and future opportunities.

The question is how we as a society deal with these types of discrimination. While the answer lies in projects of *data justice* and *data activism* (see the next section), it is crucial to acknowledge the limitations of the anti-discrimination discourse and assess and rethink the role of technology in it. In an article entitled 'Where Fairness Fails', Hoffmann (2019) writes that it is critical to identify bias in algorithmic decision-making. Efforts to achieve fairness and combat algorithmic discrimination often fail to address the hierarchical logic that produces advantaged and disadvantaged subjects in the first place, thereby risking worsening existing injustices. Hoffman (2019) discusses three specific shortcomings of the anti-discrimination discourse:

- The law is often too focused on *bad actors*, and there is a risk that by tackling them, they are replaced by *bad data/algorithms*, which might be biased too (or worse).
- The problem of *single-axis thinking* must be addressed by taking intersectionality seriously.
- The tendency to focus on disadvantages linked to limited goods, such as rights, opportunities and resources. As a solution, anti-discrimination should go beyond mere distribution and aim for structural change.

Beyond the weaknesses of the anti-discrimination discourse, Gangadharan and Niklas (2019) also advocate decentring technology in discrimination discourses. They argue that anti-discrimination initiatives require more than technical tweaks and must be part of broader social justice concerns. Their research highlights the importance of understanding that fairness and discrimination have different meanings according to people's normative understanding of equality. Decentring technology includes prioritising the specific experiences of marginalised groups and acknowledging the connection between (algorithmic) discrimination and larger systems of institutionalised oppression.

Data Harm and Violence

While discrimination is terrible and should never be underestimated, we must also talk about other negative consequences of datafication. Data harm and violence are certainly on a spectrum of negative impacts, so it is worthwhile to try conceptualising what they mean. *Harm* is not straightforward to define, but we agree it can include damage, injury and other adverse effects. Citron and Pasquale (2014) refer to *data harm* as a situation in which data (or algorithmic) systems negatively impact an individual, community or society. Redden (2022) proposes a helpful *data harm* taxonomy, which includes exploitation, discrimination, privacy loss, surveillance (including control and physical injury), manipulation, exclusion from necessities for life, and injustice. This is quite a comprehensive overview of what can include data harm and includes aspects discussed above, such as discrimination.

We also need to explain what data violence is. *Data violence* is a container concept that unites different types of violence in the age of big data. Hoffmann (2021) stresses that it refers to violence enabled by both public and private data technologies and their associated discourses. It operates by diffusing resistance, deepening dependence on oppressive structural conditions, and preserving the potential of other forms of violence. Where data can play a role in direct and physical violence (e.g., riots and militias), we must also distinguish data-mediated and structural violence:

- *Data-mediated* violence refers to the negative impact of policing and surveillance operations targeting vulnerable groups in society.
- *Structural violence* includes state violence and bio-politics.

Here, it is essential to refer to Achille Mbembe, whose work on necropolitics is highly relevant in data worlds. Mbembe (2003) argues that power exists asymmetrically in all aspects of society, which includes the ultimate power – power over who lives or dies. In his definition of *necropolitics*, Mbembe (2003: 38) writes that 'death and freedom are irrevocably interwoven', but death and freedom can be linked to various forms of exclusion and violence. The Covid-19 pandemic and the use of data systems for tracking individuals who got infected (but also people and communities who are excluded/invisible) illustrate how data violence can have deadly consequences.

Finally, artist and researcher Onuoha (2018) has coined the term *algorithmic violence* (which she considers part of structural violence, too) to refer to the complex and myriad types of violence that influence the production and outcomes of algorithms. Structural violence can happen through algorithms or automated decision-making systems that prevent people from meeting their basic needs.

Data Justice, Activism and How to Fight Back

The main question of this chapter is how we deal with data colonialism, discrimination, harm and violence. We must understand what is at stake here and think about how to fight back. In the field of *critical data studies*, we can identify three approaches for doing this:

- Data ethics
- Data justice
- Data activism.

Let us start by explaining what *data ethics* entails.

Conceptualising Data Ethics

Data ethics is part of a broader field of study (i.e., ethics). We review some key concepts here. First, *ethics* or *moral philosophy* is a branch of philosophy that questions what is (morally) good or bad and systematically evaluates right and wrong behaviour (Arendt, 2003). Of course, good/right and bad/wrong are subjective categories that can vary according to people, situations and contexts. Some scholars refer to *virtue ethics*, which involves moving towards accomplishing a *good life* and *living well* (Vallor, 2016). Ever, since the start of the information technology (IT) revolution, people have started working on developing ethical principles for computers. *Computer ethics* is a philosophical field where ethics, communication/media studies and computer science intersect. It deals with the question of 'how computer technology should be used' (Moor, 1985: 266) and analyses different types of concerns (social, ethical and values) related to computing. Also, in addition to computer ethics, attention has increasingly been paid to *information ethics*. The latter has been defined as the branch of ethics that focuses on the relationship between the creation, organisation, dissemination and use of information and the ethical standards and moral codes governing human conduct in society (Capurro, 2006).

Earlier in the book, we discussed how data and information are related, so let us look here at what data ethics means and how it can be positioned *vis-à-vis* information ethics. In simple terms, *data ethics* is concerned with moral problems in data (Floridi and Taddeo, 2016). It is a relatively new and interdisciplinary field, both critical and computational, to address ethical issues that emerge from our increasing reliance on data-driven systems (D'Ignazio and Klein, 2020). This includes questions and problems about data (its collection, curating, dissemination, generation, processing, recording, sharing and use), algorithms (including AI, artificial agents, machine learning and robots), and corresponding practices (such as hacking, programming, responsible innovation, and professional codes). Data ethics builds on the foundations provided by computer and information ethics, but at the same time it refines the approach endorsed so far in this research field by shifting the level of abstraction of ethical enquiries from information-centric to data-centric.

Data Ethics in Practice

Let us look into data ethics in practice. The Open Data Institute (2021) defines *data ethics* as 'a branch of ethics that evaluates data practices with the potential to adversely impact people and society – in data collection, sharing and use'. Data ethics focuses on accountability, bias, consent, equality, fairness, privacy, rights, security, transparency, and the formulation of and compliance with regulations and laws (Floridi and Taddeo, 2016). It asks questions about what type of datafication or data-driven society we want, how it should be governed, and how people and their data can be treated respectfully. It also seeks to identify data-related harms and denote ways to address this while recognising that different stakeholders might have diverse views and perspectives on the nature and effect of harm and potential interventions (Kitchin, 2022).

Data ethics is concerned with a range of ethical issues and problems. This can be related to the ethical problems posed by the collection and analysis of large datasets, as well as issues related to the use of big data in research, advertising, the context of open data, profiling and data philanthropy. In this context, key points concern the potential identification of individuals through practices of data mining, linking, merging or reusing of large datasets. In addition to *individual* privacy, there also exist concerns about so-called *group* privacy, when the identification of individuals leads to severe ethical problems, from group discrimination (e.g., based on race/ethnicity or gender) to group-targeted forms of violence (Taylor et al., 2016).

While ethics in data and AI are crucial to thinking about what type of data society we want and how we can organise governance and policies around this, ethics initiatives also have limitations:

- Experts develop ethical guidelines; the question is how representative of society these experts are. There is a risk of exclusion and lack of diversity if expert panels are not representative. In addition, while there are good examples of expert panels (e.g., the European Union high-level expert group on AI), there are pressures from government and industry (particularly big tech) to influence these ethics initiatives.
- There is the aspect of time and the pace of technological development. Formulating ethical guidelines requires time, and there is a risk that ethics initiatives cannot keep up with the rapid development of digital technology (Boddington, 2017).
- Another problem surrounding ethics initiatives is the so-called *ethics washing*, which refers to exaggerating an organisation's interest in promoting beneficial data technologies while simultaneously abandoning legal obligations (e.g., around data protection) (Wagner, 2018).
- Finally, moving from ethics to concrete policies is not always straightforward. There are questions about who should be involved in leading this and what exactly should be done. As such, critical data studies must consider what policy and legal approaches are available to enact data ethics and avoid discrimination, harm and violence (Kitchin, 2022).

How Data Ethics Leads Us to Data Justice

The next question we must ask ourselves is how data ethics can lead to justice. *Data justice* is – similar to data ethics – concerned with data-related discrimination, harms or violence, but rather than seeking interventions to ensure ethical practice within an existing frame or system, it is focused on the normative questions that surround the relationship between data and society and, notably, how those relations can be fundamentally reconfigured or dismantled to create a more just set of arrangements (Kitchin, 2022). Linnet Taylor (2017: 1) defines *data justice* as 'fairness in the way people are made visible, represented and treated as a result of their production of digital data', thereby referring to the power of data to produce social categorisations and interventions in the world as a by-product of people's use of digital technologies. Dencik et al. (2016) trace the roots of *data justice* in the resistance against surveillance capitalism and refer to how awareness around data-driven surveillance and the resulting decision-making and governance need to be linked to an agenda of social justice.

Where data ethics frames the source and solutions of data-related discrimination, harms or violence to *data assemblages* and their elements and apparatus, data justice frames them within a broader framework of structural power in terms of how society is organised and functions and how forms of inequalities and oppression are reproduced within it. The notion of *data assemblages* deserves some more elaboration: it is 'a complex socio-technical system composed of many apparatuses and elements that are thoroughly entwined, whose central concern is the production, management, analysis and translation of data for a particular purpose', writes Kitchin (2022: 23). A data assemblage consists of more than the data system or infrastructure itself (such as an open data repository or data archive) but also includes all the technological, political, economic and social apparatuses that frame their nature, operation and work. Critical data studies must unpack data assemblages and analyse how they shape policy and regulation.

Data justice is linked to societal power issues and an agenda of social justice. It is interested in how social justice can be advanced concerning datafication and how data-driven processes define and construct social justice itself. Dencik (2022b: 124) argues that our analysis of media and communication systems, including data systems, is often scrutinised using frameworks of moral ethics rather than justice. She stresses: 'Data is both a matter in and of justice; it embodies not only processes and outcomes of (in)justice, but also its own justifications.' Thinking about justice in the data context is often linked to an agenda of equal rights and opportunities for everyone, especially fairness, as in a fair distribution of resources and opportunities. Data justice aims to broaden the discussion of the impact of the datafied society beyond single-issue approaches but rather encompassing scholarship that addresses a variety of issues, including democratic procedures, the entrenchment and introduction of inequalities, discrimination and exclusion of certain groups, deteriorating working conditions, and the dehumanisation of decision-making and interaction around sensitive issues (Dencik et al., 2019).

Data Justice in Practice

More than a concept or framework, data justice should be seen as a research agenda. It aims to advance a research agenda that examines the intricate relationship between datafication and social justice by foregrounding and highlighting the politics and impact of (big) data-driven processes. While interdisciplinary in nature, the underlying philosophy of data justice is heavily inspired by feminist and Marxist frameworks. Its mission is to map out patterns and practices of data discrimination, harm and violence and imagine inspiring alternatives regarding what a just data world could look like (Kitchin, 2022). Data justice is central in bringing researchers, activists and civil society together to work on a joint project of developing a *good* society, which is based on three dimensions: redistribution (economic), recognition (cultural) and representation (political), to borrow Nancy Fraser's (2003) theory of social justice. In addition, within data justice studies, there is increasing attention to the manifest global inequalities in the hidden infrastructure of data systems and their industries and how this furthers patterns of colonialism, exploitation and oppression in the Global South (Couldry and Mejias, 2019a; Taylor, 2017). To deal with this, Milan and Treré (2019) call for a de-Westernisation of critical data studies and foreground a *big data from the South* approach that moves beyond *data universalism*.

Having explained *why* and *how* data justice research can be organised, let us now turn to the question of *what* exactly should be the focus of any inquiry. Taylor (2017) proposes a framework focusing on representation, autonomy and protection from data-driven discrimination. In concrete, she suggests an approach based on three pillars:

- *Visibility*. This first dimension deals with privacy and representation. It calls for research that focuses on privacy but beyond the individual focus, as is often the case in the Global North. Instead, visibility and privacy for groups and communities in the margins or at risk of collective profiling are an important focus.
- *(Dis)engagement with technology*. Rather than focusing solely on who engages with digital technologies and for what purpose(s), it is suggested to include a perspective on how to create the freedom *not* to participate and how to create autonomy for groups and communities to decide against participation in data processing, analysing and profiling.
- *Non-discrimination*. This third dimension deals with people's ability to be aware of and protect themselves against discrimination. It includes the power to identify and challenge bias in data use and the freedom not to be discriminated against.

What is powerful about this framework is that it not only centralises asking questions about data discrimination, harm and violence but also considers what can be done about it in terms of thinking about answers and other solutions. This brings us to data activism and how we can implement data justice.

What Is Data Activism?

How does data activism fit in the picture alongside data ethics and data justice? Milan and van Der Velden (2016: 57) see *data activism* as 'new forms of civic engagement and political action' that respond to the paradigm shift created by how datafication progressively invades and impacts all spheres of contemporary society. Data activism can simultaneously be seen as a theoretical construct, a method, a heuristic tool and an emerging field of research:

- As a theoretical construct, data activism is a variation of related concepts such as cyber/digital activism or *hacktivism* (McCaughey and Ayers, 2003; Jordan and Taylor, 2004). Data activism explores the possibilities of data for mobilisation and resistance but also understands the risks and challenges related to data. 'It bears the promise to incorporate a wider set of tactical responses' to those risks, write Milan and van Der Velden (2016: 61), which 'position themselves in a continuum between contestation and recognition.' It is another manifestation of activism in the digital society and reflects on the ubiquity of digital communication and evolving activism and protest configurations. Its theoretical underpinnings are inspired by combining science and technology studies and social movement studies.
- Gutiérrez (2018: 4) frames data activism as 'activism that utilises the data infrastructure as an enabling method'. While this refers to a method to bring about social change (and the opportunities that data can offer), she also writes about the challenges that need to be overcome, mainly in governmental and corporate surveillance data infrastructure.
- Rather than a method that activists can use, data activism can also be a 'valuable heuristic tool for the study of political participation and civil engagement in the age of datafication,' argue Milan and van Der Velden (2016: 65) in the sense that it can serve as a lens to observe and analyse how activism develops and evolves concerning datafication.
- Finally, Lehtiniemi and Ruckenstein (2019: 1) refer to data activism as an emerging field of research that is interested in 'the harnessing of the capacities of data technology to promote social justice, new forms of agency and political participation, meanwhile challenging accepted norms, practices and ideological projects'. An important objective is creating alternative social imaginaries that help foster social justice and responsible data futures.

With the mention of social justice, how exactly are data activism and data justice connected? Data justice seeks to challenge data power relations and to mobilise groups and communities to enhance social justice. Data activism can be seen as a practical application of the ideas of data ethics and data justice and how they are enacted as an expression of counter-hegemonic data politics (Kitchin, 2022). This means challenging and resisting *data power*. For example, this can be done by helping (vulnerable) groups and communities develop data counter-strategies to provide alternative datasets and analytics, like those offered by governments and companies. Ultimately, data activists aim to produce data imaginaries, assemblages and practices that benefit communities and challenge data practices that create unjust and pernicious effects (Gutiérrez, 2018). A vital aspect of this is to conduct political and legal campaigns to assert data rights and to prevent/limit data discrimination, harm and violence.

Data Activism in Practice

Looking at data activism in practice, Milan and van der Velden (2016) argue that it is concerned and engages with new forms of information and knowledge, how they are produced, and how activism can challenge dominant understandings of datafication. As such, we need to distinguish *proactive* and *reactive* data activism:

- *Proactive* data activism considers the increasing availability of data – whether from government or corporate origin – as an opportunity to seek political action and social change.
- *Reactive* data activism concerns activists resisting existing data collection patterns and how data systems are created and organised. They aim to challenge existing regimes of data power and seek to undermine them.

In the same vein, Segura and Waisbord (2019) talk about *social* data activism, focused on awareness raising and online and offline mobilisation, and *data rights* activism, which centralises social movements that promote policies aimed at data protection and limiting *data extractivism* by governments and corporations. Data rights activism thus follows the path of communication and cultural rights to demand change and propose alternative policies in the digital society.

Gutiérrez (2018) stresses that any mobilisation around data activism should be self-organised, citizen-controlled, self-managed and non-commercial. The activism can depart from different perspectives, incorporating several theoretical approaches and transitions. More specifically, she discusses the following perspectives:

- *Communicative action*. Following Habermas's (1984) theory, data activism is a meaning-building process whereby people's mutual understanding of their objective, social and subjective worlds generates social change using the knowledge from datasets.

- *Journalism and alternative media studies*. Just as we discussed *data journalism*, this type of activism uses analysis of datasets to hold power to account and expose the truth. The alternative media perspective is focused on altering the relationships between citizens and data collection, giving them a more prominent voice in the production of data systems.
- *International relations studies*. This perspective considers local and global dimensions of data activism and argues that collaboration across borders is necessary.
- *Social movement studies*. Data activists inspired by this perspective are working towards long-term change and are primarily interested in using data and other digital technologies to form a collective identity, mobilise, demonstrate and act.
- *Monitorial and public sphere*. While this perspective partly overlaps with others, the primary approach here is influenced by the idea of the *monitorial citizen* and how data activism can contribute to the development of alternative public spheres better suited for collaboration and action.
- *Tech activism*. The final perspective links to *proactive* data activism but should find new ways to mobilise its followers and intensify its impact by diversifying its actions.

Above all, whatever perspective(s) data activists choose to use as their framework as a starting point for organisation and mobilisation, Kennedy (2018) stresses that any activism projects and initiatives should be rooted in and inspired by the everyday experience of datafication, especially by how non-expert citizens express and articulate what would be ways to live better with data. This everyday life experience is central and needs to inform the conceptualisation and implementation of data activism.

The Future of Data and Society

Now we'll consider how data and power can be rethought to incorporate greater fairness.

Rethinking Data and Power

Having discussed data and politics and looked into negative aspects of datafication such as data discrimination, harm and violence, this chapter provides an overview of frameworks, tactics and strategies that can inspire resistance and how to fight against an unjust datafied society. What must be apparent from the discussion is that we simultaneously need to engage in projects of data ethics, data justice and data activism. While data ethics might not solve inequalities and harm, it can offer a starting point to improve things. But then again, ethics must be complemented with data justice projects, which also must be embedded into data activism. Above all, if we want to create a fairer data world, we ultimately need to talk about data power and its concentration in the hands of a small number of wealthy and powerful companies and countries. Beyond data ethics and governance approaches and initiatives inspired by data justice and activism, we need to imagine alternatives that provide hope and guide us towards a more just data society. These alternatives are essential in the discourses surrounding data and the inspiration they offer for concrete projects and actions. This section examines concepts that inspire the imagination and conceptualisation of alternatives.

Envisioning the Alternatives for a Fairer Data World

I conclude this book with eight concepts that we can use to propose alternatives for a fairer data world.

While there is no commonly accepted definition of *data governance*, it is used in fields such as information management. It broadly refers to a comprehensive framework of procedures, rules, policies, standards and processes which ensure the effective and efficient use of data (assets). The concept is often deployed in the context of how organisations (should) collect, analyse, store and use data, and therefore a lot of focus is on data quality and security. A critical take on data governance includes analysing how data systems are part of histories of structural inequality and domination and how these systems can be dismantled (Redden, 2022).

Data literacy can be seen as applying (media) literacy to the context of datafication, which then asks how we can define *media literacy*. According to Livingstone (2004), this encompasses access to, analysis and evaluation of media and content creation. D'Ignazio (2017) elaborates on this and argues that *data literacy* includes *reading* data (understanding what it is and what it represents), *working with* data (collecting, creating, cleaning, etc.), *analysing* data (comparing, aggregating, sorting, etc.) and *arguing with* data (using data to support a narrative and communicate a message to particular audiences). Data literacy is an essential prerequisite to participating in datafied societies.

Data ownership refers to the rights and responsibilities related to the collection, analysis, use and sharing of data. Within this are questions about different types of ownership (e.g., personal, corporate or government data), the challenges of defining and enforcing data ownership rights and the impact of data ownership on innovation, privacy, social justice, etc. As discussed in this book, one of the main problems is the concentration of data ownership, and this is why scholars argue about alternative models, such as *data commons* (Hicks, 2023), which can be a means to redistribute the value generated by data.

While *data sharing* can refer to making research data and materials available to the broader scientific community (and sometimes even beyond that, as in *open science*), it can also be a starting point to rethink the concentration of data ownership. Just as data commons is one approach to conceptualising how more people, communities and organisations can benefit from data, there are other alternative ways of *democratising our data* (Lane, 2021). Delacroix and Lawrence (2019) advocate an approach of bottom-up *data trusts*, which is essentially a legal framework whereby individuals and organisations can decide in what context and for what purposes their data can be accessed and used by organisations.

Data solidarity is another principle for data governance that could help overcome the limitations of the concentration of ownership and inspire new approaches in sharing data. Bunz and Vrikki (2022) propose this concept as a principle for creating datasets that could help companies and governments rethink practices around making datasets available, not just as economic opportunities but also as democratic resources that offer possibilities for giving back to society and advancing the public good. They see data solidarity as an essential step in making data processes more visible and argue that this is indispensable to creating more equal AI futures.

The idea of *data sovereignty* has its roots in the claims of indigenous people and communities, who have leveraged the concept to protect the intellectual property of their heritage (Kukutai and Taylor, 2016). It has evolved into an overarching demand for giving communities and users power over their data, wrestling back control over what has been surrendered by the colonisers, such as big tech. Data sovereignty is a means to protect against exploitation and demands that everyone has a say in the mechanisms by which data are collected, extracted, analysed and exploited.

As part of a broader decolonising movement, there have been calls for *decolonising data*. Kukutai and Taylor (2016) argue that achieving data sovereignty cannot happen without dismantling and decolonising settler states' knowledge, data and statistical systems and reinstating the ones of indigenous communities. Decolonising data thus needs to go beyond asserting rights to control and ownership and include decolonising the infrastructures of *empire* (Aouragh and Chakravartty, 2016). The call for decolonising data should be broadened to tackling (data) injustices that exist in both the Global South and North, involving marginalised communities around gender, race/ethnicity, caste and other patterns of exclusion and oppression (Ricaurte, 2019).

Finally, *resisting data capitalism* is something we can all engage in: we have the power to determine our place in the data world. Being involved in the project of fighting against and overcoming the oppression and exploitation of data capitalism, and seeking refuge in strategies of resistance might be a good way forward. Thatcher and Dalton (2022) discuss the potential of resistance in tactics that contest the everyday practices of data collection, production and extraction, for example, by feeding incorrect data into targeted advertising systems or pursuing other *obfuscation* strategies (Brunton and Nissenbaum, 2016). If we want to achieve a society that is based on equality/fairness, democracy/freedom and community/solidarity, the late Marxist sociologist Erik Olin Wright (2019) teaches us that resisting capitalism should be a combined effort of smashing, dismantling, taming, resisting and escaping (data) capitalism.

Learning Takeaways

- In the world of data, we must remember that data manifests itself through material things, language and people.
- Data politics exists not only as an object of power but also as an object of knowledge.
- Data ethics is a branch of philosophy concerned with moral problems in data, algorithms and corresponding practices.
- Data justice is a research agenda that examines the relationship between datafication and social justice by highlighting the politics and impact of data-driven processes.
- Data activism consists of new forms of civic engagement and political action in the age of datafication.

Recommended Reading

Dencik, L., Hintz, A., Redden, J. and Treré, E. (2022). *Data Justice*. London: SAGE.

Gutiérrez, M. (2018). *Data Activism and Social Change*. Cham: Springer.

Hepp, A., Jarke, J. and Kramp, L. (2022). N*ew Perspectives in Critical Data Studies: The Ambivalences of Data Power*. Cham: Springer.

Jackson, S. J. (2020). *#HashtagActivism: Networks of Race and Gender Justice*. Cambridge, MA: MIT Press.

McIlwain, C. D. (2019). *Black Software: The Internet & Racial Justice, From The Afronet To Black Lives Matter*. Oxford: Oxford University Press.

Recommended Listening

Tech Won't Save Us is a podcast series hosted by Paris Marx, which critically examines the tech industry, its big promises, and the people behind them. https://www.techwontsave.us/

References

Adorno, T. and Horkheimer, M. (1972). *Dialectic of Enlightenment*. trans. J. Cummings. New York: Herder & Herder.

Agrawal, A., Gans, J. and Goldfarb, A. (2018). *Prediction Machines: The Simple Economics of Artificial Intelligence*. Boston: Harvard Business School Publishing.

Albrecht, S. (2006). Whose voice is heard in online deliberation? A study of participation and representation in political debates on the internet. *Information, Communication & Society*, 9(1), 62–82.

Alpaydin, E. (2016). *Machine Learning. The New AI*. Cambridge, MA: MIT Press.

Altheide, D.L. and Snow, R.P. (1979). *Media Logic*. Beverly Hills, CA: Sage.

Amrute, S., Singh, R. and Guzmán, R.L. (2022). A primer on AI in/from the majority world: An empirical site and a standpoint. SSRN Scholarly Paper 4199467.

Ananny, M. and Crawford, K. (2018). Seeing without knowing: Limitations of the transparency ideal and its application to algorithmic accountability. *New Media & Society*, 20(3), 973–989.

Anderson, A.A. and Huntington, H.E. (2017). Social media, science, and attack discourse: How Twitter discussions of climate change use sarcasm and incivility. *Science Communication*, 39(5), 598–620.

Anderson, C. (2008). The end of theory: The data deluge makes the scientific method obsolete. *Wired, 16.07*. http://statlit.org/pdf/2008EndOfTheory-DataDelugeMakesScientificMethodObsolete-WiredMagazine.pdf

Anderson, C.W. (2013). Towards a sociology of computational and algorithmic journalism. *New Media & Society*, 15(7), 1005–1021.

Anderson, C.W. (2018). *Apostles of Certainty: Data Journalism and the Politics of Doubt*. Oxford: Oxford University Press.

Anderson, A. A., & Huntington, H. E. (2017). Social Media, Science, and Attack Discourse: How Twitter Discussions of Climate Change Use Sarcasm and Incivility. *Science Communication*, 39(5), 598–620.

Andrejevic, M. (2007). *iSpy: Surveillance and Power in the Interactive Era*. Lawrence, KS: University Press of Kansas.

Andrejevic, M. (2013). *Infoglut: How Too Much Information Is Changing the Way We Think and Know*. London: Routledge.

Andrejevic, M. (2014). The big data divide. *International Journal of Communication*, 17.

Andrejevic, M. (2019a). Automating surveillance. *Surveillance & Society*, 17(1/2), 7–13.

Andrejevic, M. (2019b). *Automated Media*. London and New York: Routledge.

Anstead N., Chadwick A. 2009. Parties, election campaigning and the internet: Toward a comparative institutional approach. In P.N. Howard and A. Chadwick (eds), *Routledge Handbook of Internet Politics* (pp. 56–71). Abingdon: Routledge.

Aouragh, M. and Chakravartty, P. (2016). Infrastructures of empire: Towards a critical geopolitics of media and information studies. *Media, Culture & Society*, 38(4), 559–575.

Appadurai, A. (1996). *Modernity at Large: Cultural Dimensions of Globalization*. Minneapolis, MN: University of Minnesota Press.

Arendt, H. (1951). The decline of the nation-state and the end of the rights of man. In *The Origins of Totalitarianism* (pp. 266-298). New York: Harcourt, Brace and Company.

Arendt, H. (2003). Some questions of moral philosophy. In J. Kohn (ed.), *Responsibility and Judgment* (pp. 49–146). New York: Schocken Books.

Arrieta, A.B., Díaz-Rodríguez, N., Del Ser, J., Bennetot, A., Tabik, S., Barbado, A., Garcia, S., Gil-Lopez, S., Molina, D., Benjamins, R., Chatila, R. and Herrera, F. (2020). Explainable artificial intelligence (XAI): Concepts, taxonomies, opportunities and challenges toward responsible AI. *Information Fusion*, 58, 82–115.

Arora, P. (2016). The bottom of the data pyramid: Big data and the Global South. *International Journal of Communication*, 10, 1681–1699.

Arvidsson, A. and Colleoni, E. (2012). Value in informational capitalism and on the internet. *The Information Society*, 28(3), 135–150.

Asaro, P. (2019). What is an 'artificial intelligence arms race' anyway? *I/S: A Journal of Law and Policy for the Information Society*, 15(1–2). https://peterasaro.org/writing/Asaro_AIArmsRace.pdf

Autor, D. H. (2015). Why are there still so many jobs? The history and future of workplace automation. *Journal of Economic Perspectives*, 29(3), 3–30.

Bagdikian, B. H. (2004). *The New Media Monopoly*. Boston: Beacon Press.

Baker, C. E. (2006). *Media Concentration and Democracy: Why Ownership Matters*. Cambridge: Cambridge University Press.

Bakir, V. and McStay, A. (2018). Fake news and the economy of emotions. *Digital Journalism*, 6(2), 154–175.

Banet-Weiser, S. (2018). *Empowered. Popular Feminism and Popular Misogyny*. Durham, NC: Duke University Press.

Barbrook, R. and Cameron, A. (1996). The Californian ideology. *Science as Culture*, 6(1), 44–72.

Barnett, S. (2002). Will a crisis in journalism provoke a crisis in democracy? *Political Quarterly*, 73(4), 400–408.

Bastos, M. T. and Mercea, D. (2019). The Brexit botnet and user-generated hyperpartisan news. *Social Science Computer Review*, 37(1), 38–54.

Bauman, Z. (2000). *Liquid Modernity*. Cambridge: Polity Press.

Bayes, T. (1763). An essay toward solving a problem in the doctrine of chances. *Philosophical Transactions of the Royal Society of London*, 53, 370–418.

Beck, U. (1999). *What Is Globalization?* Cambridge: Polity Press.

Beck, U, Giddens, A and Lash, S. (1994). *Reflexive Modernization: Politics, Tradition and Aesthetics in the Modern Social Order*. Stanford, CA: Stanford University Press.

Beer, D. (2019). *The Data Gaze: Capitalism, Power and Perception*. London: SAGE.

Bekey, G. A. (2005). *Autonomous Robots: From Biological Inspiration to Implementation and Control*. Cambridge, MA: MIT Press.

Belk, R. (2010). Sharing. *Journal of Consumer Research*, 36(5), 715–734.

Bell, D. (1973). *The Coming of the Post-Industrial Society: A Venture in Social Forecasting*. New York: Basic Books.

Beller, J. (2021). *The World Computer: Derivative Conditions of Racial Capitalism*. Durham, NC: Duke University Press.

Benanav, A. (2020). *Automation and the Future of Work*. London: Verso Books.

Bender, E. M., Gebru, T., McMillan-Major, A. and Shmitchell, S. (2021). On the dangers of stochastic parrots: Can language models be too big? *In Proceedings of the 2021 ACM Conference on Fairness, Accountability, and Transparency* (pp. 610–623). New York; Association for Computing Machinery.

Benjamin, R. (2019). *Race After Technology: Abolitionist Tools for the New Jim Code*. Cambridge: Polity Press.

Benkler Y. (2006). *The Wealth of Networks: How Social Production Transforms Markets and Freedom*. New Haven, CT: Yale University Press.

Bennett W.L., Lawrence R.G. and Livingston S. (2007). *When the Press Fails*. Chicago: University of Chicago Press.

Bennett, W.L. and Livingston, S. (2018). The disinformation order: Disruptive communication and the decline of democratic institutions. *European Journal of Communication*, 33(2), 122–139.

Bennett, W. L. and Pfetsch, B. (2018). Rethinking political communication in a time of disrupted public spheres. *Journal of Communication*, 68(2), 243–253.

Bennett, W.L. and Segerberg, A. (2013). *The Logic of Connective Action: Digital Media and the Personalization of Contentious Politics*. New York: Cambridge University Press.

Bigo, D., Esin, E. and Ruppert, E. (2019). *Data Politics: Worlds, Subjects, Rights*. London: Routledge.

Birkinbine, B.J. (2017). Microsoft Corporation. In B.J. Birkinbine, R. Gomez and J. Wasko (eds), *Global Media Giants* (pp. 383–397). New York: Routledge.

Birkinbine, B. J., Gomez, R. and Wasko, J. (2017). *Global Media Giants*. New York: Routledge.

Boddington, P. (2017). *Towards a Code of Ethics for Artificial Intelligence*. Cham: Springer.

Boden, M. E. (2016). *AI: Its Nature and Future*. Oxford: Oxford University Press.

Boole G. (1854). *An Investigation of the Laws of Thought: On Which Are Founded the Mathematical Theories of Logic and Probabilities*. London: Walton and Maberly.

Borgman, C.L. (2016). *Big Data, Little Data, No Data: Scholarship in the Networked World*. Cambridge, MA: MIT Press.

Bostrom, N. (2014). *Superintelligence: Paths, Dangers, Strategies*. Oxford: Oxford University Press.

Botsman, R. and Rogers, R. (2010). *What's Mine Is Yours: The Rise of Collaborative Consumption*. London: HarperCollins.

Bounegru, L. and Gray, J. (eds) (2021). *The Data Journalism Handbook: Towards a Critical Data Practice*. Amsterdam: Amsterdam University Press.

Bounegru, L., Gray, J., Venturini, T. and Mauri, M. (2018). A field guide to 'fake news' and other information disorders. SSRN Scholarly Paper 3097666.

Bourdieu, P. (1986/2011). The forms of capital. In I. Szeman and T. Kaposy (eds), *Cultural Theory: An Anthology* (pp.81–93). Malden MA: Wiley-Blackwell Publishers.

Bowker, G. C. (2014). Big data, big questions: The theory/data thing. *International Journal of Communication*, 8.

boyd, d. and Crawford, K. (2012). Critical questions for big data. *Information, Communication & Society*, 15(5), 662–679.

Brevini, B. (2021). *Is AI Good for the Planet?* Cambridge: Polity Press.

Brevini, B. and Pasquale, F. (2020). Revisiting the Black Box Society by rethinking the political economy of big data. *Big Data & Society*, 7(2), 2053951720935146.

Brock, A. Jr. (2020). *Distributed Blackness: African American Cybercultures*. New York: New York University Press.

Broussard, M. (2018). *Artificial Unintelligence: How Computers Misunderstand the World*. Cambridge, MA: MIT Press.

Browne, S. (2015). *Dark Matters: On the Surveillance of Blackness*. Durham, NC: Duke University Press.

Bruns, A. (2008). *Blogs, Wikipedia, Second Life, and Beyond: From Production to Produsage*. New York: Peter Lang.

Bruns, A. (2019). *Are Filter Bubbles Real?* Cambridge: Polity Press.

Bruns, A., Enli, G., Skogerbö, E., Larsson, A. and Christensen, C. (eds) (2016). *Routledge Companion to Social Media and Politics*. New York: Routledge.

Bruns, A., Hurcombe, E. and Harrington, S. (2022). Covering conspiracy: Approaches to reporting the COVID/5G conspiracy theory. *Digital Journalism*, 10(6), 930–951.

Brunton, F. and Nissenbaum, H. (2016). *Obfuscation: A User's Guide for Privacy and Protest*. Cambridge, MA: MIT Press.

Brynjolfsson, E. and McAfee, A. (2014). *The Second Machine Age: Work, Progress, and Prosperity in a Time of Brilliant Technologies*. New York: W. W. Norton.

Bucher, T. (2018). *If...Then: Algorithmic Power and Politics*. Oxford: Oxford University Press.

Bunz M. (2014). *The Silent Revolution: How Digitalization Transforms Knowledge, Work, Journalism and Politics without Making Too Much Noise*. Basingstoke: Palgrave Macmillan.

Bunz, M. and Vrikki, P. (2022). From big to democratic data. In M. Filimowicz (eds), *Democratic Frontiers* (pp. 47–62). London: Routledge.

Buolamwini, J. (2016). InCoding – In the beginning was the coded gaze. *Medium*. https://medium.com/mit-media-lab/incoding-in-the-beginning-4e2a5c51a45d

Burgess, J., Albury, K., McCosker, A. and Wilken, R. (2022). *Everyday Data Cultures*. Cambridge: Polity.

Burrell, J. (2016). How the machine 'thinks': Understanding opacity in machine learning algorithms. *Big Data & Society*, 3(1), 2053951715622512.

Calabrese, A. and Rollins, T. (2017). Amazon.com. In B. J. Birkinbine, R. Gomez and J. Wasko (eds), *Global Media Giants* (pp. 413–427). New York: Routledge.

Calhoun, C. (1993). Introduction: Habermas and the public sphere. In C. Calhoun (ed.), *Habermas and the Public Sphere* (pp. 1–48). Cambridge, MA: MIT Press.

Calzada, I. (2022). How digital citizenship regimes are rescaling European nation-states. *Space and Polity*, 26(1), 44–52.

Calzati, S. (2021). Decolonising 'data colonialism' propositions for investigating the realpolitik of today's networked ecology. *Television & New Media*, 22(8), 914–929.

Cant, C. (2020). *Riding for Deliveroo: Resistance in the New Economy*. Cambridge: Polity.

Capurro, R. (2006). Towards an ontological foundation of information ethics. *Ethics and Information Technology*, 8(4), 175–186.

Carah, N. and Louw, E. (2015). *Media & Society: Production, Content & Participation*. London: SAGE.

Carlson, M. (2015). The Robotic Reporter. *Digital Journalism*, 3(3), 416–431.

Carpentier, N. (2011). *Media and Participation: A Site of Ideological-Democratic Struggle*. Basingstoke: Intellect.

Castells, M. (1996). *The Rise of the Network Society*. Malden, MA: Blackwell

Castells, M. (1997). *The Power of Identity*. Malden, MA: Blackwell

Castells, M. (1998). *End of Millennium*. Malden, MA: Blackwell

Castells, M. (2001). *The Internet Galaxy*. New York: Oxford University Press.

Castells, M. (2009). *Communication Power*. Oxford: Oxford University Press.

Chadwick, A. (2006). *Internet Politics: States, Citizens, and New Communication Technologies*. Oxford: Oxford University Press.

Chadwick, A. (2013). *The Hybrid Media System: Politics and Power*. Oxford: Oxford University Press.

Chan J., Selden M. and Ngai, P. (2020). *Dying for an iPhone: Apple, Foxconn, and the Lives of China's Workers*. London: Pluto.

Chatfield, T. (2018). *Critical Thinking*. London: Sage.

Chen, J.Y. (2018). Thrown under the bus and outrunning it! The logic of Didi and taxi drivers' labour and activism in the on-demand economy. *New Media & Society*, 20(8), 2691–2711.

Chen, Y., Mao, Z. and Qiu, J.L. (2018). *Super-Sticky WeChat and Chinese Society*. Bingley: Emerald Publishing.

Cheney-Lippold, J. (2016). Jus algoritmi: How the National Security Agency remade citizenship. *International Journal of Communication*, 10, 1721–1742

Cheney-Lippold, J. (2017). *We Are Data: Algorithms and the Making of Our Digital Selves*. New York: New York University Press.

Christin, A. (2020). *Metrics at Work: Journalism and the Contested Meaning of Algorithms*. Princeton, NJ: Princeton University Press.

Chun, W.H.K. (2009). Introduction: Race and/as technology; or, How to do things to race. *Camera Obscura*, 24(1).

Citron, D.K. and Pasquale, F. (2014). The scored society: Due process for automated predictions. *Washington Law Review*, 89(1), 1–34.

Clarke, R. (1988). Information technology and dataveillance. *Communications of the ACM*, 31(5), 498–512.

Coeckelbergh, M. (2020). *AI Ethics*. Cambridge, MA: MIT Press.

Cohen, N. S. (2015). From pink slips to pink slime: Transforming media labor in a digital age. *Communication Review*, 18(2), 98–122.

Coleman, B. (2009). Race as technology. *Camera Obscura*, 70(24), 177–207.

Coleman, F. (2019). *A Human Algorithm: How Artificial Intelligence Is Redefining Who We Are*. Berkeley, CA: Counterpoint.

Coleman, S. and Blumler, J.G. (2009). *The Internet and Democratic Citizenship*. Cambridge: Cambridge University Press.

Costera Meijer, I. and Groot Kormelink, T. (2015). Checking, sharing, clicking and linking. *Digital Journalism*, 3(5), 664–679.

Couldry, N. (2008). Mediatization or mediation? Alternative understandings of the emergent space of digital storytelling. *New Media & Society*, 10(3), 373–391.

Couldry N. and Hepp A. (2017). *The Mediated Construction of Reality*. Cambridge: Polity Press.

Couldry, N. and Mejias, U. (2019a). *The Costs of Connection: How Data Is Colonizing Human Life and Appropriating It for Capitalism*. Stanford, CA: Stanford University Press.

Couldry, N. and Mejias, U. (2019b). Data colonialism: Rethinking big data's relation to the contemporary subject. *Television & New Media*, 20(4), 336–349.

Courtois, C. and Verdegem, P. (2016). With a little help from my friends: An analysis of the role of social support in digital inequalities. *New Media & Society*, 18(8), 1508–1527.

Coyle, D., Diepeveen, S., Wdowin, J., Tennison, J., and Kay, L. (2020). *The Value of Data. Policy Implications*. Bennet Institute for Public Policy, University of Cambridge. https://www.bennettinstitute.cam.ac.uk/wp-content/uploads/2020/12/Value_of_data_Policy_Implications_Report_26_Feb_ok4noWn.pdf

Crain, M. (2016). The limits of transparency: Data brokers and commodification. *New Media & Society*, 20(1), 88–104.

Crawford, K. (2021). *Atlas of AI: Power, Politics, and the Planetary Costs of Artificial Intelligence*. New Haven, CT: Yale University Press.

Crawford, K. and Joler, V. (2018). Anatomy of an AI system. An anatomical case study of the Amazon echo as a artificial intelligence system made of human labor. https://anatomyof.ai/

Cukier, K. and Mayer-Schoenberger, V. (2013). The rise of big data: How it's changing the way we think about the world. *Foreign Affairs*, 92(3), 28–40.

Curran, J. (2002). *Media and Power*. London and New York: Routledge.

Curran, J. (2011). *Media and Democracy*. London and New York: Routledge.

Curran, J. (2012). Rethinking Internet History. In: J. Curran, N. Fenton, and D. Freedman, D. (eds). *Misunderstanding the Internet* (pp. 34-65). London & New York: Routledge.

Curran, J. (2019). Triple crisis of journalism. *Journalism*, 20(1), 190–193.

Curran, J., Fenton, N. and Freedman, D. (2016). *Misunderstanding the Internet* (2nd edn). New York: Routledge.

Curran, J. and Seaton, J. (2018). *Power Without Responsibility* (8th edition). London & New York: Routledge.

Dahlberg, L. (1998). Cyberspace and the public sphere: Exploring the democratic potential of the net. *Convergence: The International Journal of Research into New Media Technologies*, 4(1), 70–84.

Dahlberg, L. (2001). Computer-mediated communication and the public sphere: A critical analysis. *Journal of Computer-Mediated Communication*, 7(1), JCMC714.

Dahlberg, L. (2007). Rethinking the fragmentation of the cyberpublic: From consensus to contestation. *New Media & Society*, 9(5), 827–847.

Dahlgren, P. (2004). Theory, boundaries and political communication: The uses of disparity. *European Journal of Communication*, 19(1), 7–18.

Dahlgren, P. (2009). *Media and Political Engagement: Citizens, Communication, and Democracy*. New York: Cambridge University Press.

Dahlgren, P. (2018). Media, knowledge and trust: The deepening epistemic crisis of democracy. *Javnost – The Public*, 25(1–2), 20–27.

Dalton, C.M. and Thatcher, J. (2014). What does a critical data studies look like, and why do we care? *Society and Space*. https://www.societyandspace.org/articles/what-does-a-critical-data-studies-look-like-and-why-do-we-care

Daly, A., Devitt, K.S. and Mann, M. (2018). *Good Data*. Amsterdam: Institute of Network Cultures.

Davis, M. and Xiao, J. (2021). De-Westernizing platform studies: History and logics of Chinese and U.S. platforms. *International Journal of Communication*, 15, 103–122.

Delacroix, S. (2019). Beware of 'algorithmic regulation'. Available at SSRN: https://ssrn.com/abstract=3327191

Delacroix, S. and Lawrence, N. D. (2019). Bottom-up data trusts: Disturbing the 'one size fits all' approach to data governance. *International Data Privacy Law*, 9(4), 236–252.

de-Lima-Santos, M.-F. and Ceron, W. (2022). Artificial intelligence in news media: Current perceptions and future outlook. *Journalism and Media*, 3(1), Article 1.

Della Porta, D. (2015). *Social movements in times of austerity. Bringing capitalism back into protest analysis*. Cambridge: Polity Press

Dencik, L. (2022a). Data and capitalism. In L., Dencik, A., Hintz, J., Redden and E. Treré (eds), *Data Justice* (pp. 11–24). London: SAGE.

Dencik, L. (2022b). Data and social justice. In L. Dencik, A. Hintz, J. Redden & E. Treré (eds), *Data Justice* (pp. 123–137). London: SAGE

Dencik, L., Hintz, A. and Cable, J. (2016) Towards data justice? The ambiguity of anti-surveillance resistance in political activism. *Big Data & Society*, 3(2), 1–12.

Dencik, L., Hintz, A., Redden, J. and Treré, E. (2019). Exploring data justice: Conceptions, applications and directions. information, *Communication & Society*, 22(7), 873–881.

Dencik, L., Hintz, A., Redden, J. and Treré, E. (2022). *Data Justice*. London: SAGE.

Denisova, A. (2022). Viral journalism. Strategy, tactics and limitations of the fast spread of content on social media: Case study of the United Kingdom quality publications. *Journalism*, 24(9), 1919–1937.

De Stefano, V. (2016). The rise of the just-in-time workforce: On-demand work, crowdwork, and labor protection in the gig-economy. *Comparative Labor Law & Policy Journal*, 37(3), 471–504.

Deuze, M. (2019). What journalism is (not). *Social Media + Society*, 5(3).

Devereux, E. (2014). *Understanding the Media*. London: SAGE

D'heer, E. and Verdegem, P. (2014). Conversations about the elections on Twitter: Towards a structural understanding of Twitter's relation with the political and the media field. *European Journal of Communication*, 29(6), 720–734.

Diakopoulos, N. (2019). *Automating the News: How Algorithms Are Rewriting the Media*. Cambridge, MA: Harvard University Press.

Diakopoulos, N. and Koliska, M. (2017). Algorithmic transparency in the news media. *Digital Journalism*, 5(7), 809–828.

D'Ignazio, C. (2017). Creative data literacy: Bridging the gap between the data-haves and data-have nots. *Information Design Journal*, 23(1), 6–18.

D'Ignazio, C. and Klein, L. F. (2020). *Data Feminism*. Cambridge, MA: MIT Press.

Dignum, V. (2019). *Responsible Artificial Intelligence: How to Develop and Use AI in a Responsible Way*. Cham: Springer Nature.

DiNucci, D. (1999). Fragmented future. *Print Magazine* 53(4), 220–222.

Dörr, K.N. (2016). Mapping the field of algorithmic journalism. *Digital Journalism*, 4(6), 700–722.

Doyle, G. (2013). *Understanding Media Economics* (2nd edn). London: Sage.

Dubois, E. and Blank, G. (2018). The echo chamber is overstated: The moderating effect of political interest and diverse media. *Information, Communication & Society*, 21(5), 729–745.

Dyer-Witheford, N. (1999). *Cyber-Marx: Cycles and Circuits of Struggle in High-Technology Capitalism*. Urbana, IL: University of Illinois Press.

Dyer-Witheford, N., Kjøsen, A. M. and Steinhoff, J. (2019). *Inhuman Power. Artificial Intelligence and the Future of Capitalism*. London: Pluto Press.

Economist (2017). *The world's most valuable resource is no longer oil, but data*. https://www.economist.com/leaders/2017/05/06/the-worlds-most-valuable-resource-is-no-longer-oil-but-data

Elliott, A. (2019). *The Culture of AI*. London: Routledge.

Enli, G. (2017). Twitter as arena for the authentic outsider: Exploring the social media campaigns of Trump and Clinton in the 2016 US presidential election. *European Journal of Communication*, 32(1), 50–61.

Ensmenger, N. (2010). *The Computer Boys Take Over: Computers, Programmers, and the Politics of Technical Expertise*. Cambridge, MA & London: MIT Press.

Eubanks, V. (2018). *Automating Inequality: How High-Tech Tools Profile, Police, and Punish the Poor*. New York: St. Martin's Publishing Group.

European Commission (2018). *A Multi-Dimensional Approach to Disinformation: Report of the Independent High Level Group on Fake News and Online Disinformation*. Luxembourg: Publications Office of the European Union.

Farkas, J. and Schou, J. (2020). *Post-Truth, Fake News and Democracy: Mapping the Politics of Falsehood*. New York and Abingdon: Routledge.

Favaretto, M., De Clercq, E. and Elger, B.S. (2019). Big Data and discrimination: Perils, promises and solutions. A systematic review. *Journal of Big Data*, 6(1), 12.

Fenton, N., Freedman, D., Schlosberg, J. and Dencik, L. (2020). *The Media Manifesto*. Cambridge: Polity.

Fink, K. and Anderson, C.W. (2015). Data journalism in the United States. *Journalism Studies*, 16(4), 467–481.

Flew, T. (2007). *New Media: An Introduction*. Oxford: Oxford University Press.

Flew, T. (2018). *Understanding Global Media*. London: Bloomsbury Publishing.

Floridi, L. (2010). *Information: A Very Short Introduction*. Oxford: Oxford University Press.

Floridi, L. (2020). AI and its new winter: From myths to realities. *Philosophy & Technology*, 33, 1–3.

Floridi, L. and Taddeo M. (2016). What is data ethics? *Philosophical Transactions of the Royal Society*, 374(2083), 20160360.

Forbes (2021). *Forbes' 35th Annual World's Billionaires List: Facts And Figures 2021*. https://www.forbes.com/sites/kerryadolan/2021/04/06/forbes-35th-annual-worlds-billionaires-list-facts-and-figures-2021/?sh=1abf00445e58

Ford, M. (2015). *Rise of the Robots: Technology and the Threat of a Jobless Future*. New York: Basic Books.

Foucault, M. (1979). *Discipline and Punish*. Harmondsworth: Penguin

Foucault, M. (1980). *Power/Knowledge: Selected Interviews and Other Writings 1972–1977*. Hemel Hempstead: Harvester Wheatsheaf.

Foucault, M. (1983). The subject and power: Afterword. In H. Dreyfus and P. Rabinow (eds), *Michel Foucault: Beyond Structuralism and Hermeneutics* (pp. 208–227). Chicago: University of Chicago Press.

Foucault, M. (1988). Technologies of the self. In L.H. Martin, H. Gutman and P.H. Hutton (eds), *Technologies of the Self: A Seminar with Michel Foucault* (pp. 16–49). Amherst, MA: University of Massachusetts Press.

Foucault, M. (1991). Governmentality. In G. Burchell, C. Gordon and P. Miller (eds), *The Foucault Effect: Studies in Governmentality*. Chicago: University of Chicago Press.

Franklin, B. (2014). The future of journalism. *Journalism Studies*, 15(5), 481–499.

Fraser, N. (2003). Social justice in the age of identity politics: Redistribution, recognition, and participation. In N. Fraser and A. Honneth (eds), *Redistribution or Recognition? A Political-Philosophical Exchange* (pp. 7–109). London: Verso.

Freedman, D. (2014). *The Contradictions of Media Power*. London: Bloomsbury.

Freelon, D. and Wells, C. (2020). Disinformation as political communication. *Political Communication*, 37(2), 145–156.

Frenken, K. and Schor, J. (2017). Putting the sharing economy into perspective. *Environmental Innovation and Societal Transitions*, 23, 3–10.

Frey, C. B. and Osborne, M. A. (2017). The future of employment: How susceptible are jobs to computerisation? *Technological Forecasting and Social Change*, 114, 254–280.

Fuchs, C. (2010). Labor in informational capitalism and on the internet. *The Information Society*, 26 (3): 179–196.

Fuchs, C. (2014a). *Digital Labour and Karl Marx*. New York: Routledge.

Fuchs, C. (2014b). *Social Media: A Critical Introduction*. London: SAGE.

Fuchs, C. (2017a). *Social Media: A Critical Introduction* (2nd edn). London: SAGE.

Fuchs, C. (2017b). From digital positivism and administrative big data analytics towards critical digital and social media research! *European Journal of Communication*, 32(1), 37–49.

Fuchs, C. (2017c). Facebook. In B. J. Birkinbine, R. Gomez and J. Wasko (eds), *Global Media Giants* (pp. 428–444). New York: Routledge.

Fuchs, C. (2020). *Marxism: Karl Marx's Fifteen Key Concepts for Cultural and Communication Studies*. New York: Routledge.

Fuchs, C. (2021). *Social Media. A Critical Introduction* (3rd edn). London: SAGE.

Fuchs, C. and Sevignani, S. (2013). What is digital labour? What is digital work? What's their difference? And why do these questions matter for understanding social media? *tripleC: Communication, Capitalism & Critique*, 11(2), 237–293.

Fukuyama, F. (2018). *Identity: Contemporary Identity Politics and the Struggle for Recognition*. London: Profile Books.

Galloway, A. R. (2006). *Gaming: Essays on Algorithmic Culture*. Minneapolis, MN: University of Minnesota Press.

Galtung, J. and Ruge, M. (1965). The structure of foreign news: The presentation of the Congo, Cuba and Cyprus crises in four Norwegian newspapers. *Journal of International Peace Research*, 2, 64–90.

Gandini, A. (2021). Digital labour: An empty signifier? *Media, Culture & Society*, 43(2), 369–380.

Gandomi, A. and Haider, M. (2015). Beyond the hype: Big data concepts, methods, and analytics. *International Journal of Information Management*, 35(2), 137–144.

Gandy, O.H. Jr. (1993). *The Panoptic Sort: A Political Economy of Personal Information*.Boulder, CO: Westview.

Gangadharan, S.P. (ed.) (2014). *Data and Discrimination: Selected Essays*. Washington, DC: Open Technology Institute, New America Foundation. www.newamerica.org/oti/data-and-discrimination

Gangadharan, S.P. and Niklas, J. (2019). Decentering technology in discourse on discrimination. *Information, Communication & Society*, 22(7), 882–899.

Gao, Y. (2012). *China as the Workshop of the World: An Analysis at the National and Industry Level of China in the International Division of Labor*. London: Routledge.

Gibson, W. (1984). *Neuromancer*. New York: Ace Books.

Giddens, A. (1984). *The Constitution of Society: Outline of a Theory of Structuration*. Cambridge: Polity.

Giddens, A. (1990). *The Consequences of Modernity*. Cambridge: Polity.

Giddens, A. (1991). *Modernity and Self-Identity*. Stanford, CA: Stanford University Press.

Gilbert, J. (2020). *Twenty-First Century Socialism*. Blackwell, MA: Wiley.

Gill, R. (2007). *Technobohemians or the New Cybertariat?* Amsterdam: Institute of Network Cultures.

Gillespie, T. (2010). The politics of 'platforms'. *New Media & Society*, 12(3), 347–364.

Gillespie, T. (2018). *Custodians of the Internet: Platforms, Content Moderation, and the Hidden Decisions That Shape Social Media*. New Haven, CT: Yale University Press.

Gitelman, L. (ed.) (2013). *'Raw Data' Is an Oxymoron*. Cambridge, MA: MIT Press.

Goffman, E. (1956). *The Presentation of Self in Everyday Life*. Edinburgh: University of Edinburgh, Social Sciences Research Centre.

Goggin, G. (2006). *Cell Phone Culture*. London: Routledge.

Golding, P. (2000). Forthcoming features: Information and communications technologies and the sociology of the future. *Sociology*, 34(1), 165–184.

Gordon, E. & de Souza e Silva, A. (2011). *Net Locality: Why Location Matters in a Networked World*. Malden, MA: Wiley-Blackwell.

Graefe, A. (2016). Guide to automated journalism. https://doi.org/10.7916/D80G3XDJ

Gray, J., Chambers, L. and Bounegru, L. (2012). *The Data Journalism Handbook: How Journalists Can Use Data to Improve the News*. Sebastopol, CA: O'Reilly Media.

Gray, M.L. and Suri, S. (2019). *Ghost Work: How to Stop Silicon Valley from Building a New Global Underclass*. Boston: Houghton Mifflin Harcourt.

Grint, K. (2005). *The Sociology of Work: Introduction*. Cambridge: Polity.

Gunitsky, S. (2015). Corrupting the cyber-commons: Social media as a tool of autocratic stability. *Perspectives on Politics*, 13(1), 42–54.

Gurevitch, M., Coleman, S. and Blumler, J. G. (2009). Political communication: Old and new media relationships. *Annals of the American Academy of Political and Social Science*, 625, 164–181.

Gurstein, M.B. (2011). Open data: Empowering the empowered or effective data use for everyone? First Monday, 16(2).

Gurumurthy, A. (2018). Where is the 'struggle' in communications for social progress? *Global Media and Communication*, 14(2), 193–200.

Gutiérrez, M. (2018). *Data Activism and Social Change*. Cham: Springer.

Habermas, J. (1962/1989). *The Structural Transformation of the Public Sphere*. Cambridge, MA: MIT Press.

Habermas, J. (1984). *The Theory of Communicative Action, Volume I: Reason and the Rationalization of Society*. Boston: Beacon.

Hacking, I. (1983/2015). Biopower and the avalanche of printed numbers. In V.W. Cisney and N. Morar (eds), *Biopower: Foucault and Beyond* (pp. 65–80). Chicago: University of Chicago Press.

Hague, B.N. and Loader, B.D. (eds) (1999). *Digital Democracy: Discourse and Decision Making in the Information Age*. New York: Routledge.

Hall, S. (1997). The Centrality of Culture: Notes on the Cultural Revolutions of Our Time. In K. Thompson (Eds.) *Media and Cultural Regulation* (217–238). London: Sage.

Hao K. (2022). Artificial intelligence is creating a new colonial world order. *MIT Technology Review*, 19 April. https://www.technologyreview.com/2022/04/19/1049592/artificial-intelligence-colonialism/

Hao, K. (2023). The human toll of making ChatGPT safe for users. *Wall Street Journal Podcasts*, 25 July. https://www.wsj.com/podcasts/tech-news-briefing/the-human-toll-of-making-chatgpt-safe-for-users/76788cbf-cf72-4f36-9dd6-afc1f07cebc2

Haraway, D.J. (1985/2016). A cyborg manifesto: science, technology, and socialist-feminism in the late twentieth century. In D.J. Haraway (ed.), *Manifestly Haraway* (pp. 3–90). Minneapolis, MN: University of Minnesota Press.

Harcup, T. and O'Neill, D. (2001). What is news? Galtung and Ruge revisited. *Journalism Studies*, 2(2), 261–280.

Harcup, T. and O'Neill, D. (2017). What is news? *Journalism Studies*, 18(12), 1470–1488.

Hardy, J. (2014). *Critical Political Economy of the Media*. London: Routledge.

Hargittai, E. (2002). Second-level digital divide: Differences in people's online skills. *First Monday*, 7(4).

Harvey, D. (1989). *The Condition of Postmodernity*. Oxford: Blackwell.

Hassan, R. (2008). *The Information Society*. Cambridge: Polity Press.

Hay, J. and Couldry, N. (2011). Rethinking convergence/culture. *Cultural Studies*, 25(4–5), 473–486. https://doi.org/10.1080/09502386.2011.600527

Helmond, A. (2015). The platformization of the web: Making web data platform ready. *Social Media + Society*, 1(2), 2056305115603080.

Helsper, E. (2021). *The Digital Disconnect*. London: SAGE.

Hepp, A., Jarke, J. and Kramp, L. (eds) (2022). *New Perspectives in Critical Data Studies: The Ambivalences of Data Power*. Cham: Springer.

Hesmondhalgh, D. (2010). User-generated content, free labour and the cultural industries. *Ephemera*, 10 (3/4): 267–284.

Hicks, J. (2023). The future of data ownership: An uncommon research agenda. *Sociological Review*, 71(3), 544–560.

Hicks, M. (2017). *Programmed Inequality: How Britain Discarded Women Technologists and Lost Its Edge in Computing*. Cambridge, MA & London: MIT Press.

Hildebrandt, M. (2008). Defining profiling: A new type of knowledge? In M. Hildebrandt and S. Guthwirth (eds), *Profiling the European Citizen. Cross-Disciplinary Perspectives* (pp. 17–30). Berlin: Springer.

Hildebrandt, M. (2018). Algorithmic regulation and the rule of law. *Philosophical Transactions of the Royal Society A: Mathematical, Physical and Engineering Sciences*, 376(2128), 20170355. https://royalsocietypublishing.org/doi/abs/10.1098/rsta.2017.0355

Hinton, S. and Hjorth, L. (2019). *Understanding Social Media* (second edition). London: Sage.

Hintz, A., Dencik, L. and Wahl-Jorgensen, K. (2019). *Digital Citizenship in a Datafied Society*. Cambridge: Polity Press.

Hobbes T. (1651/1996). *Leviathan* (R. Tuck, ed.). Cambridge: Cambridge University Press.

Hoffmann, A. L. (2019). Where fairness fails: Data, algorithms, and the limits of antidiscrimination discourse. *Information, Communication & Society*, 22(7), 900–915.

Hoffmann, A. L. (2021). Terms of inclusion: Data, discourse, violence. *New Media & Society*, 23(12), 3539–3556.

Howard, P.N. (2020). *Lie Machines: How to Save Democracy from Troll Armies, Deceitful Robots, Junk News Operations, and Political Operatives*. New Haven, CT: Yale University Press.

Howard, P.N. and Hussain, M.M. (2011). The upheavals in Egypt and Tunisia: The role of digital media. *Journal of Democracy*, 22(3), 35–48.

Hu, M. (2020). Cambridge Analytica's black box. *Big Data & Society*, 7(2), 2053951720938091.

Huberman, J. (2022). *The Spirit of Digital Capitalism*. Cambridge: Polity.

Huws, U. (2003). *The Making of a Cybertariat: Virtual Work in a Real World*. New York: Monthly Review Press.

Huws, U. (2014). *Labor in the Global Digital Economy: The Cybertariat Comes of Age*. New York: New York University Press.

Ibrahim, Y. (2021). *Posthuman Capitalism: Dancing with Data in the Digital Economy*. Abingdon: Routledge.

Iliadis, A. and Russo, F. (2016). Critical data studies: An introduction. *Big Data & Society*, 3(2).

Internet World Stats (2023). *World Internet Usage and Population Statistics. 2023 Year Estimates*, https://www.internetworldstats.com/stats.htm

Irani, L. (2015). The cultural work of microwork. *New Media & Society*, 17(5), 720–739.

Jamieson, K. H. and Cappella, J. N. (2008). *Echo Chamber: Rush Limbaugh and the Conservative Media Establishment*. Oxford: Oxford University Press.

Jarrett, K. (2016). *Feminism, Labour and Digital Media: The Digital Housewife*. New York & London: Routledge.

Jarrett, K. (2022). *Digital Labor*. Cambridge: Polity.

Jenkins, H. (2006). *Convergence Culture: Where Old and New Media Collide*. New York: New York University Press.

Jenkins, H., Ford, S. and Green, J. (2013). *Spreadable Media*. New York: New York University Press.

Jia, L. and Winseck, D. (2018). The political economy of Chinese internet companies: Financialization, concentration, and capitalization. *International Communication Gazette*, 80(1), 30–59.

Jones, B. and Jones, R. (2019). Public service chatbots. *Digital Journalism*, 7(8), 1032–1053.

Jones, P. (2021). *Work Without the Worker: Labour in the Age of Platform Capitalism*. London: Verso.

Jordan, T. (2020). *The Digital Economy*. Cambridge: Polity.

Jordan, T. and Taylor, P. A. (2004). *Hacktivism and Cyberwars: Rebels with a Cause?* New York: Routledge.

Kaluža, J. (2022). Habitual generation of filter bubbles: Why is algorithmic personalisation problematic for the democratic public sphere? *Javnost – The Public*, 29(3), 267–283.

Kaplan, A. and Haenlein, M. (2020). Rulers of the world, unite! The challenges and opportunities of artificial intelligence. *Business Horizons*, 63(1), 37–50.

Karpf, D. (2012). *The MoveOn Effect: The Unexpected Transformation of American Political Advocacy*. New York: Oxford University Press.

Karpf D. (2016). *Analytic Activism: Digital Listening and the New Political Strategy*. New York: Oxford University Press.

Katz, E. (1996). And deliver us from segmentation. *Annals of the American Academy of Political and Social Science*, 546, 22–33.

Katz, M.L. and Shapiro, C. (1985). Network externalities, competition, and compatibility. *American Economic Review*, 75(3), 424–440.

Kelleher, J.D. and Tierney, B. (2018). *Data Science*. Cambridge, MA: MIT Press.

Kennedy, H. (2018). Living with data: Aligning data studies and data activism through a focus on everyday experiences of datafication. *Krisis: Journal for Contemporary Philosophy*, 2018(1), 18–30.

Kennedy, H., Poell, T. and van Dijck, J. (2015). Data and agency. *Big Data & Society*, 2(2), 2053951715621569.

Keynes, J.M. (1930/1963). Economic possibilities for our grandchildren. In *Essays in Persuasion* (pp. 358–373) New York: W.W. Norton & Co.

Kidd, D. (2019). Extra-activism: Counter-mapping and data justice. Information, *Communication & Society*, 22(7), 954–970.

Kitchin, R. (2014a). *The Data Revolution*. London: Sage.

Kitchin, R. (2014b). Big Data, new epistemologies and paradigm shifts. *Big Data & Society*, 1(1), 2053951714528481.

Kitchin, R. (2022). *The Data Revolution* (2nd edn). London: Sage.

Kitchin, R. and Lauriault, T. (2014). Towards critical data studies: Charting and unpacking data assemblages and their work. In J. Thatcher, J. Eckert and A. Shears (eds), *Thinking Big Data in Geography. New Regimes, New Research* (pp. 83–94). Lincoln, NE: University of Nebraska Press.

Kitchin, R. and Lauriault, T. P. (2015). Small data in the era of big data. *GeoJournal*, 80(4), 463–475.

Komlosy, A. (2018). *Work*. London: Verso.

Kreiss, D. (2012). *Taking Our Country Back: The Crafting of Networked Politics from Howard Dean to Barack Obama*. New York: Oxford University Press.

Kreiss, D. (2016). *Prototype Politics: Technology-Intensive Campaigning and the Data of Democracy*. New York: Oxford University Press.

Kreiss, D. and McGregor, S.C. (2018). Technology firms shape political communication: The Work of Microsoft, Facebook, Twitter, and Google with campaigns during the 2016 U.S. presidential cycle. *Political Communication*, 35(2), 155–177.

Kukutai, T. and Taylor, J. (eds) (2016). *Indigenous Data Sovereignty: Toward an Agenda*. Canberra: Australian National University Press.

Kurzweil, R. (2005). *The Singularity Is Near: When Humans Transcend Biology*. London: Penguin.

Lane, J. (2021). *Democratizing Our Data*. Cambridge, MA: MIT Press

Laney, D. (2001). 3D data management: Controlling data volume, velocity and variety. *META Group Research Note 6*. https://www.scirp.org/reference/ReferencesPapers?ReferenceID=1611280

Larson, R. (2020). *Bit Tyrants: The Political Economy of Silicon Valley*. Chicago: Haymarket Books.

Larsson, A. O. and Moe, H. (2012). Studying political microblogging: Twitter users in the 2010 Swedish election campaign. *New Media & Society*, 14(5), 729–747.

Lazarsfeld, P.F. (1941) Remarks on administrative and critical communications research. *Studies in Philosophy and Science*, 9, 3–16.

Lazer, D.M.J., Baum, M.A., Benkler, Y., Berinsky, A.J., Greenhill, K.M., Menczer, F., Metzger, M.J., Nyhan, B., Pennycook, G., Rothschild, D., Schudson, M., Sloman, S.A., Sunstein, C.R., Thorson, E.A., Watts, D.J. and Zittrain, J.L. (2018). The science of fake news. *Science*, 359(6380), 1094–1096.

LeCun, Y., Bengio, Y. and Hinton, G. (2015). Deep learning. *Nature*, 521, 436–444

Lee, K.-F. (2018). *AI Superpowers*. Boston: Houghton Mifflin.

Lee, M. (2017). Google: Information organizer. In B.J. Birkinbine, R. Gomez and J. Wasko (eds), *Global Media Giants* (pp. 398–412). New York: Routledge.

Lee, M.K. (2018). Understanding perception of algorithmic decisions: Fairness, trust, and emotion in response to algorithmic management. *Big Data & Society*, 5(1).

Lehdonvirta, V. (2016). Algorithms that divide and unite: Delocalisation, identity and collective action in 'microwork' (pp. 53–80). In J. Flecker (eds) *Space, Place and Global Digital Work*. Basingstoke: Palgrave Macmillan.

Lehdonvirta, V. (2018). Flexibility in the gig economy: Managing time on three online piecework platforms. *New Technology, Work and Employment*, 33(1), 13–29.

Lehtiniemi, T. and Ruckenstein, M. (2019). The social imaginaries of data activism. *Big Data & Society*, 6(1), 2053951718821146.

Lehuedé, S. (2022). *Big Tech's New Headache: Data Centre Activism Flourishes Across the World*, https://blogs.lse.ac.uk/medialse/2022/11/02/big-techs-new-headache-data-centre-activism-flourishes-across-the-world/

Lessig, L. (2008). *Remix: Making Art and Commerce Thrive in the Hybrid Economy*. London: Penguin Press.

Levinson, P. (2004). *Cellphone: The Story of the World's Most Mobile Medium and How It Has Transformed Everything!* Basingstoke: Palgrave Macmillan.

Leurs, K. and Shepherd, T. (2017). Datafication and discrimination. In K. Van Es and M.T. Schafer (eds), *The Datafied Society: Studying Culture through Data*. Amsterdam: Amsterdam University Press.

Lewin, K. (1951). *Field Theory in Social Sciences*. New York: Harper & Row.

Linden, C.-G. (2017). Decades of automation in the newsroom. *Digital Journalism*, 5(2), 123–140.

Liu, W. (2020). *Abolish Silicon Valley: How to Liberate Technology from Capitalism*. London: Repeater Books.

Livingstone, S. (2004). Media literacy and the challenge of new information and communication technologies. *Communication Review*, 7(1), 3–14.

Loosen, W., Reimer, J. and De Silva-Schmidt, F. (2020). Data-driven reporting: An on-going (r)evolution? An analysis of projects nominated for the Data Journalism Awards 2013–2016. *Journalism*, 21(9), 1246–1263.

Luitse, D. and Denkena, W. (2021). The great transformer: Examining the role of large language models in the political economy of AI. *Big Data & Society*, 8(2), 20539517211047736.

Lupton, D. (2020). *Data Selves: More-than-Human Perspectives*. Cambridge: Polity.

Lyon, D. (1998). The world wide web of surveillance: The internet and off-world power-flows. *Information, Communication & Society*, 1(1), 91–105.

Lyon, D. (2001). *Surveillance Society: Monitoring Everyday Life*. Berkshire: Open University Press.

Lyon, D. (2002a). Surveillance studies: Understanding visibility, mobility and the phenetic fix. *Surveillance & Society*, 1(1), 1–7.

Lyon, D. (2002b). Everyday surveillance: Personal data and social classifications. *Information, Communication & Society*, 5(2), 242–257.

Lyon, D. (2003). *Surveillance as Social Sorting*. London: Routledge.

Lyon, D. (2014). Surveillance, Snowden, and Big Data: Capacities, consequences, critique. *Big Data & Society*, 1(2), 2053951714541861.

Mann, M. and Daly, A. (2019). (Big) Data and the North-in-South: Australia's informational imperialism and digital colonialism. *Television & New Media*, 20(4), 379–395.

Mann, M. and Matzner, T. (2019). Challenging algorithmic profiling: The limits of data protection and anti-discrimination in responding to emergent discrimination. *Big Data & Society*, 6(2), 2053951719895805.

Manovich, L. (2012). Trending: The promises and the challenges of big social data. In M. Gold (ed.), *Debates in the Digital Humanities*. Minneapolis, MN: University of Minnesota Press.

Mansell, R. and Steinmueller, W.E. (2020). *Advanced Introduction to Platform Economics*. Cheltenham: Edward Elgar.

Margolis, M. and Resnick, D. (2000). *Politics as Usual: The Cyberspace 'Revolution'*. London: Sage.

Marwick, A. and Lewis, R. (2017). Media Manipulation and Disinformation Online. New York: Data and Society Research Institute.

Marx, G.T. (2002). What's new about the 'New Surveillance'? Classifying for change and continuity. *Surveillance & Society*, 1(1), 9–29.

Marx, K. (1859/1975). Preface to A Contribution to the Critique of Political Economy. In *Marx & Engels Collected Works*, Volume 29 (pp. 261–265). London: Lawrence & Wishart.

Marx, K. (1867/1976). *Capital Volume 1*. London: Penguin.

Marx, K. (1973). *The Grundrisse: Foundations of the Critique of Political Economy*. Harmondsworth: Penguin.

Marx, K. and Engels, F. (1848/1976). The manifesto of the Communist Party. In *Marx & Engels Collected Works*, Volume 6. London: Lawrence & Wishart

Mayer-Schoenberger, V. and Cukier, K. (2013). *Big Data: A Revolution That Will Transform How We Live, Work, and Think*. London: John Murray.

Mayer-Schoenberger, V. and Ramge, T. (2018). *Reinventing Capitalism in the Age of Big Data*. London: John Murray.

Mbembe, A. (2003). Necropolitics. *Public Culture*, 15(1), 11–40.

McAfee, A. and Brynjolfsson, E. (2017). *Machine, Platform, Crowd: Harnessing Our Digital Future*. New York: W. W. Norton.

McCarthy, J., Minsky, M., Rochester, N. and Shannon, C. (1955/2006). A proposal for the Dartmouth Summer Research Project on Artificial Intelligence. *AI Magazine*, 27(4).

McCaughey, M. and Ayers, M. D. (2003). *Cyberactivism: Online Activism in Theory and Practice*. New York: Routledge.

McChesney, R. (2000). The political economy of communication and the future of the field. *Media, Culture & Society*, 22(1), 109–116.

McChesney, R. (2015). *Rich Media, Poor Democracy*. New York: New Press.

McIlwain, C. D. (2019). *Black Software: The Internet & Racial Justice, From The Afronet To Black Lives Matter*. Oxford: Oxford University Press.

McLuhan, M. (1962). *The Gutenberg Galaxy*. London: Routledge & Kegan Paul.

McLuhan, M. (1964). *Understanding Media*. Berkeley, CA: Gingko Press.

McQuail D. (2010). *McQuail's Mass Communication Theory*. London: Sage

McQuail, D. and Deuze, M. (2020). *McQuail's Media and Mass Communication Theory* (7th edn). London: Sage.

McQuillan, D. (2022). *Resisting AI: An Anti-Fascist Approach to Artificial Intelligence*. Bristol: Bristol University Press.

Meikle, G. (2016). *Social Media: Communication, Sharing and Visibility*. New York: Routledge.

Meikle, G. (2022). *Deepfakes*. Cambridge: Polity.

Milan, S. and Treré, E. (2019). Big Data from the South(s): Beyond data universalism. *Television & New Media*, 20(4), 319–335.

Milan, S. and Treré, E. (2020). The rise of the data poor: The COVID-19 pandemic seen from the margins. *Social Media + Society*, 6(3).

Milan, S. and van der Velden, L. (2016). The alternative epistemologies of data activism. *Digital Culture & Society*, 2(2), 57–74.

Miller, T. and Maxwell, R. (2017). Apple. In B. J. Birkinbine, R. Gomez and J. Wasko (eds), *Global Media Giants* (pp. 369–382). New York: Routledge.

Mittelstadt, B. (2016). Automation, algorithms, and politics: Auditing for transparency in content personalization systems. *International Journal of Communication*, 10.

Moazed, A. and Johnson, N. L. (2016). *Modern Monopolies*. New York: St. Martin's Press.

Moll, I. (2021). The myth of the fourth industrial revolution. *Theory: A Journal of Social and Political Theory*, 68(167), 1–38.

Montal, T. and Reich, Z. (2017). I, robot. You, journalist. Who is the Author? *Digital Journalism*, 5(7), 829–849.

Moor, J.H. (1985). What is computer ethics? *Metaphilosophy*, 16(4): 266–275.

Moore, M. and Tambini, D. (2018). *Digital Dominance. The Power of Google, Amazon, Facebook, and Apple*. Oxford University Press.

More, M. (2013). The philosophy of transhumanism. In M. More and N. Vita-More (eds), *The Transhumanist Reader: Classical and Contemporary Essays on the Science, Technology, and Philosophy of the Human Future* (pp. 3–17). Hoboken, NJ: John Wiley & Sons.

Morozov, E. (2011). *The Net Delusion: The Dark Side of Internet Freedom*. New York: Public Affairs.

Morozov, E. (2013). *To Save Everything, Click Here: The Folly of Technological Solutionism*. New York: Public Affairs.

Morozov, E. (2014). Don't believe the hype. The sharing economy masks a failing economy. *The Guardian*, 28 September. https://www.theguardian.com/commentisfree/2014/sep/28/sharing-economy-internet-hype-benefits-overstated-evgeny-morozov

Mosco, V. (2005). *The Digital Sublime: Myth, Power, and Cyberspace*. Cambridge, MA: MIT Press.

Mosco, V. (2009). *The Political Economy of Communication* (2nd edn). London: SAGE.

Mosco, V. (2014). *To the Cloud*. Boulder, Co: Paradigm.

Mueller, G. (2021). *Breaking Things at Work: The Luddites Are Right About Why You Hate Your Job*. London: Verso.

Muldoon, J. (2022). *Platform Socialism: How to Reclaim Our Digital Future from Big Tech*. London: Pluto Press.

Mumford, D. (2022). Data colonialism: Compelling and useful, but whither epistemes? *Information, Communication & Society*, 25(10), 1511–1516.

Munn, L. (2022). *Automation Is a Myth*. Stanford, CA: Stanford University Press.

Murdock, G. and Golding, P. (1973). For a political economy of mass communications. *Socialist Register*, 10, 205–234.

Murdock, G. and Golding, P. (2005). Culture, Communications and Political Economy. In J. Curran and M. Gurevitch (eds), *Mass Media and Society* (pp. 60–83). London: Hodder.

Nakamura, L. (2002). *Cybertypes: Race, Ethnicity, and Identity on the Internet*. New York: Routledge.

Nakamura, L. (2008). *Digitizing Race: Visual Cultures of the Internet*. Minneapolis, MN: University of Minnesota Press.

Nath, R. and Manna, R. (2023). From posthumanism to ethics of artificial intelligence. *AI & Society*, 38, 185–196.

National Telecommunications and Information Administration (NTIA) (1999). *Falling through the Net: Defining the Digital Divide. A Report on the Telecommunications and Information Technology Gap in America*. Washington, DC: US Department of Commerce.

Nieborg, D.B. and Poell, T. (2018). The platformization of cultural production: Theorizing the contingent cultural commodity. *New Media & Society*, 20(11), 4275–4292.

Nielsen, R.K. and Ganter, S.A. (2022). *The Power of Platforms: Shaping Media and Society*. New York: Oxford University Press.

Noble, S. U. (2018). *Algorithms of Oppression: How Search Engines Reinforce Racism*. New York: New York University Press.

Oates, S. (2008). *An Introduction to Media and Politics*. London: Sage.

Omi, M. and Winant, H. (1986). *Racial Formation in the United States: From the 1960s to the 1990s*. New York: Routledge.

O'Neil, C. (2016). *Weapons of Math Destruction*. New York: Crown.

Onuoha, M. (2018) Notes on algorithmic violence. https://github.com/MimiOnuoha/On-Algorithmic-Violence

Open Data Institute (2021). The Data Ethics Canvas. https://www.theodi.org/article/the-data-ethics-canvas-2021

O'Reilly, T. (2007). What is Web 2.0? Design patterns and business models for the next generation of software. *Communications & Strategies*, 65, 17–37.

O'Reilly, T. (2013) Open data and algorithmic regulation. In B. Goldstein, and L. Dyson (eds), *Beyond Transparency: Open Data and the Future of Civic Innovation* (pp. 289–300). San Francisco: Code for America Press.

Papacharissi, Z. (2002). The virtual sphere: The internet as a public sphere. *New Media & Society*, 4(1), 9–27.

Papacharissi, Z. (2010). *A Networked Self: Identity, Community, and Culture on Social Network Sites*. New York and London: Routledge.

Papacharissi, Z. (2015). *Affective Publics: Sentiment, Technology, and Politics*. New York: Oxford University Press.

Papacharissi, Z. and de Fatima Oliveira, M. (2012). Affective news and networked publics: The rhythms of news storytelling on #Egypt. *Journal of Communication*, 62(2), 266–282.

Pariser, E. (2011). *The Filter Bubble*. New York: Penguin Press.

Pasquale, F. (2015). *The Black Box Society: The Secret Algorithms That Control Money and Information*. Cambridge, MA: Harvard University Press.

Pavlik, J. V. (2013). Innovation and the future of journalism. *Digital Journalism*, 1(2), 181–193.

Perez, C. C. (2019). *Invisible Women: Data Bias in a World Designed for Men*. New York: Abrams.

Pickard, V. (2019). *Democracy without Journalism? Confronting the Misinformation Society*. Oxford: Oxford University Press.

Plantin, J.-C., Lagoze, C., Edwards, P.N. and Sandvig, C. (2016). Infrastructure studies meet platform studies in the age of Google and Facebook. *New Media & Society*, 20(1), 293–310.

Poell, T. (2014). Social media and the transformation of activist communication: Exploring the social media ecology of the 2010 Toronto G20 protests. *Information, Communication & Society*, 17(6), 716–731.

Postman, N. (1986). *Amusing Ourselves to Death: Public Discourse in the Age of Show Business*. Harmondsworth: Penguin.

Prassl, J. (2018). *Humans as a Service: The Promise and Perils of Work in the Gig Economy*. Oxford: Oxford University Press.

Qiu, J. L. (2009). *Working-Class Network Society*. Cambridge, MA: MIT Press.

Qiu J.L. (2015). Locating worker-generated content (WGC) in the world's factory. In R. Maxwell (ed.), *The Routledge Companion to Labor and Media* (pp. 303–314). New York: Routledge.

Qiu, J. L. (2016). *Goodbye iSlave: A Manifesto for Digital Abolition*. Chicago: University of Illinois Press.

Raboy, M. (2002). *Global Media Policy in the New Millennium*. Luton: University of Luton Press.

Ragnedda, M. (2017). *The Third Digital Divide: A Weberian Approach to Digital Inequalities*. London: Routledge.

Ragnedda, M. and Ruiu, M.L. (2020). *Digital Capital: A Bourdieusian Perspective on the Digital Divide*. Bingley: Emerald Publishing.

Rainie, L. and Wellman, B. (2012). *Networked: The New Social Operating System*. Cambridge, MA: MIT Press.

Raley, R. (2013). Dataveillance and countervailance. In L. Gitelman (ed.), *'Raw Data' is an Oxymoron* (pp. 121–146). Cambridge, MA: MIT Press.

Rantanen, T. (2005). *The Media and Globalization*. London: Sage.

Resnick, D. (1998). Politics on the Internet: The normalization of cyberspace. In C. Toulouse and T.W. Luke (eds), *The Politics of Cyberspace*. London and New York: Routledge.

Redden, J. (2022). Data harms. In L. Dencik, A. Hintz, J. Redden and E. Treré (eds), *Data Justice* (pp. 59–72). London: SAGE.

Rheingold, H. (1993). *The Virtual Community in a Computerised World*. London: Secker & Warburg.

Ricaurte, P. (2019). Data epistemologies, the coloniality of power, and resistance. *Television & New Media*, 20(4), 350–365.

Ricaurte, P. (2022). Ethics for the majority world: AI and the question of violence at scale. *Media, Culture & Society*, 44(4), 726–745.

Richterich, A. (2018). *The Big Data Agenda: Data Ethics and Critical Data Studies*. London: University of Westminster Press.

Ritzer, G. (1993). *The McDonaldization of Society*. Thousand Oaks, CA: Sage.

Ritzer, G. (2007). *The Globalization of Nothing 2*. London: Sage

Roberts, S.T. (2019). *Behind the Screen: Content Moderation in the Shadows of Social Media*. New Haven, CT: Yale University Press.

Robinson, C. J. (2020). *Black Marxism* (3rd edn). Chapel Hill, NC: University of North Carolina Press.

Rogers, E.M. (1995), *Diffusion of Innovations* (4th edn). New York: Free Press.

Rogers, S. (2016). Data journalism matters more now than ever before. https://simonrogers.net/2016/03/07/data-journalism-matters-more-now-than-ever-before/

Rosenberg, D. (2013). Data before the fact. In L. Gitelman (ed.), *'Raw Data' is an Oxymoron* (pp. 15–40). Cambridge, MA: MIT Press.

Rosenblat, A. (2018). *Uberland: How Algorithms Are Rewriting the Rules of Work*. Berkeley, CA: University of California Press.

Rouvroy, A. (2013). The end(s) of critique: Data behaviourism versus due process. In M. Hildebrandt and K. de Vries (eds), *Privacy, Due Process and the Computational Turn: The Philosophy of Law Meets the Philosophy of Technology* (pp. 157–182). London: Routledge.

Ruppert, E., Isin, E. and Bigo, D. (2017). Data politics. *Big Data & Society*, 4(2).

Russell, S.J. (2019). *Human Compatible: Artificial Intelligence and the Problem of Control*. London: Viking.

Russell, S.J. and Norvig, P. (2016). *Artificial Intelligence: A Modern Approach* (3rd edn). Harlow: Pearson Education.

Sadowski, J. (2019). When data is capital: Datafication, accumulation, and extraction. *Big Data & Society*, 6(1), 2053951718820549.

Sadowski, J. (2020). *Too Smart: How Digital Capitalism is Extracting Data, Controlling Our Lives, and Taking Over the World*. Cambridge, MA: MIT Press.

Sadowski, J. (2021). I'm a Luddite. You should be one too. *The Conversation*, 9 August. http://theconversation.com/im-a-luddite-you-should-be-one-too-163172

Sandoval, M. (2020). Entrepreneurial activism? Platform cooperativism between subversion and co-optation. *Critical Sociology*, 46(6), 801–817.

Schäfer, M.T. (2016). Challenging citizenship: Social media and big data. *Computer Supported Cooperative Work*, 25, 111–113.

Schiller, D. (2000). *Digital Capitalism: Networking the Global Market System*. Cambridge, MA: MIT Press.

Scholz, T. (ed.) (2013). *Digital Labor: The Internet as Playground and Factory*. London: Routledge.

Scholz, T. (2016). *Uberworked and Underpaid: How Workers Are Disrupting the Digital Economy*. Cambridge: Polity.

Schor, J. (2016). Debating the sharing economy. *Journal of Self-Governance and Management Economics*, 4(3), 7–22.

Schudson, M. (1998). *The Good Citizen: A History of American Civic Life*. New York: Free Press.

Schwab, K. (2016). *The Fourth Industrial Revolution*. New York: Crown Business.

Searle, J.R. (1980). Minds, brains, and programs. *Behavioral and Brain Sciences*, 3(3), 417–424

Segura, M. S. and Waisbord, S. (2019). Between data capitalism and data citizenship. *Television & New Media*, 20(4), 412–419.

Selwyn, N. (2004). Reconsidering political and popular understandings of the digital divide. *New Media & Society*, 6(3), 341–362.

Shen, H. (2021). *Alibaba: Infrastructuring Global China*. New York: Routledge.

Siegel, J. and Pappas, G. (2023). Morals, ethics, and the technology capabilities and limitations of automated and self-driving vehicles. *AI & Society*, 38, 213–226.

Simon, F.M. (2022). Uneasy bedfellows: AI in the news, platform companies and the issue of journalistic autonomy. *Digital Journalism*, 10(10), 1832–1854.

Šimunjak, M. (2022). *Tweeting Brexit: Social Media and the Aftermath of the EU Referendum*. Abingdon: Routledge.

Smythe, D.W. (1977). Communications: Blindspot of Western Marxism. *Canadian Journal of Political and Social Theory*, 1(3), 1–27.

Smythe, D.W. (1981/2006). *Dependency Road*. Norwood, NJ: Ablex.

Srnicek, N. (2017). *Platform Capitalism*. Cambridge: Polity Press.

Standing, G. (2011). *The Precariat. The New Dangerous Class*. London: Bloomsbury.

Steinberg, M. (2019). *The Platform Economy. How Japan Transformed the Consumer Internet*. Minneapolis, MN: University of Minnesota Press.

Stilgoe, J. (2018). Machine learning, social learning and the governance of self-driving cars. *Social Studies of Science*, 48(1), 25–56.

Striphas, T. (2015). Algorithmic culture. *European Journal of Cultural Studies*, 18(4–5), 395–412.

Su, C. and Flew, T. (2021). The rise of Baidu, Alibaba and Tencent (BAT) and their role in China's Belt and Road Initiative (BRI). *Global Media and Communication*, 17(1), 67–86.

Sundararajan, A. (2017). *The Sharing Economy: The End of Employment and the Rise of Crowd-Based Capitalism*. Cambridge, MA: MIT Press.

Sunstein, C.R. (2001). *Republic.com*. Princeton, NJ: Princeton University Press.

Sunstein, C. R. (2009). *Going to Extremes: How Like Minds Unite and Divide*. Oxford: Oxford University Press.

Susskind, R.E. and Susskind, D. (2015). *The Future of the Professions: How Technology Will Transform the Work of Human Experts*. Oxford: Oxford University Press.

Tajfel, H. and Turner, J.C. (1986). The social identity theory of intergroup behaviour. In S. Worchel and W.G. Austin (eds), *Psychology of Intergroup Relations*. Chicago: Nelson-Hall.

Tandoc, E.C. (2014). Journalism is twerking? How web analytics is changing the process of gatekeeping. *New Media & Society*, 16(4), 559–575.

Tandoc, E.C., Lim, Z.W. and Ling, R. (2018). Defining 'fake news'. *Digital Journalism*, 6(2), 137–153.

Tang, M. (2020). *Tencent: The Political Economy of China's Surging Internet Giant*. London: Routledge.

Taylor, L. (2017). What is data justice? The case for connecting digital rights and freedoms globally. *Big Data & Society*, 4(2).

Taylor, L., Floridi, L., & Sloot, B. van der. (eds) (2016). *Group Privacy: New Challenges of Data Technologies*. Cham: Springer.

Terranova, T. (2004). *Network Culture. Politics for the Information Age*. London: Pluto Press.

Thatcher, J.E. and Dalton, C.M. (2022). *Data Power: Radical Geographies and Resistance*. London: Pluto Press.

Thompson, J. B. (1995). *The Media and Modernity*. Cambridge: Polity Press.

Thompson, N. and Bremmer, I. (2018) The AI cold war that threatens us all. *Wired*. https://www.wired.com/story/ai-cold-war-china-could-doom-us-all/

Tichenor, P.J., Donohue, G.A. and Olien, C.N. (1970) Mass media flow and differential growth in knowledge. *Public Opinion Quarterly*, 34(2), 159–170.

Toffler A. (1980). *The Third Wave*. New York: Bantam.

Tucker, J., Guess, A., Barbera, P., Vaccari, C., Siegel, A., Sanovich, S., Stukal, D. and Nyhan, B. (2018). Social media, political polarization, and political disinformation: A review of the scientific literature. *SSRN Electronic Journal*.

Tufekci, Z. (2014). Engineering the public: Big data, surveillance and computational politics. *First Monday*, 19(7). https://doi.org/10.5210/fm.v19i7.4901

Turing, A.M. (1950). Computing machinery and intelligence. *Mind*, 59, 433–460.

Turow, J. (2006). *Niche Envy: Marketing Discrimination in the Digital Age*. Cambridge, MA: MIT Press.

Turow, J. (2011). *The Daily You: How the New Advertising Industry Is Defining Your Identity and Your Worth*. New Haven, CT: Yale University Press.

Urry, J. (2016). *What is the Future?* Cambridge: Polity.

Vaccari, C. and Chadwick, A. (2020). Deepfakes and disinformation: Exploring the impact of synthetic political video on deception, uncertainty, and trust in news. *Social Media + Society*, 6(1), 2056305120903408.

Valenzuela, S., Halpern, D., Katz, J.E. and Miranda, J.P. (2019). The paradox of participation versus misinformation: Social media, political engagement, and the spread of misinformation. *Digital Journalism*, 7(6), 802–823.

Vallas, S. and Schor, J. B. (2020). What do platforms do? Understanding the gig economy. *Annual Review of Sociology*, 46(1), 273–294.

Vallor, S. (2016). *Technology and the Virtues: A Philosophical Guide to a Future Worth Wanting*. Oxford: Oxford University Press.

van Dalen, A. (2012). The algorithms behind the headlines. *Journalism Practice*, 6(5–6), 648–658.

van Deursen, A. and van Dijk, J. (2011). Internet skills and the digital divide. *New Media & Society*, 13(6), 893–911.

van Deursen, A.J. and van Dijk, J.A. (2014). The digital divide shifts to differences in usage. *New Media & Society*, 16(3), 507–526.

van Deursen, A.J.A.M. and Helsper, E.J. (2015), The third-level digital divide: Who benefits most from being online? In *Communication and Information Technologies Annual* (Studies in Media and Communications, Vol. 10, pp. 29–52). Bingley: Emerald Group Publishing.

van Dijck, J. (2009). Users like you? Theorizing agency in user-generated content. *Media, Culture & Society*, 31(1), 41–58.

Van Dijck, J. (2014). Datafication, dataism and dataveillance: Big data between scientific paradigm and ideology. *Surveillance & Society*, 12(2), 197–208.

Van Dijck, J. and Poell, T. (2013). Understanding social media logic. *Media and Communication*, 1(1), 2–14.

Van Dijck, J., Poell, T. and de Waal, M. (2018). *The Platform Society*. Oxford University Press.

van Dijk, J. (1999). *The Network Society*. London: Sage.

van Dijk, J. (2005). *The Deepening Divide*. Thousand Oaks: Sage.

van Dijk, J. (2006). *The Network Society* (2nd edn). London: Sage.

van Dijk, J. (2020). *The Digital Divide*. Cambridge: Polity Press.

van Dijk, J. and Hacker, K. (2003). The digital divide as a complex and dynamic phenomenon. *The Information Society*, 19(4), 315–326.

van Dijk, T. (2008). *Discourse and Power*. Basingstoke: Palgrave.

van Doorn, N. (2017). Platform labor: On the gendered and racialized exploitation of low-income service work in the 'on-demand' economy. *Information, Communication & Society*, 20(6), 898–914.

Verdegem, P. (ed.) (2021). *AI for Everyone? Critical Perspectives*. London: University of Westminster Press.

Verdegem, P. (2022). Dismantling AI capitalism: The commons as an alternative to the power concentration of big tech. *AI & Society*. https://doi.org/10.1007/s00146-022-01437-8

Verdegem, P. and Verhoest, P. (2009). Profiling the non-user: Rethinking policy initiatives stimulating ICT acceptance. *Telecommunications Policy*, 33(10), 642–652.

Wachter-Boettcher, S. (2017). *Technically Wrong: Sexist Apps, Biased Algorithms, and Other Threats of Toxic Tech*. New York: W.W. Norton.

Waddell, T. F. (2018). A robot wrote this? *Digital Journalism*, 6(2), 236–255.

Wagner, B. (2018). Ethics as an escape from regulation: From 'ethics-washing' to ethics-shopping? In E. Bayamliogu, I. Baraliuc, L.A.W. Janssens and M. Hildebrandt (eds), *Being Profiled: Cogitas Ergo Sum* (pp. 84–90). Amsterdam: Amsterdam University Press.

Waisbord, S. (2018). Truth is what happens to news. *Journalism Studies*, 19(13), 1866–1878.

Wajcman, J. (2004). *Techno Feminism*. Cambridge: Polity Press.

Wajcman, J. (2017). Automation: Is it really different this time? *British Journal of Sociology*, 68(1), 119–127.

Wallerstein, I. M. (2004). *World-Systems Analysis: An Introduction*. Durham, NC: Duke University Press.

Warschauer, M. (2003). *Technology and Social Inclusion: Rethinking the Digital Divide*. Cambridge, MA: MIT Press.

Wardle, C. and Derakhshan, H. (2017). *Information Disorder: Toward an Interdisciplinary Framework for Research and Policymaking*. Council of Europe Report DGI(2017)09. Strasbourg: Council of Europe.

Warwick, K. (2012). *Artificial Intelligence*. New York: Routledge.

Wasserman, H. (2009). Tabloidization of the news. In K. Wahl-Jorgensen and T. Hanitzsch (eds), *The Handbook of Journalism Studies* (pp. 277–289). New York: Routledge.

Webb, A. (2019). *The Big Nine. How The Tech Titans & Their Thinking Machines Could Warp Humanity*. New York: Hachette Book Group.

Weber, M. (1904/1949). Objectivity in social science and social policy. In E.A. Shils and H.A. Finch (eds), *The Methodology of the Social Sciences*. New York: Free Press.

Weber, M. (1924/1947). *The Theory of Social and Economic Organization*. New York: Free Press.

Weber, M. (1978). *Economy and Society* (2 vols, G. Roth and C. Wittich, eds). Berkeley, CA: University of California Press.

Webster, F. (2014). *Theories of the Information Society* (4th edn). Abingdon: Routledge.

Webster, J. (2023). The promise of personalisation: Exploring how music streaming platforms are shaping the performance of class identities and distinction. *New Media & Society*, 25(8), 2140–2162.

Wernimont, J. (2019). *Numbered Lives: Life and Death in Quantum Media*. Cambridge, MA: MIT Press.

West, S. M. (2019). Data capitalism: Redefining the logics of surveillance and privacy. *Business & Society*, 58(1), 20–41.

Williams, R. (1958/1989). *Resources of Hope: Culture, Democracy, Socialism*. London: Verso.

Williams, R. (1980). Base and superstructure in Marxist cultural theory. In *Problems in Materialism and Culture: Selected Essays* (pp. 31–49). London: Verso.

Williams, R. (1983). *Keywords*. Oxford & New York: Oxford University Press.

Wilson, D. H. (2011). *Robopocalypse*. London: Simon and Schuster.

Winfield, A. (2012). *Robotics: A Very Short Introduction*. Oxford: Oxford University Press.

Winseck, D. (2008). The State of Media Ownership and Media Markets: Competition or Concentration and Why Should We Care? *Sociology Compass*, 2(1), 34–47.

Winterson, J. (2021). *12 Bytes: How Artificial Intelligence Will Change the Way We Live and Love*. London: Penguin.

Wired (2014). Data is the new oil of the digital economy. https://www.wired.com/insights/2014/07/data-new-oil-digital-economy/

Wood, A. J., Graham, M., Lehdonvirta, V. and Hjorth, I. (2019). Good gig, bad gig: Autonomy and algorithmic control in the global gig economy. *Work, Employment and Society*, 33(1), 56–75.

Woodcock, J. and Graham, M. (2020). *The Gig Economy: A Critical Introduction*. Cambridge: Polity.

Wright, E.O. (2010). *Envisioning Real Utopias*. London: Verso.

Wright, E. O. (2015). *Understanding Class*. London: Verso.

Wright, E. O. (2019). *How to Be an Anticapitalist in the 21st Century?* London: Verso.

Wyatt, S. (2008). Technological determinism is dead; long live technological determinism. In E.J. Hackett, O. Amsterdamska, M.E. Lynch and J. Wajcman (eds), *The Handbook of Science and Technology Studies* (3rd edn, pp. 165–180). Cambridge, MA: MIT Press.

Yeo, S. (2023). *Baidu. Geopolitical Dynamics of the Internet in China*. New York: Routledge.

Yeung, K. (2018). Algorithmic regulation: A critical interrogation. *Regulation & Governance*, 12(4), 505–523.

Zeleny, M. (1987). Management support systems: Towards integrated knowledge management. *Human Systems Management*, 7(1), 59–70.

Zhao, Y. (2008). *Communication in China: Political Economy, Power, and Conflict*. London: Rowman & Littlefield.

Zillien, N. and Hargittai, E. (2009). Digital distinction: Status-specific types of internet usage. *Social Science Quarterly*, 90(2), 274–291.

Zimmer, M. (2010). 'But the data is already public': On the ethics of research in Facebook. *Ethics and Information Technology*, 12(4), 313–325.

Zuboff, S. (2019). *The Age of Surveillance Capitalism*. New York: Public Affairs.

Index

Page numbers followed by "f" indicate figures; those followed by "t" indicate tables.

12 Bytes (Winterson), 23

abstraction and generalisation, 19
A/B testing, 69–70
access and infrastructure inequalities, 136–137
action research, 11
Ada Lovelace Institute, 155
administrative research, 8
Adorno, T., 5
Advanced Research Projects Agency Computer
    Network (ARPANET), 16
advertising platforms, 48
Affective Publics (Papacharissi), 68
affective publics, 68
agency/structure, 76
Airbnb, 183, 184
AI Superpowers (Lee), 125
Albrecht, S., 58
Alexander, M., 151
Al Gore, 116
algorithmic activism, 191
algorithmic auditing, 140
algorithmic authorship, 167
algorithmic citizenship, 86–90
algorithmic culture, 6, 29–31
algorithmic governmentality, 88–89
algorithmic identities, 84–85
algorithmic inequity, 145, 149
algorithmic management, 186
algorithmic oppression, 152
algorithmic power, 29
algorithmic profiling, 85–86
algorithmic regulation, 88–89, 90
algorithmic transparency, 166
algorithmic violence, 204
algorithms, 28–29, 93
    from citizens to, 87–88
    conceptualising, 13
    and data, 6, 74
    as gatekeepers, 163
    opportunities and challenges of, 157
Algorithms of Oppression (Noble), 152
Alibaba, 35, 43, 46, 125, 126, 128–129
Alipay app, 128
Allen, P., 123
Alpaydin, E., 28

Alphabet Workers Union, 191
AlphaGo, 96
Amazon, 29, 35, 43, 46, 119t, 120–121, 189
Amazon Mechanical Turk (AMT), 189
Amazon Web Services (AWS), 120
American Association of Artificial
    Intelligence, 94
analytic activism, 69–70
Analytic Activism: Digital Listening and the New
    Political Strategy (Karpf), 69
Analytical Engine, 92–93
analytics frontier, 70
'Anatomy of an AI System', 107, 189
Anderson, C., 26, 163
Andrejevic, M., 79, 84, 153–154
anti-Black box, 151–152
anti-discrimination discourse, 203
antitrust, 127
Apple, 62, 119t, 122–123
Arendt, H., 87–88
Aristotle, 11
Arora, P., 131, 154
artificial intelligence (AI), 31–32
    AI capitalism, 53
    AI cold war, 133
    AI journalism, 165
    AI pipelines, 104
    AI winters, 94–95
    'Anatomy of an AI System', 107, 189
    applications, 53, 100–105
    bias and injustice, 106–107
    breakthroughs, 94–96
    challenges and controversies, 105–109
    classifications of subfields, 100–101t
    comprehensive conceptualisation of, 99–100
    computer vision, 101
    emergence of, 93–94
    environmental impact, 107
    ethics in data and, 206
    explainable AI (XAI), 105
    general versus narrow AI, 96–97
    history of, 92–93
    imperfect technologies, 105–106
    industrial infrastructures of, 99
    McCarthy's definition, 94
    natural language processing, 98, 102–103

power, inequalities and injustices, 108–109
rise in mainstream media, 91–92
self-driving cars, 95, 103–105
services, 4
singularity and superintelligence, 108
social practices of, 99
speech recognition, 102
strong and weak, 96–97
technicalities underlying, 97–99
transparency and trust, 106
artificial neural networks, 95, 99, 101
artificial neurons, 99
Artificial Unintelligence: How Computers Misunderstand the World (Broussard), 140
Arvidsson, A., 179
Associated Press, 165
Association for Computing Machinery (ACM), 141
Atlas of AI (Crawford), 43
attention hacking, 168
attribute data, 22
audience building, 49
audience commodity, 38, 42, 178
audiences, 38, 59
authorship, 167
automated algorithmic profiling, 86
automated content production, 165
automated journalism
    challenges presented by, 167
    opportunities for, 166–167
    types of, 165–166
automated reasoning, 98
automatic machine. *See* Turing machine
Automating Inequality (Eubanks), 144
automating surveillance, 79–80
automation
    critiques of hyperbole with, 187
    and data work, 186–190
    and future of work, 187, 190
    as ghost work, 188–189
    in newsroom, 165, 173
    and robots, 146
    sharing economy to, 175–176
    technological unemployment, 189–190
Automation and the Future of Work (Benanav), 188
Automation is a Myth (Munn), 188
Autor, D. H., 165

Babbage, C., 92
Baidu, 29, 46, 125, 126, 127–128
Bakir, V., 168
Barbrook, R., 117
BAT companies, 4, 46, 50, 126–127
Bayes, T., 92
Bayes' theorem, 92
Beck, U., 76

Becoming Data podcast, 18
Beer, D., 51, 147
Bekey, G. A., 97
Belk, R., 182
Bell, D., 36
Beller, J., 151
Benanav, A., 188
Benjamin, R., 151–152
Benkler Y., 65
Benn, T., 199
Bezos, J., 120, 144
bias and injustice, 106–107
big data
    capitalism, 51–52
    characteristics of, 25
    conceptualising, 13
    versus datafication, 27–28
    defining, 24
    provocations, 27
    revolution, 4, 26
    rise of, 24–28
    Vs for, 24–25
Big Data (Mayer-Schoenberger and Cukier), 24
big data divide, conceptualising, 153–154
Big Data from the South(s) project, 154
Bigo, D., 198
big tech companies, 4, 118, 127, 197
Birkinbine, B. J., 144
black boxes, 106, 141, 151
The Black Box Society (Pasquale), 53
Black Lives Matter (BLM) movement, 135
Black Marxism: The Making of the Black Radical Tradition (Robinson), 150
Blackness, 150
Blank, G., 66
blue-collar jobs, 182
Boden, M. E., 101
Boolean logic, 92
Boole, G., 92
Bostrom, N., 96, 97
Botsman, R., 182, 183
Bounegru, L., 164, 172
Bourdieu, P., 6, 142
bourgeois public sphere, 64
boyd, d., 24, 27, 153
Brevini, B., 107
Brexit referendum, 169
BRICS countries, 131
Brin, S., 119, 144
Brock, A., 150
Broussard, M., 140
Browne, S., 150
browser wars, 124
Bruns, A., 40, 171
brute force methods, 96
Brynjolfsson, E., 188
Bucher, T., 29

Bunz, M., 66, 213
Buolamwini, J., 148–149
Burgess, J., 6
ByteDance, 126

Californian ideology, 117–118
Calzada, I., 88
Calzati, S., 132
Cambridge Analytica scandal, 23, 42, 63, 170
Cameron, A., 117
capital accumulation, 40, 42, 151
capitalism, 39–40, 179
capitalist and working classes, 191
Cappella, J. N., 163
Carpentier, N., 139
Castells, M., 14, 36, 38, 57, 58, 76
censorship, 65–66, 67
Ceron, W., 100–101t
Chadwick, A., 56, 67, 172
Chan, J., 43
chatbots, 166
ChatGPT, 91, 97, 108, 123, 175, 189, 197
Cheney-Lippold, J., 83–85, 87, 90
Chen, J.Y., 191
Chenye, Xu, 129
China
    BAT companies, 126–130
    manufacturing powerhouse to tech
        superpower, 125
    rise as (tech) superpower, 124–130
    as workshop of the world, 125
Chun, W., 151
citizen journalism, 160, 169
citizenship, 87–88
Citron, D.K., 204
Clarke, R., 81
class
    and digital capital, 142–143
    and labour, 179–180
class conflict, 180
classification, 19
class position, 180
clickbait and listicles, 161
climate change, 171
Clinton, H., 168
cloud platforms, 48
co-decision, 139
Coded Bias documentary, 149
#CodedGaze hashtag, 148–149
code-driven regulation, 88
coercive power, 59
cold war, 113
cold war 2.0, 113
Coleman, B., 151
collaborative consumption, 182
Colleoni, E., 179
colonisation, 47

combinatorial explosion, 94
commodification, 37–38, 42, 43, 44, 48, 178
communication
    cooperation and, 6
    global media and, 115–116
    impact on democracy, 60–61
    media and, 37
    political economy of, 37, 39, 65
    revolution, 83
Communication Power (Castells), 76
communicative action, 210
Communist Manifesto, 179
computational journalism, 165
computational racial capital, 151
computer-assisted reporting, 164
The Computer Boys Take Over
    (Ensmenger), 146
computer ethics, 205
computer girls, 145
computer science, 145
computer vision, 101, 149
'Computing Machinery and Intelligence'
    (Turing), 93
concentration of ownership, in media and
    communications, 46
confirmation bias, 171
connectivity, 31
conspiracy theories, 157, 171
constant capital, 52
contact tracing, 73
content, 38, 59
    moderation, 49
    optimisation, 166
    platforms, 47
content-related internet skills, 138
Convergence Culture (Jenkins), 41
convergence culture, 41
cooperation and communication, 6
corporate surveillance, 80–81
'Corrupting the Cyber-Commons: Social
    Media as a Tool of Autocratic Stability'
    (Gunitsky), 70
Cosmopolitan magazine, 145
The Costs of Connection (Couldry and
    Mejias), 131
Couldry, N., 131, 132
counter-mobilisation, 70
Covid-19 pandemic, 4, 43, 58, 63, 73, 118,
    155, 204
Cramer, J., 118
Crawford, K., 24, 27, 43, 107, 153, 189
crisis of journalism, 159
critical data studies, 200–201
critical political economy
    commodification, 37–38
    contribution of, 37
    ownership in media and communications, 46

spatialisation, 38–39
structuration, 39
'Critical Questions for Big Data' (boyd and
    Crawford), 153
critical techno-cultural discourse analysis, 150
critical thinking, 7–8
cross-subsidisation, 51
crowd-based capitalism, 182, 184
crowdsourcing, 164
crowd work, 184
Cukier, K., 4, 24, 26, 27
cultural capital, 142
cultural globalisation, 115
culture
    of algorithms, 29
    industry, 5–6
    meanings of, 5–6
    reasons for studying, 3–7
    using critical thinking, 7–11
Curran, J., 60, 159
cyber-libertarianism, 118
cyberspace, 16, 58, 71
cybertariat, 181–182
Cybertypes (Nakamura), 149
cybertypes, 149
A Cyborg Manifesto (Haraway), 146–147

Dahlberg, L., 65
Dahlgren, P., 56
DALL-E, 91, 108
Dalton, C.M., 200, 213
Daly, A., 131
Dark Matters (Browne), 150
DARPA Grand Challenge, 95, 103
Dartmouth College, 92, 93–94
Dartmouth Summer Research Project on
    Artificial Intelligence, 93
data
    and age of datafication, 4
    and AI industries, 133
    and algorithms, 6, 74
    analytic activism, 69–70
    analytics, 25
    categories of, 21–22
    collection, 4, 19
    commodification of, 43, 44
    conceptualising, 18–24
    contexts of, 22–23
    definition of, 18
    dictatorship of, 140
    and discrimination, 202–203
    economy, 35
    explosion of, 24
    extraction, 43, 44–45, 52, 132
    and information, 19
    and knowledge, 19–21
    mining, 165

misuse of, 62
and oil, 13, 23–24
perspectives for, 22–23
and politics, 198–201
and power, 62–63, 211–212
qualitative, 21
quantitative, 21
raw material of, 18–19
reasons for studying, 3–7
rise in journalism, 164–165
semi-structured, 21
and social class, 142
and society, 9, 211–213
structured, 21
and technology as gatekeeper, 162–163
three dimensions in management,
    24–25
understanding of, 198
unstructured, 21
using critical thinking, 7–11
value creation with, 52–53
as watchdog, 61–63
See also big data; specific entries
data (infrastructure/centre) activism, 197, 201,
    203, 209–211
data analytics, 69
data assemblages, 200–201, 207
data as the new oil metaphor, 13, 23–24
data behaviourism, 89
data capitalism, 51–52
data collectors, 153
data colonialism, 131–132
data commons, 212
data divides, 153, 155–156
data-driven campaigning and elections, 66–71
    corrupting the cyber-commons, 70–71
    data/analytic activism, 69–70
    dynamics of digital campaigning, 68–69
    participation and engagement in
        digital era, 67
    Politics as Usual, 71
data-driven regulation, 88–89
data economy
    business model of, 43
    deconstructing, 43–47
    winner-takes-all risk of, 46
data ecosystem, 201
data ethics, 205–206
data extractivism, 131, 210
Data Feminism (D'Ignazio and Klein), 148
data feminism, 148
datafication, 24, 31, 48
    age of, 4
    big data versus, 27–28
    and commodification, 44
    and computation, 151
    and dataveillance, 83

concerning discrimination and violence,
   202–204
and life mining, 82
in practice, 28–32
process of, 80
and social justice, 208
of society, 62, 66
and subjectivity, 82–86
datafied identities, in pandemic, 73
datafied public sphere, 66
data gaze, 51, 147
data governance, 212
data harm, 203–204
dataism, 28, 82
data journalism, 63, 163
data justice, 148, 203, 207–209
data literacy, 212
data-mediated violence, 204
data ownership, 212
Data Politics (Bigo), 198
data politics, 199–200
data poverty, 155
data power, 201, 210
data privacy, 127
data relations, 131
The Data Revolution (Kitchin), 18
data revolution, 4, 198
data-rich markets, 51
data rights, 199
data rights activism, 210
data selves, 83–84
data sharing, 212
data solidarity, 213
data sovereignty, 213
data subjects, 198–199
data trusts, 212
dataveillance, 28, 74, 131
data(sur)veillance, 81–82, 83
data violence, 203–204
data worlds, 198
decentring technology, 203
decolonising data, 213
deductive reasoning, 92
deepfakes, 157, 171–172
deep learning, 95–96, 99, 103, 171
DeepMind, 107, 119
   AlphaGo, 96
default male, 147
Delacroix, S., 89, 212
de-Lima-Santos, M.-F., 100–101t
democracy
   crisis of, 56–57
   media impact on, 60–61
Dencik, L., 207
Denisova, A., 161
derived data, 22
Descartes, R., 74, 92

De Stefano, V., 184
Deuze, M., 83, 159
Development Plan for a New Generation of
   Artificial Intelligence, 125
Devereux, E., 7
Diakopoulos, N., 167
Dialectic of Enlightenment (Adorno and
   Horkheimer), 5
Didi Chuxing, 126
digital campaigning, dynamics of, 68–69
digital capital, 143
digital capitalism, 35, 40, 116, 192
digital citizenship, 87
The Digital Disconnect (Helsper), 137
digital divide, 136
The Digital Divide (van Dijk), 137
Digital Dominance (Moore and Tambini), 119
The Digital Economy (Jordan), 118
digital housewife metaphor, 147
digital inequalities, 136–139, 152
   access and infrastructure, 136–137
   participation and inclusion, 139
   skills and usage, 137–138
digitalisation, 44–45
digital labour, 42, 177–179
   change and reform in, 190–191
digital platforms, growth of, 45
digital poorhouse, 145
digital positivism, 200
digital revolution. See third industrial revolution
digital selves, 83–84
digital storytelling, 68
digital technologies, interdisciplinary
   perspectives in, 9
Digitizing Race (Nakamura), 150
D'Ignazio, C., 148, 212
DIKW pyramid, 20–21, 20f
DiMaggio, P., 137
DiNucci, D., 16
direct discrimination, 202
Discipline and Punish (Foucault), 9
discourse, 60
discourse framing, 70
discrimination, 135, 202
discursive formations, 5
disinformation, 157
   conceptualising, 168–169
   in context of pandemics and climate
      change, 171
   countering false information, 172
   and deepfakes, 171–172
   as part of human communication, 169–170
   and political polarisation, 170
   tackling, 172
   and trust crisis, 167–172
Distributed Blackness (Brock), 150
diversity and inclusivity in tech, 149

division of labour, 6
dominant cultural expectations, 6
DoubleClick, 119
doxing, 169
Dubois, E., 66
Durkheim, E., 6
Dyer-Witheford, N., 42

echo chamber, 66, 163
economic benefits, of sharing economy, 183
economic capital, 142
economic decoupling, 128
economic globalisation, 114
economic power, 59
economies of scale, 45, 116
The Economist (2017), 23
economy
    political/data, 35
    versus society, 36
    thinking about, 36–39
elite coordination, 70
elite/plutocracy, 181
ELIZA, 94
Engels, F., 179
Ensmenger, N., 145–146
entrepreneurial activism, 192
environmental impact, AI's, 107
epistemology, 23
ethics/moral philosophy, 205
ethics washing, 206
Eubanks, V., 144, 145
European Commission, 172
exhaust data, 22
expert systems, AI, 94
explainable AI (XAI), 105
exploitation, 42–43, 131, 178–179
extraction of resources, 197

Facebook/Meta, 29, 43, 46, 62, 119t, 121–122,
    160, 178
facial recognition, 149
Fairmondo, 192
fair work, collective action for, 191
Fairwork project, 191
fake news, 168
Falling Through the Net studies, 136
false information, 168
feedback data, 104
feminism, 146
Fifth Generation Computer Systems project,
    94–95
filter bubble, 163
The Filter Bubble (Pariser), 29, 30, 66
Fink, K., 163
first industrial revolution, 17
first-level digital divide, 136–137
Floridi, L., 19

Foucault, M., 5, 9, 77, 89
fourth estate, 60
fourth industrial revolution, 17–18, 186–187
Frankfurt School, 63–64
Fraser, N., 208
free labour, 42
free market, 62
Frenken, K., 183
Frey, C. B., 187
Fuchs, C., 8, 16, 38, 41–43, 52, 65, 80, 122, 144,
    176, 178
The Future of Professions (Susskind and
    Susskind), 187

GAFAM companies, 4, 46, 50, 118–119
Galtung, J., 158
Gandini, A., 179
Gandy, O. Jr., 79
Gangadharan, S., 202, 203
Ganter, S.A., 68
gatekeeper, data and technology as, 162–163
Gates, B., 123, 144
Gebru, T., 103
gender, class and, 146
gender stereotypes, 106
generative adversarial networks, 171
generative artificial intelligence (generative
    AI/GenAI), 97, 175
ghost work, 189
Gibson, W., 16
Giddens, A., 38, 39, 76
gig economy, 184
gig work
    forms of, 184
    sharing economy to, 182–186
Gillespie, T., 47
Gill, R., 182
Gitelman, L., 19
glamorised millennial labour, myth of, 186
global data divide, 154–155
global data industries and data colonialism,
    130–133
globalisation, 114–115
    and digital (data) revolution, 116–117
global media and communication, 115–116
Global Media Giants (Birkinbine), 144
Go (board game), 96
Goffman, E., 75
Golding, P., 18, 37
good old-fashioned artificial intelligence
    (GOFAI), 95
Google/Alphabet, 29, 43, 46, 62, 103, 107,
    119–120, 119t, 160, 189
government accountability, 63
GPT4, 103
GPT (Generative Pre-trained Transformer)
    software, 123

Graham, M., 184
Gramsci, A., 60
Gray, J., 164
Gray, M. L., 189
group of individuals, 6
group privacy, 206
Gunitsky, S., 70
Gurstein, M., 153
Gurumurthy, A., 66
Gutenberg printing press, 169
Gutiérrez, M., 209, 210

Habermas, J., 63, 64, 159, 210
hacktivism, 209
Hall, S., 5
Hao, K., 133, 189
Haraway, D., 146
Harcup, T., 158–159, 160
Hargittai, E., 137
harm, 204
Harvey, D., 38
Hassan, R., 14
healthy scepticism, 7
hegemony, 60
Helmond, A., 50
Helsper, E., 137, 139–140
Hepp, A., 201
Hicks, M., 146
Hildebrandt, M., 88
Hinton, G., 99
Hintz, A., 87
Hobbes, T., 92
Hoffmann, A. L., 203, 204
Hoggart, R., 5
horizontal integration, 46
Horkheimer, M., 5
Huateng, Ma, 129
Huawei, 125, 126
human labour, 40
human-level machine intelligence, 97
Humans as a Service, 186, 189
Huws, U., 181–182
hybridity, 67
The Hybrid Media System (Chadwick), 67
hybrid posthumans, 108

ideal types, 84
identity(ies), 74–75
    data and algorithms impacting, 74–77
    and modernity, 76
    and performance, 75
    politics, 68
    and self-communication, 76–77
    and subjectivity, 77
ideology, 60
if and *then*, 28
ImageNet, 95

InCoding, 149
Independent Workers of Great Britain labour
    union, 191
indexal data, 22
indirect discrimination, 202
industrial infrastructures of AI, 99
industrialisation, 176
industrial platforms, 48
Industry 4.0, 17
inequalities
    access and infrastructure, 136–137
    in digital sphere, 136
    and discrimination, 135
    outcome, 139
    skills and usage, 137–138
    technology role in reproducing social,
        139–141
infodemic, 58, 171
Information Age trilogy, 14
informational politics, 58
information and communication
        technologies (ICT)
    production of, 143
    sector, 127
information disorder, 168
information ethics, 205
information fabrication, 169
information overload, 159
information paradox, 159
information society, 14–15
information superhighway, 116, 136
information, types of, 19
input data, 104
intelligence explosion, 97
interdisciplinary approaches, 9–10
international relations studies, 211
internet, 15–16, 150
    as communication medium, 82
    as democratising technology, 57
    features of, 82–83
    limitations, to serve as public sphere,
        65–66
    rise, in China, 125
    and social media, 160
interval attributes, 21
Irani, L., 189
iSlavery, 143

Jamieson, K. H., 163
Jarrett, K., 147, 179, 191
JD.com, 126
Jenkins, H., 41, 76, 161
Jennings, K., 96
Jia, L., 130
Jobs, S., 122
Johnson, N. L., 49
Joler, V., 189

Jones, P., 188
journalism
  and alternative media studies, 211
  automated, 165, 166–167
  crisis of, 159
  defining, 159
  and digital technologies, 157
  rise of data in, 164–165
  social media impact on, 160
jus algoritmi, 87

Kaluža, J., 66
Karpf, D., 69
Katz, E., 60
Kelleher, J.D., 21
Kennedy, H., 201, 211
Keynes, J.M., 190
killer robots, 105
Kitchin, R., 18, 21, 22, 25, 200
Klein, L. F., 148
knowledge
  four types of knowing, 21
  information and, 19
  pyramid, 20–21, 20f
  representation, 98
  types of, 11
knowledge gap theory, 138
Kormelink, G., 161
Kreiss, D., 69
Kukutai, T., 213
Kurzweil, R., 97

labour, 38
  capital and, 190
  class and, 179–180
  digital, 177–179
  power, 177
  as valorisation process, 177–178
  work and, 176–177
labour theory of value, 42
Laney, D., 24
large language models, 103
Lash, S., 76
Lauriault, T., 200
Lawrence, N. D., 212
Lazarsfeld, P., 8
lean platforms, 48
Lee, K.-F., 125
Lehtiniemi, T., 209
Leibniz, G., 92
Lenovo, 125
Lessig, L., 182
Leviathan (Hobbes), 92
Levinson, P., 17
Lewin, K., 11
lidar (light detection and ranging), 104
life mining, 28

Linden, C.-G., 165
LinkedIn, 123
liquid modernity, 76
Li, R., 127
Livingstone, S., 212
Living, Z., 129
lock-in, 119
Loomio, 192
Loosen, W., 164
Los Angeles Times, 165
Lovelace, A., 92–93
lumpen-precariat (underclass), 181
Lupton, D., 83
Lyon, D., 78, 79, 81

machine learning, 31, 92, 98
Machine, Platform, Crowd (McAfee and
  Brynjolfsson), 188
machine translation, 100
Made in China 2025, 125
Ma, J., 128–129
male gaze, 147
mal-information, 169
Mann, M., 131
Manovich, L., 153
Mao Zedong, 125
marketing campaigns, 80
Marx, G., 78
Marxian class analysis, 142
Marx, K., 6, 36, 38, 39, 177, 178, 179–180
mass communication, 82
Mass Communication Theory (McQuail), 82
mass media, evolution to mass customisation,
  82–83
mass self-communication, 57, 76–77
mass surveillance, 88
matchmaking, 49
Mayer-Schoenberger, V., 4, 24, 26, 27, 51
Mbembe, A., 204
McAfee, A., 188
McCarthy, J., 93–94
The McDonaldization of Society (Ritzer), 41
McLuhan, M., 74
McQuail, D., 10, 82
McStay, A., 168
means of production, 177
measurable types, 84–85, 87
Mechanical Turk, 186, 189
media
  acting as voice of the people, 61, 66–67
  and communication, 37, 88
  content, 38
  credibility for institutions, 172
  democratic role of, 59–61
  digital, 66, 67, 71, 150, 178
  impact on democracy, 60–61
  literacy, 172, 212

logic, 30
manipulation, 168–169
old and new, 67
pluralism, 172
scrutiny, 63
spreadable, 161
traditional, 83
as watchdog, 60–61
mediatisation, 56, 68
medium-related skills, 138
Meijer, C., 161
Meikle, G., 16
Meituan, 126
Mejias, U., 131, 132
metadata, 22, 85
Microsoft, 119t, 123–124
microwork, 189
middle class, 180
Milan, S., 154, 155, 208, 209, 210
Mill, J.S., 36
Minsky, M., 93
misinformation, 169
Moazed, A., 49
mobile media, 4, 17, 160
mobile revolution, 17
modernity, and identity, 76
modes of production, 179
monitorial and public sphere, 211
monitorial citizens, 159
monopolisation, risk of, 46–47
Moore, M., 119
Morozov, E., 140, 184
Mosco, V., 37–39
Motorola Mobility, 119
Mueller, G., 193
Muldoon, J., 192
Mumford, D., 132
Munn, L., 188
Murdock, G., 37
Musk, E., 55

Nakamura, L., 149–150
National Telecommunications and Information
    Administration (NTIA), US, 136
natural language generation, 103
natural language processing, 98, 102–103
necropolitics, 204
neo-Luddite movement, 192–193
Netflix, 29
Networked (Rainie and Wellman), 4
networked democracy
    challenges of, 58
    crisis of democracy, 56–57
    early promises of, 57
    expectations of, 57
    freedom and facilitating empowerment, 58–59
networked individualism, 4

networked public sphere, 65
network effects, 45, 50–51
network folding, 69
network society, 14, 76
Neuromancer (Gibson), 16
New Jim Code, 151
New Left counterculture, 118
New Perspectives in Critical Data Studies
    (Hepp), 201
news dissemination, 166
new social operating system, 4
news production, and consumption, 59
    automated journalism, 165–167
    automating the newsroom, 165
    changes in, 158–163
    changing news consumption, 161–162
    commercial pressures versus news values,
        160–161
    data and technology as gatekeeper, 162–163
    information and news paradox, 158–160
    news values, 158–159t
news values, 158–159t, 160
New Yorker magazine, 75
Nielsen, R.K., 68
Niklas, J., 203
Nissenbaum, H., 90
Noble, S., 152
nominal attributes, 21
non-discrimination, 208
normalisation of cyberspace, 71
Norvig, P., 97–98
numbered lives, 84

Obama campaign, 69–70
obfuscation, 90
object recognition and movement tracking, 101
old 'core' working class (proletariat), 181
O'Neil, C., 145
O'Neill, D., 158–159, 160
online advertising, 100
online content, 127
online news consumption, 161
ontology, 23
Onuoha, M., 204
OpenAI, 91, 103, 108, 123, 175
Open Data Institute, 205
ordinal attributes, 21
O'Reilly, T., 16, 88
Osborne, M. A., 187
outcome inequalities, 139

Page, L., 119, 144
Panama Papers, 164
Papacharissi, Z., 68
Pariser, E., 29, 66
Parsons, T., 6
participation and inclusion, 139

participatory media culture, 41
participatory openness, 164
Pasquale, F., 53, 141, 204
Perez, C.C., 147–148
performance/stage metaphor, 75
personalisation, 49, 85
Platform Capitalism (Srnicek), 47
platform capitalism, characteristics of, 50–51
platform cooperativism, 192
platform ecosystem, 47–50
platformisation, 43
    of society, 49–50
platform labour, 179
platforms, 44, 47
    functions of, 49
    mechanisms, 48–49
    power of, 68
    typology of, 47–48
platform socialism, 192
platform society, 50
Poell, T., 30
political authority, 6
political deepfakes, 172
political economy, 35
    of communication, 37, 39, 65
    as framework and critique, 36–37
political globalisation, 114–115
political power, 59, 199
politics and economy, influence over culture, 5
popularity, 30–31
positive identity, 74
posthumanism, 108
Postman, N., 159
power
    in AI context, 108–109
    balance, from media, 83
    and critical approaches, 8–9
    and data, 62–63, 211–212
    dynamics in media and politics, 59
    holding, to account, 62–63
    and identity, 77
    interrogating, 199
    of networks, 58
    and struggle for resources, 59–60
    types of, 59
practice, 11
precariat, 181
prediction products, 52
preference divulgence, 70
The Presentation of Self in Everyday Life
    (Goffman), 75
Press Gazette, 63
primary data, 22
print media, 82
proactive data activism, 210
productive forces, 177
product platforms, 48

product-technology platforms, 47
produsage, 40
professionalisation, 56
proficians, 181
profilisation, 85
programmability, 30
programmable machines, 92
Programmed Inequality (Hicks), 146
programmed sociality, 29
proletariat (working class), 180–181
propaganda, as news, 169
prosumer commodity, 38, 41–42, 81t, 122, 178
prosumers' big data commodity, 80
prosumption and prosumer capitalism, 40–41
prototype campaigning, 69
Prototype Politics (Kreiss), 69
prototyping and network folding, 69
public infrastructure, 43
public service broadcasting, 60
public sphere
    datafied, 66
    Habermas's concept of, 64
    myth of, 55
    potential and limits of internet as, 65–66

Qiu, J.L., 43, 143
QQ, 129
QQ Games, 129
Quakebot, 165, 166
qualitative data, 21
quantitative data, 21
quasi-monopolies, 46
Qzone, 129

Raboy, M., 88
race
    in digital media, 149–150
    as technology, 151–152
Race After Technology (Benjamin), 151
race-critical code studies, 152
racial bias, 106
racial capitalism, 150–151
racial formation, 151
racialism, 150
Ragnedda, M., 143
Rainie, L., 4
Raley, R., 81
Ramge, T., 51
ratio scales, 21
raw data, 19, 25
reactive data activism, 210
Reagan, R., 116
Redden, J., 204
reflexive modernity, 76
reinforcement learning, 98–99
relational platforms, 47
relevance paradox, 30

Remix (Lessig), 182
Reporters Without Borders, 63
reproductive labour, 147
reputations and user trends, 49
resisting data capitalism, 213
Resnick, D., 71
revolutionary change, 71
Rheingold, H., 57
Ricardo, D., 36
Ricaurte, P., 132
Richterich, A., 201
The Rise of the Network Society (Castells), 58
The Rise of the Robots (Ford), 187
Ritzer, G., 41
Robinson, C., 150
Robopocalypse (Wilson), 108
robots, 97, 187
Rogers, R., 182, 183
Rogers, S., 163
Rosenblat, A., 185, 186
Rothkopf, D., 171
Rouvroy, A., 89
Ruckenstein, M., 209
Ruge, M., 158
Ruiu, M.L., 143
Ruppert, E., 199
Russell, S.J., 97–98
Rutter, B., 96

Sadowski, J., 45, 52, 53
salariat, 181
sales data, 22
Sandoval, M., 192
scepticism, 7
Schiller, D., 40, 116
Scholz, T., 42, 185, 192
Schor, J., 183, 185
Schudson, M., 159
Schwab, K., 17
science and technology studies, 146
Searle, J.R., 93
secondary data, 22
second industrial revolution, 17
second-level digital divide, 137–138
Second Life, 75
The Second Machine Age (Brynjolfsson and McAfee), 187
Segura, M. S., 132, 210
selection mechanism, 49
self, 75
self-communication, and identity, 76–77
self-driving cars, 95, 103–105
self-employed entrepreneurs, 186
self-identity, 76
self-presentation, 75, 76
semi-structured data, 21
Sevignani, S., 176

Shannon, C., 93
sharing economy, 48, 176
  and automation, 175–176
  categories and examples, 183t
  and gig work, 182–186
Simon, H., 93
singularity, 97, 108
skills and use inequalities, 137–138
Skype, 123
slave work, 43
Smith, A., 36
Smythe, D.W., 42
Snowden revelations, 23, 42, 62, 79, 88, 165
social action, 39
social benefits, 183
social capital, 142
social class, 142, 179
social identity theory, 74
social inequalities, technology role in reproducing, 139–141
social justice, 208
social media, 4, 16, 160
  co-opting, 70
  in EU referendum, 67
  listening through, 70
  logic, 30, 162
  in proliferation of disinformation, 169
  sharing as essential characteristic of, 160–161
  users, 42
  See also media
social movement studies, 211
social practices of AI, 99
social shaping and feminism, 146
social sorting, 86
social stratification, 142
social web, 16
society
  datafication of, 62, 66
  economy versus, 36
  information and data play in, 15
  platformisation of, 49–50
  reasons for studying, 3–7
  and structures of human organisation, 6–7
  using critical thinking, 7–11
socio-digital inequalities, 139
software as a service, 189
spam filtering, 100
spatialisation, 38–39
speech recognition, 100, 102
spreadability, 161
Spreadable Media (Jenkins), 41
spreadable media, 41
Srnicek, N., 47–50
Standing, G., 180–181
Stanford University, 95
Steinberg, M., 47
Stop Killer Robots, 106

stratification class analysis, 142
Striphas, T., 6, 29
Strong AI (artificial general intelligence), 96–97
The Structural Transformation of the Public Sphere (Habermas), 64, 159
structural violence, 204
structuration, in critical political economy of communication, 39
structuration theory, 76
structured data, 21
subjectification, 131
subjectivity
    and datafication, 82–86
    and identity, 77
Sundararajan, A., 182–183, 184
Sunstein, C.R., 163
superintelligence, 96, 97, 108
supervised learning, 98
Suri, S., 189
surplus labour, 178
surplus value, 39–40, 177, 178
surveillance
    censorship and, 67
    corporate, 80–81
    culture, 77–82
    data(sur)veillance, 81–82
    defining, 78
    perspectives on, 78–80
    prosumer commodity and, 41–42
    as social sorting, 79
surveillance capitalism, 42, 82, 201
sustainability, 183
switching cost, 119
symbolic capital, 142
symbolic power, 59
synthetic media, 171

tabloidisation, 160
Tajfel, H., 74
Tambini, D., 119
Tandoc, E.C., 168
Taobao, 29, 128
Taylor, J., 213
Taylor, L., 207, 208
tech activism, 211
Technically Wrong (Wachter-Boettcher), 145
technical revolution. *See* second industrial revolution
techno bohemians, 182
technochauvinism, 140
technofeminism and digital housewife, 146–147
technological determinism, 118, 190, 200
technological exceptionalism, 186
technological unemployment, 189–190
techno logic surveillance perspective, 79
technologies of the self, 77
technosolutionism, 140
Tencent, 43, 46, 125, 126, 129–130

Tenpay, 129
tertiary data, 22
Tesla, 103, 105
Thatcher, J., 200, 213
Thatcher, M., 116
theory versus practice, 10–11
third industrial revolution, 17
third-level digital divide, 139
the third wave, 40
Thompson, J. B., 199, 201
Thomson Reuters, 165
three Vs, 24–25
Tierney, B., 21
Tmall, 128
Toffler, A., 40
To Save Everything, Click Here (Morozov), 140
toy problems, 94
training data, 104
transhumanism, 108
transient data, 22
transnational media corporation, 116
transparency and trust, in AI, 106
Treré, E., 154, 155, 208
Trump, D., 67, 168
Tucker, J., 170
Turing, A., 93–94
Turing machine, 93
Turing test, 93, 98
Turner, J.C., 74
Twitter/X, 55

Uber, 35, 184, 186, 189
Uberisation of work, 185
Uberland: How Algorithms Are Rewriting the Rules of Work (Rosenblat), 185
uncritical thinking, 7
underclass (lumpen-precariat), 181
unemployed, 181
unstructured data, 21
unsupervised learning, 98
Urry, J., 188
user profiling, advantages and disadvantages of, 81t
use values, 177, 178
US National Telecommunications and Information Administration (NTIA), 136
us versus them attitude, 75

Vaccari, C., 172
Vallas, S., 185
value, 25
van der Velden, L., 209, 210
van Deursen, A., 138
van Dijck, J., 28, 30, 43, 47, 48, 50, 82, 131
van Dijk, J., 14, 136–138
variability, 25
variety, 25
Veblen, T., 140

velocity, 25
veracity, 25
vertical integration, 46
violence, 204
viral content, 161
viral news, 161
virtual space, 14
virtue ethics, 205
visibility and privacy, 208
volume, 24–25
Vrikki, P., 213
Vs (three), 24–25

Wachter-Boettcher, S., 145, 149
Waisbord, S., 132, 210
Wajcman, J., 146–147, 187
Wallerstein, I., 130–131
watchdog role for media, 61–62
Watson, 96
weak AI (artificial narrow intelligence), 96–97
Weapons of Math Destruction (O'Neil), 145
We Are Data: Algorithms and the Making of our Digital Selves (Cheney-Lippold), 84, 87
Web 1.0, 58
Web 2.0, 16, 58, 76, 182
Web 3.0, 59
Weberian class analysis, 142
Weber, M., 6, 79, 84
Webster, F., 15
WeChat, 29, 129
Weibo, 29, 178
Weizenbaum, J., 94
Wellman, B., 4
Wernimont, J., 83
West, S.M., 51
'Where Fairness Fails' (Hoffmann), 203
white-collar jobs, 182
whizz-kid computer boys, 146
Williams, R., 5
Wilson, D. H., 108

Winfield, A., 97
winner-takes-all markets, 119
winner-takes-all risk, 46
Winseck, D., 130
Winterson, J., 23
Wired magazine, 23, 26, 133
wisdom, 20
Wood, A. J., 186
Woodcock, J., 184
Wood, G., 59
work
    on demand via apps, 184
    future of, 187, 190
    and labour, 176–177
    object and product of, 177t
worker self-management, 192
working class (proletariat), 180–181
working-class network society, 143
Work Without the Worker (Jones), 188
World Computer (Beller), 151
World Health Organisation (WHO), 171
world-systems theory, 130
Wozniak, S., 122
Wright, E.O., 8, 142, 180, 199, 201, 213
Wylie, C., 63

Xiaomi, 126
Xi Jinping, 113
Xu, E., 127

Yeung, K., 88
Yiran, C., 129
Youku, 29
you loop, 29
YouTube, 29, 119, 178

Zeleny, M., 21
Zhidong, Z., 129
Zuboff, S., 42, 51, 52, 82
Zuckerberg, M., 30, 121, 144

www.ingramcontent.com/pod-product-compliance
Lightning Source LLC
Chambersburg PA
CBHW081144020426
42333CB00021B/2663